THE WRITINGS OF

ISAAC

PENINGTON

VOLUME 2

EDITED BY JASON R. HENDERSON

This and other publications
are available FREE upon request
by contacting:

MARKET STREET FELLOWSHIP
981 W. Market Street   Akron, Ohio 44313
email: MSFPrinting@gmail.com
phone: 330-419-1527

www.marketstreetfellowship.com

Contents

Chapter I
Spiritual Knowledge

"This is life eternal, that they might know you, the only true God, and Jesus Christ whom you have sent." —John 17:3

I sought and traveled (from my childhood) after the true knowledge of God, and of his Christ, and was satisfied with nothing that I ever could meet with. But having at length (through the tender mercy of the Lord, and guidance of his Spirit) met with it and been satisfied, finding it to be the eternal life, the true food, the living power, the pure rest, the joy and salvation of my soul, I cannot help but testify of it to those that spend their money on that which is not bread, and their wages on that which does not satisfy.

We (some of us at least) have spent just as much of our money and labor as they[1] who now despise us have done. And some of us (I speak it in the fear of the Lord, and in a true sense, without boasting) have had just as much of what they feed upon, and what they call bread, as they have now. Yet when the Lord brought us to the true balance, we found it not to be bread, nor able to give the soul true satisfaction.

---

[1] He speaks of professing Christians, and more particularly their leaders and priests who were educated in schools of higher learning, and who held Quakers in contempt.

The true bread was not what we then called bread, but was a bread which we had overlooked and not known. For the eternal life which is hid with the Father, and is manifested in the Son, and made known to the soul—this is true bread which does not perish. Such bread will endure when all literal and outward knowledge of God fails and falls short of satisfying the hunger of the soul which seeks the substance itself.

Now, it is my heart's desire to draw men's minds to a sense of truth, to a sense of that which is the substance itself, that they might know the bread indeed, know the living waters, come to them and drink, and find Christ in them a well of water springing up to eternal life. Therefore, it was in my heart to give forth the ensuing question, and the inquiries that follow. He that can rightly answer these questions must indeed know the substance. But he that cannot answer may thereby discover that he does not rightly know, and so may wait upon God to receive the knowledge of it, and come to him for the eternal life which he freely gives.

The Jews were puzzled about the Messiah to come because of their literal knowledge of the law and prophets. Indeed, they were kept from the true knowledge of him by their own understanding of the prophecies concerning him. Most sorts of men who now profess Christ are similarly puzzled about a knowledge concerning the outward body, flesh, and blood of Christ, according as they apprehend the Scriptures to speak. Thus the veil remains over their hearts as well, and they cannot see the eternal life and substance any more than the Jews, but by their outward and literal knowledge they are kept back from the substance.

Now the breathing of my heart to the Lord is this: to take away the veil from all hearts that sincerely desire the truth, and to open the true eye in them, that they may see the desire and beloved of their souls, and be led by him into the true travel, out of self and towards the kingdom. Oh that they may travel into the very land of the living, where the food of life is fed upon and where the living springs flow. There are the vineyards which we planted not, and dwelling places which we built not, where the fruit of God's planting (the wine of the kingdom) is drunk, even drunk anew in the kingdom with the Father and Son in the Spirit, who are One and all there.

A Question to Professors of Christianity

The question is not whether they know what is said of Christ in the Scriptures, but whether they know it savingly, truly, livingly, and powerfully. Yes, they may know what is said of him, and yet not know him of whom those things are said. So it was with the Scribes and Pharisees, for they knew what was said of Christ in the law and prophets, but they knew him not when he appeared in that body of flesh. So men may now know what the apostles and the evangelists have said concerning his appearance in a body of flesh (concerning his birth, circumcision, baptism, preaching, doctrine, miracles, death, resurrection, ascension, intercession, etc.), and yet not know him of whom these things are said. Yes, they may know what is said concerning the Word which was from the beginning, and yet not know the Word, the power, the life itself.

Since the prevailing of the apostles' testimony, the way of the enemy has not been directly to deny Christ, but to bring men into such a knowledge of Christ that does not save. And as the enemy did acknowledge Christ when he appeared in that body of flesh, saying: "I know who you are, the Holy One of God;" so he has found it to his advantage (ever since) to acknowledge that outward appearance. This outward appearance he does not oppose, nor men's knowledge and understanding of Scriptures that confirm them in this. But the saving knowledge, the true knowledge, the living knowl - edge, the powerful knowledge of truth—*that* he always opposes; for that alone overturns and destroys his kingdom in man, and brings man from out of his reach.

Now there is a vast difference between knowing the descriptions concerning a thing, and knowing the thing described. And there is also a great deal of difference between believing the descriptions concerning a thing, and believing in the thing which is described.

Spiritual things cannot be savingly known except by a union with them, by a receiving of them. A man can never truly know the Spirit of God by words that are said concerning it. Rather, he must first experience something of it in order to truly know it. So the peace, the joy, the life, the power—these pass the understanding. Thus a man can never rightly know them by reading or comprehending ever so much concerning them, but rather by coming out of himself, and traveling to where they are given and made manifest. Only in this way may he come into acquaintance with them. And if the peace which Christ gives, the joy, the life, the power, cannot be known by literal descriptions, how could Christ himself, who is the fullness of all, the fountain of them all, the treasury of all perfection, in whom are hid all the riches and treasures of wisdom and knowledge—how could he be known by outward and literal descriptions?

True knowledge is in a seed, in which man can receive a capacity of knowing, and wherein the Father (from whom the seed came) does teach. And this is his way of teaching us: by making us one with the thing he teaches. In this way we learn Christ—by being born of him, by putting him on. In this way we know his righteousness, his life, his wisdom, his power—by receiving a proportion of them, which gives an ability to discern and acknowledge the fullness. And in this we receive the understanding of the Scriptures, and know the seed of the woman (which bruises the serpent's head), by receiving the seed, by feeling its growth in us, and its power over the enemy. Then we know the thing itself.

Likewise, we know the woman that brings forth this seed after the Spirit, which is the Jerusalem above. And we know also, and singly acknowledge, the seed that was brought forth outwardly after the flesh. This seed we know to be the seed of Abraham, the seed of David after the flesh, and the seed of God after the power of the endless life. And we are taught of God to give the due honor to each—to the seed of God in the first place, to the seed of David in the second place.[2] There was the seed that wrought the thing, which seed was the life itself; and the seed in which he wrought it, which was formed into a vessel like ours, but without sin. In this vessel the pure Lamb appeared in the pure power of life, which kept the vessel pure; and so he (who was to be the first fruits) had the honor above all his brethren, being anointed with the oil of gladness above his fellows.

But we also are born of the same seed. He is formed in us; we are formed of him; we are as well of his flesh and blood, as he was of ours. And by being thus formed, and feeling him grow up in us, and receiving an understanding from him, and in him, thus we come to know him, and to understand the words of Scripture concerning him. By experiencing and knowing the Lamb in our vessels, we know also what the Lamb was in his vessel.

---

[2] Here Penington speaks of the two natures of Christ, who was fully God according to the seed of God, and fully man according to the seed of Abraham and David.

Thus we know things in the certainty and demonstration of God's Spirit, even in the light which shines from him, and in the life which he begets. And we speak of things as they are, and as we feel them to be in the true life, which the Spirit of Christ has begotten in us. And we can truly say concerning the Scriptures that now we believe, not so much because of the relation of things concerning Christ which we have found in them, but because we have seen and received the thing of which the Scriptures speak. And we find this to be the very substance indeed, the very Christ of God, the spotless one, the living garment of righteousness and salvation, wherein God finds no fault, and in which the soul appears without blame before him. And concerning this, can we speak words of its nature, words of its virtue, words of its life, power, and righteousness. These are words that the flesh cannot hear, but he that is born of God does naturally acknowledge and understand. Why so? Because he knows the nature of the thing, and receives the words in the savor thereof. Can life deny life? Can the birth of life deny that which springs out of the same womb? No, no. The children which are born of wisdom do justify wisdom in its several sproutings-forth and appearances. But that which denies it is a birth after the letter, a birth after the literal and outward knowledge of things, a birth of man's comprehending wisdom. This birth indeed reproaches and blasphemes the incomprehensible wisdom in its incomprehensible ways, and would restrain life to be what they can apprehend or comprehend by the letter concerning it.

And this may be a great evidence to professors[3] that they indeed do not know Christ in his nature, Spirit, life, and power, because they do not speak of him as persons who

---

[3] The word *professor* will be used throughout to refer to those who *profess* faith in Christ. Here the word has nothing to do with teachers or educators.

experience the substance, nor speak from the present sense and acquaintance with it, but only as persons that bring forth a notion which they have received into their understanding. And yet they fail in this also, for they speak not of Christ according as the Scriptures truly present him (when compared one with another), but only what they have grossly apprehended concerning him from some Scriptures, even as the outward Jews did.

Now friends, if you have this living spiritual knowledge, and if you hold it in him who is true, then own and acknowledge it (as it is expressed in the Scriptures, and as God has now brought it forth in his people), so that you may manifest yourselves as being of him. There is an understanding and wisdom of man, and there is a witness of God which gives true judgment. Man (at his best) judges only according as things appear to him from the Scriptures. But the witness of God judges the things of God in the demonstration of the Spirit, according as they are felt and known to be in him.

But if you do not have this spiritual knowledge, but have long given out your money and labor for that which is not bread, nor can yield the true satisfaction, then oh, come to the waters, and receive that which is given freely, without money and without price! Oh, sell all for the pearl, for the knowledge which is of life, for the knowledge which is life! "I am the way, the truth, and the life," said Christ; to know this is eternal life. So wait to feel the rock laid as a foundation in you, even the seed of God, the life of Christ, the Spirit of Christ revealed in you, and your souls born of it, and built upon it. Oh that you could come out of your own under-standing, that you might feel and receive the love of my heart, and know the travail of my soul for you—that you might be born of the truth, and know and receive it as it is in Jesus, and as it is felt in the Spirit, and its own pure power!

Christ Known Outwardly and Inwardly

Now a little further, to remove the scruples and prejudices out of the minds of those who at times have been touched with the power of truth, and have had the witness of God reached to in their hearts, but afterwards the enemy has raised a mist, and cast blocks in their way, stirring up in them hard thoughts against us; I say, to remove this out of the minds of the honest-hearted (who in the guidance of God might chance upon this paper), I shall open my heart nakedly: [4]

1. We do indeed acknowledge that the Word of God (the only begotten of the Father) did take up a body of the flesh of the virgin Mary, who was of the seed of David, according to the Scriptures, and did the will of the Father therein, in holy obedience unto him, both in life and death.

2. That he did offer up the flesh and blood of that body (though not only this, but he poured out his soul, he poured out his life) a sacrifice or offering for sin, a sacrifice unto the Father, and in it tasted death for every man. And it is upon God's consideration and acceptance of this sacrifice for sin that the sins of believers are pardoned, so that God might be just and the justifier of him who believes in Jesus, or who is of the faith of Jesus.

3. What is attributed to Christ's body we do acknowledge in its place, according as the Scripture attributes it, which is

---

[4] The following assertions are made in response to what was a common (though false) criticism against Penington and the early Quakers, namely, that they taught Christ to be only an inward life or light that worked in the heart, but denied or neglected the outward work of Christ accomplished in His natural body.

through and because of that which dwelt and acted in it. But that which sanctified and kept the body pure (and made all acceptable in him) was the life, holiness, and righteousness of the Spirit. And the same thing that kept his vessel pure is that which now cleanses us. For man was shut out from this living virtue and power by the fall; but through the true knowledge of the death of Christ, the way is made open for it again, and man is brought to it to be baptized, washed, cleansed, sanctified, fitted for, and filled with life.

Now of this thing we might speak yet more clearly and plainly, if men could hear our words. But if we have spoken to you earthly things (in parables and figures) suitable to your understanding, and you believe not, how shall you believe if we speak to you heavenly things, or if we tell you plainly of the Father, in whom is all the life of the Son, and all the virtue and salvation that ever the Son had from him? The Jews were to learn in types, figures, and shadows, till Christ came. And after Christ came, he also taught them in resemblances and similitudes of things. And the apostles wrote and spoke much to persons who were just coming out of that state, in a language suited to that state. But he that comes into the substance itself, and is taught there by the Spirit, after he is grown up and made capable, he is taught plainly the nature of the heavenly things. Then the words of the apostles (concerning the deep things of God) which are mysterious to others, are manifest and plain to him. Yes, the Lord teaches him things that words cannot utter. The peace of God, the joy of his Spirit, the life and power of the Lord Jesus Christ, his wisdom, righteousness, and pure, precious ways of sanctifying the heart, the tender mercy, faithfulness, and rich love of the Father, etc., these are known in such a way as cannot be uttered to any man. Indeed, they are not learned (nor could ever be learned) from words about the things, but rather by the sense and experience of the thing itself. The Lord (in whom are the depths of life, and who gives the sense and understanding of the deep things of the Spirit) opens these things in him, and manifests them to him.

Indeed, this is the right and excellent way of knowledge: to come into union, to come into the thing itself, to learn in the union, to see and know in the thing. This is the way that the Lord teaches all his children in the new covenant, by the inward life, by the pure light within, by the inward demonstration of his Spirit, by the power and virtue of the truth itself. And he that is in the Son has some measure of this life. But he that does not have some measure of this life is not in the Son, but only in a talk and a wise knowledge of things according to the flesh, which will perish, and he with it who abides there. For no man can be saved, but by coming into the knowledge which is of a pure, eternal, living, saving nature. Can an opinion which a man takes up concerning Christ from the Scriptures save him? No, for it is no more than an opinion or judgment of man, unless he be in the life and power of the thing itself. Only then is it truth indeed to him, and right knowledge in him. Otherwise it is but a false knowledge, a knowledge that will not subdue his heart to truth, for its seat is not in the heart, but rather in his head, making him wise and able there to oppose truth. Such false knowledge brings man into a state of condemnation, wrath, and misery beyond the heathen, and makes him harder to be wrought upon by the light and power of the truth than the very heathen.

Therefore, consider your ways O professors of Christianity! Do not despise the hand which is stretched forth to you in the love of God, and in the motion and guidance of his Spirit, who condescends to you exceedingly. Let him reach to his own in you and scatter your apprehensions, imaginations, and conceivings about the meanings of Scriptures (which are like many chains of death and darkness upon you), so that you might come to him in whom is life, and who gives life freely to all who come to him. Oh, observe what iron bars were in the way of the Scribes and Pharisees! They would not come to him that they might have life; indeed, they could not as they stood. Yet there are greater bars in your way; yes, it is harder for many of you to come to him than it was for them. My upright desire to the Lord for you is that he would remove the stumbling blocks out of your way, that he would batter and knock down the flesh in you, and that he would strip you of all your knowledge of Scriptures according to the flesh. Only then will you be capable of knowing and receiving things according to the Spirit. Only then will you know how to understand, honor, and make use of the Scriptures also. But until then you cannot help but make use of them both against your own souls and against Christ and his truth.

Now, having certainly felt and known the thing in our own hearts, and having also seen the snares and nets which the enemy lays for you, whereby he keeps you from the true bread, and from the water and wine of the kingdom (even as he kept us formerly), how can we hold our peace? How can we help but witness to you (in the love and drawings of the Spirit of the Lord) of the truth, life, and power which we have felt in Jesus, even if by doing so you become our enemies? It is not our desire or end to bring you to another opinion or outward way, but rather that you might feel the thing itself, and know assuredly what is the truth, and abide in that which was never deceived itself, nor ever deceived any. Oh, why should you wander in the dark opinions and uncertainties of the night? Why should you not rather come to that wherein the light of the day springs, and out of which it shines? Can the natural man (who has his eyes) be deceived about the light of the natural day? Does he not recognize and know the light of the day both from the light itself and also from the darkness of the night? Ten thousand times more certain and inwardly satisfied is he who is born of the spiritual day, brought forth in the light thereof, and who spiritually sees, lives, and walks therein. Indeed, there is no doubt in him who is grown up into the thing; for he has the assurance of faith (which is far above the assurance of outward sense or reason), and the assurance of understanding. Oh blessed is he who has an eye to see, an ear to hear, a heart to under-stand, the things which God has revealed by his Spirit in this our day, the living way which he has now made manifest, the seed of life that he has raised out of the grave of death.

But he that reproaches and speaks evil of this light (who will neither enter in himself, nor allow others), he is far from receiving the blessing or blessedness of this seed. Such a man grows up in the wrong nature and spirit, the spirit whose end is to be burned along with all that is in union with it and grows up from it. Therefore, come out from that spirit; come out of that dark mind and nature which never saw, nor ever can see the truth, but sets up opinions and appearances of things instead of it. Come receive the anointing which is given with and in the seed, which is raised in some, and visited in many, in this day of the Lord's love and tender mercy. Come to Him to whom the living, the sensible, the redeemed sing praises, and on whom they wait for the further manifesting of his power and glory in them daily more and more.

Now friends, if you will know aright, or believe aright, you must know and believe in him who was with the Father before the world was, who was the Savior, the Jesus, the Christ, from everlasting. For what makes him so? Is it not the power of salvation in him? His taking up a body made no alteration in him, added nothing to him; only it was necessary that he should take it up to fulfill the will of God in it, and to offer it up as a sacrifice in his own life and Spirit to the Father. This we firmly believe! And yet we cannot help but say further that the virtue, the value, the worth, the excellency of what was done by him in the body was not *of* the body, but it was in him before time, in time, and will be after time, and forever. Yes, it is he to whom the name Jesus and Christ did rightly belong before he took up the body. And he put forth in the body the saving virtue which he had before, which belonged to the nature, to the anointing in him, whether he had ever saved any with it or not. And this virtue, this life, this Spirit, this nature of his, is the food, the righteousness, the garment of life and salvation, which he (through the death of the body) made and prepared a living way for the soul to come to, to feed on, and be clothed with.

I can hardly stop speaking of these things for your sakes, that through my words you might come to feel that which is able to give you the holy understanding. Oh that you might come to the true sense and experience of the truth itself, and might see who has blinded you, and how he has blinded you, and fed you with husks and dry food, instead of that which has the true living sap in it. But while you see and judge in that which is wrong, you must of necessity judge amiss both of yourselves and others. You cannot help but judge wrongly the truth itself, and the words spoken concerning it (either formerly or now). And in this way you expose and bring yourselves under the righteous judgment of the truth itself, even of the Son, and the light of his day, which has power from the Father to judge all false appearances, deceits, and deceivers.

Rejecting the Inward Appearance of Christ

It has pleased the Lord, as he manifested his Christ gloriously before the apostasy, so to manifest him so again. For he was not only born (in the flesh) of the virgin Mary; but he was also born in the Spirit of the woman clothed with the Sun, which had the moon under her feet, and on her head a crown of twelve stars. She also brought forth the man-child, who was to rule all nations with a rod of iron. Rev. 12.

Now of this appearance and return of the Lord Jesus Christ, and of the fresh bringing-forth of his life and power in his body, the church, there are many witnesses who have seen, felt, and tasted thereof, with the eyes and senses which are of God, and of the new birth. And of this, in the love and goodwill of God, and from the drawings and requirings of his Spirit, they bear witness to others that they also might come to see the glory and brightness of his day, and rejoice therein. For indeed it is a glorious day inwardly in Spirit to those that are made alive and gathered to the living Shepherd and Bishop of the soul, by the eternal arm of his power. And happy is the eye that sees the things that they see, and the ear that hears what they hear, and the heart which understands the things which God has revealed in and unto them by his Spirit.

Glorious was the appearance of Christ in the flesh, but there were blocks in the way of the Jews so that they could not know, acknowledge, believe, and receive him. And glorious is the administration of his life in the Spirit in this day of his power, but there are now also blocks lying in the way of those to whom he is sent, which cause them to stumble and not give up to him or let him in. But blessed was he who was not offended at Christ then, and blessed is he who is not offended at him now. For he that is offended at him who is life, and gives life, and so stumbles at the present way by which God has chosen to give life, how shall he live? This is the cause that so many poor hearts lie mourning and groveling on the earth, groaning because of their sins, fearing because of the strength of the enemy and the corruptions of their own hearts which are continually ready to betray them into his hands. These do not know the one who has stretched out his arm, and has come in his power to deliver, but indeed are prejudiced against the way wherein he has and does deliver. Truly, they know not the voice that calls, "Come unto me; I am the resurrection and the life. He that believes in me shall receive my strength; and though he is ever so weak, shall become as David. And though he is ever so unclean, he shall find the waters that spring from my well to cleanse him, and nourish him to life everlasting."

How tenderly did Christ visit the Jews in the days of his flesh! How powerfully, and in the true authority of God, did he preach among them! What mighty works did he show! And yet they could not believe. Why so? The enemy had entered them with his temptations, had got something into their minds of a contrary nature so to keep out the sense, knowledge, and acknowledgment of him. So that when their hearts were even overcome with his power, and his sweet, precious doctrine, and were ready to yield that he was the Christ indeed, then the enemy raised up some argument or other to prejudice them against him and drive them back again from acknowledging or receiving him.

"This man is not of God," say some; "for he keeps not the Sabbath." He cannot be a prophet, say others, because "he is of Galilee, out of which no prophet arises." He "cannot" be Christ, says a third sort, because "we know where he is from; but when Christ comes, no man knows where he is from." He is not holy, strict, and zealous according to the law, say others; but a loose person, "a gluttonous man, and a wine-bibber, a friend of publicans and sinners." He does not teach his disciples to fast and pray, as the Pharisees did theirs, and John (who was generally looked upon as a prophet) did his. He justifies them in plucking the ears of corn on the Sabbath day, and thereby he encourages them to break it, rather than strictly to observe and keep it according to God's law. He is a "blasphemer," say some, "making himself equal with God." He reproaches the most strict and zealous men that we have, even our teachers and interpreters of the law and prophets, calling them "hypocrites, painted sepulchers, blind guides," etc., and pronounces woe upon woe against them. And those that are the children of Abraham he calls the children of the devil; and says: "He that commits sin is the servant of sin; but if the Son makes you free, you shall be free indeed." And if we will have life in us, we must believe in him, and eat his flesh, and drink his blood. (Did ever Moses or any of the prophets teach such doctrine?) Again he says: "If a man keeps my sayings, he shall never see death;" whereas Abraham and the prophets, who believed God and kept his sayings, are all dead. This made them even conclude that he had a devil. John 8:52. So how could they understand him when he said he was "the good Shepherd, and the door," etc., and "that all that ever came before him were thieves and robbers;" would they not look upon this as witnessing of himself, and endeavoring to set up himself? And when he said: "Verily, verily, before Abraham was, I am;" were they not ready to stone him for speaking a false and impossible thing (as it seemed to them), he being not yet fifty years old? And then for his miracles, having beforehand concluded that he was a bad man, a sinner, a breaker of the Sabbath, a blasphemer, a deceiver of the people, etc., how easy was it for them to harden themselves against them, and to infer that he wrought these things by the aid and assistance of the devil. Indeed many were the arguments (and some seemingly strong and unanswerable) which the wisdom and understanding in them formed against Christ, whereby they justified themselves in their refusal of him.

These things are past, and can be easily condemned by those who are now acting in the same spirit. The same spirit, under a new guise, still opposes truth in its present appearance and dispensation, and stirs men up to slight and blaspheme that holy name and power (by which they that believe are saved and sanctified).

Well, what shall I say to you? Oh that you could discern spirits! Oh that you could see what spirit you are of, and whom you serve, in opposing God's present dispensation of life! Oh that you could see how you read Scriptures outside of that light which wrote them, and bend them against him that wrote them! Thus you make yourselves wise and strong in a wrong wisdom and knowledge against the Lord, and against his Christ, whom he has set upon his holy hill of Zion, and who appears there (though you do not see it). For Zion is not now natural, or after the flesh (for the day is come, the shadows are gone). Rather, Zion is the holy hill of God in Spirit, upon which the heavenly Jerusalem was built, which is revealed, come down, and coming down from heaven, and many of the heavenly citizens dwell there already, and more are coming there to dwell. For even from the east, west, north, and south they shall be gathered to sit with Abraham, Isaac, and Jacob, in the kingdom which cannot be shaken. This kingdom was received by the Christians formerly (before the apostasy) and is now received again.

Christ Who Died at Jerusalem

We, who are commonly called Quakers, are a people whom the Lord has gathered out of wanderings, out of many professions, out of several scattered estates and conditions, and into a measure of the eternal rest where we have found that life, power, and manifestation of the eternal Spirit, with which we were never before distinctly acquainted. And now, having tasted of this, having known this, having felt this, and come to a real enjoyment of it (in some degree, according to our several measures), we could not possibly conceal this treasure. Rather, in the movings of his life and the power of the Spirit, we have been drawn to testify of it to them who are left behind, still groveling under the burden of corruption, and crying out because of the sin and bondage.

Now this we have often found: That our testimony has not been received in the same Spirit and love wherein it has gone forth. The enemy, by his subtlety, has raised up prejudices against us, as if we denied the Christ that died at Jerusalem; professing him only in words, but denying him in reality and substance.

To clear this matter, we have solemnly professed, in the sight of the Lord God, these two things:

First, that we do really in our hearts acknowledge that Christ who came in the fullness of time, in that prepared body, to do the Father's will (his coming into the world, doctrine, miracles, sufferings, death, resurrection, etc.), according as it is expressed in the letter of the Scriptures.

Secondly, that we acknowledge no other Christ than that, nor hold forth any other thing for Christ, besides him who then appeared, and was made manifest in flesh.

Now then, it should be inquired into by professors, what is the reason that their prejudices still remain concerning us. For certainly if they did know and acknowledge the same thing with us (in the Spirit, and in the power, life, and love which are of the truth), this prejudice and these hard thoughts could not remain. But if they themselves do not know Christ in the Spirit (but only according to a description in the letter), it is no wonder that they miss both the Spirit and the true intent and meaning of the letter.

And indeed the Lord has shown me in Spirit several times, that they themselves are guilty of that very charge which they cast upon us, even of denying that Christ which died at Jerusalem. For he that knows the words of Scripture according as he apprehends or conceives them in the reasonings of his mind, does not wait to have them revealed in the Spirit. Such a one sets up his own conceivings, reasonings, and imaginations, or an image in his mind concerning the things of the Spirit, but misses the thing itself.

Now, no man can in truth call Jesus the Lord except by the Spirit. However, any man that is somewhat serious, and weighs the Scriptures in the natural mind, may so learn to acknowledge his coming into the world, and that he is Lord and King, etc., and may thus call him Lord. Indeed such a man may kindle a great heat in his affections towards Christ (though without the life, without the Spirit), yet all this is but an image which man forms in his mind from his reading the Scriptures and from his own observations. But the true calling Jesus Lord is from the experience of his eternal virtue in the Spirit, and from finding the Scriptures being opened to him by the Spirit, and in a seed which is above the reason, comprehends the reason, and confounds and brings it to nothing.

Again, there is no true knowledge of Christ, no living

knowledge, no saving knowledge, no knowledge which has eternal virtue, except that which is received and retained in a measure of light given by God to the creature. Such knowledge is held in the faith which is a gift, in the grace which is supernatural and spiritual; whereas the reasoning part is but natural. And those who have received the spiritual understanding know it to be distinct from the natural. Moreover, we experientially find a very clear distinction between Scriptures searched out by the reasonings of the mind (and the practices drawn therefrom), and Scriptures opened by the Spirit, and felt in the life.

Now, professors generally have not received their knowledge of Christ from the Spirit, or from Scriptures opened in the Spirit (and so do not know the thing itself, but only a description of the thing which man's reasoning part may drink in from the letter of the Scriptures). This is manifest in that they are not able (in spirit and understanding) to distinguish the thing itself from the garment wherewith it was clothed, though the Scriptures are very clear in this. Speak of Christ according to a relation of the letter, and there they can say something. But if you speak of the substance, of the very spirit of the thing, there they stutter and stammer and show plainly that they know not what it is.

Now the Scriptures do expressly distinguish between Christ and the garment which he wore; between the one that came and the body in which he came; between the substance which was veiled, and the veil which veiled it. "Lo! I come; a body you have prepared me." There is plainly he, and the body in which he came. There was the outward vessel, and the inward life. This life we certainly know, and can never call the bodily garment Christ, but rather that which appeared and dwelt in the body. Now if you indeed know the Christ of God, tell us plainly what that is which appeared in the body, and whether that was not the Christ before it took up the body, after it took up the body, and forever.

O friends! Look to your knowledge of Christ, and to your faith and knowledge of the Scriptures, and to your prayers also! For it is easy missing the living substance in all these, and meeting with only a shadow. The shadow may please the earthly part, and make a great show in the natural understanding and affections, but it does not satisfy the soul that is born after the Spirit, which still cries out (where the soul is awakened) after truth, substance, life, virtue from God's Spirit.

A Faithful Guide to the Path of Truth

There must be something let down from God into a man's heart to change his heart and redeem it to God, or he cannot be saved. He must receive a seed, be born of a new and incorruptible seed, or he cannot be renewed from his corrupt nature and state. He must be born of water and God's Spirit, or he cannot enter into God's kingdom.

Now this is the true religion: namely, to experience and be subject to that power which redeems to God and breaks the power of the wicked one in the heart, first casting him out, and then taking possession of the vessel and filling it with the holy treasure.

Question: But how may a man meet with such a thing as this?

Answer: The Scripture, which gives a faithful testimony concerning the truth, says that Christ, the Word of faith which the apostles preached, is near. Therefore, a man need not say, 'Who shall go up or down to fetch it?' For, "The word

is very near you, in your mouth, and in your heart." This is
that Word which reconciles to God, cutting down and slaying
the enmity by the power of the cross, and bringing up the
seed.

Question: But how shall I know and receive this?

Answer: There is a seed given to the heart which is contrary
to sin, which discovers sin, which witnesses against sin, and
is drawing the mind away from it, furnishing those with a
new and holy ability who wait upon the Lord in it. Now he
that minds this seed, hearkens to it, turns from what it shows
to be evil (in its pure, unerring light), follows what it shows
to be good (in the will, strength, and ability which is of it), this
one truly receives it. And then, by waiting upon it, and
becoming daily subject to it, he shall grow up in it, increase in
the knowledge of it and acquaintance with it, and receive of it
daily more and more. Thus the man whose way was vile,
whose heart was formed in wickedness, filled with corruption, and daily bringing forth sin and fruits unto death, shall
find these things (by the pure light and holy instructions of
life) daily purged out of him. And he shall find Christ formed
in him, and the holy fruits of righteousness brought forth
through his vessel by the power and Spirit of Christ, to the
glory of God the Father.

And then, being in Christ, being in the seed of his life and
acting therein, there is peace in the soul, rest from its
enemies and God's judgments, and acceptance with the
Father in what the soul thus is and works.

Then the world will persecute and hate exceedingly,
because this soul, who thus submits to God, and is thus
changed by him, is not of the world, but of the Father, who
begat it in Christ, and formed it in his image and likeness.

But let him that once puts his hand to the plow (beginning to feel something of God, and becoming subject unto it, and tasting of the peace and pureness of it) never look back to the world, nor mind the temptations and oppositions he will meet with from that nature and spirit, either in himself or others. For if he does, he will never be able to travel on, but rather will consult with flesh and blood, and so return back into Egypt. There he will lose the crown which is laid up for those who pass on through the wilderness, through the trials, through the temptations and various exercises, to their journey's end.

This is the path of life in brief, and happy is he who experiences the one who guides into it, and faithfully follows him therein unto the end. But there is another question that springs up in my heart, which is this:

Question: How may a man come to have his sins washed away by the blood of Christ?

Answer: By coming into the light, and walking in the light which discovers the blood, and wherein alone it is sprinkled by God, and felt by the soul; there he may receive the cleansing which is by it. This is according to the testimony of Scripture; 1 John 1:7, "If we walk in the light, as he is in the light, we have fellowship one with another, and the blood of Jesus Christ, his Son, cleanses us from all sin." By the light the darkness is dispelled, and in the light the corruption and filth is washed away by the blood, and the soul (mind and conscience) is cleansed from it.

"This then is the message that we have heard of him, and declare unto you, that God is light, and in him is no darkness at all." ver. 5. What then? Then those who will know God, and walk with God, must (by the virtue of his truth) be turned from darkness to light, and from the power of Satan unto God, as in Acts 26:18. And in that light he shall meet with the Father, and with his Son Jesus Christ, and have fellowship with them, ver. 3, and shall be washed (both with the water and with the blood) and kept clean and pure thereby in the sight of God.

Question: But how shall I come into the light, and how may I walk therein?

Answer: Christ is the light. He is the light of the world, the light of men, the light of life. You need not say in your heart, "Who shall go up to heaven, or down into the deep, for him?" For he is near, in your mouth, and in your heart. This is the word of faith, which you are to believe in, love, and obey, that in the love, faith, and obedience thereof, your heart may be circumcised, and you may live. This is the gospel of our salvation, even this Christ, this word, this light, this life, which redeems from sin, which destroys the destroyer, and sets the soul free to serve and live to the Lord. This was the message the apostles had to deliver in their day, as in Rom. 10:8. And this was Moses' message too, when he spoke concerning the new covenant. For Moses did not only deliver the old covenant, but he also spoke concerning the new, even another covenant than that of Mount Horeb. Deut. 29:1. And the word of this other covenant was not the law written in tables of stone, but the word near in the mouth and heart. chap. 30:14.

Now, every man that will be sanctified, and inherit God's kingdom, must be born of the will of God. He must deny his own will (as Christ did, saying, "Not my will, but yours be done"); that will must be crucified. He must suffer in the flesh, die to the flesh, and live in and to the holy nature and

Spirit of God. By hearing the word that is near in the mouth and heart, and becoming subject to it, a man comes to be born of the pure will. This cuts down his own will day by day, and brings up the will and nature of God in him, through which he is changed and sanctified, and becomes a new creature. For the old creature is made up of the old understanding and will; but the new creature is made up of the new.

"How shall a young man cleanse his way? By taking heed according to your word," said David. What word was that? Was it the word of the old covenant, or the word near in the mouth and heart? And "your word," says he, "is a lantern to my feet, and a light to my path." What word was that, the word of the first covenant, or the word of the second? "The law of the Lord is perfect, converting the soul." What law is that? "The testimony of the Lord is sure, making wise the simple." What testimony is that? "The statutes of the Lord are right, rejoicing the heart." What statutes are they? (Were not the statutes of the old covenant heavy and burdensome?) "The commandment of the Lord is pure, enlightening the eyes." What commandment is that? Oh that men could read! Oh that men could see the thing which is pure, and makes pure; which is righteous, and makes righteous! After men have seen the thing, there is a great way to travel to it; but how far off are they who do not so much as see it, but are in the darkness and prejudices of that nature and spirit which is contrary to it!

Now if the Lord, in his tender mercy and love to your soul, brings you to a sense of this thing, and you begin to feel this precious, searching word discovering any evil to you, either in your heart or ways, oh do not dispute! Do not reason against it! Rather bless the discoverer, bow to the Son, become obedient immediately, faithfully following the

Lamb therein, lest he remove his light from you, and allow darkness and the disputing wisdom to overtake you.

Christ is not of the world, and he leads out of the world, out of its vanities, ways, customs, fashions, etc. A man cannot serve Christ and the world. Can any man be born of the Father, be begotten by him out of the spirit of the world, and yet live in that, walk in that, which is not of the Father? Can a man be born of God and yet still live in that which is of the world, which came from the worldly part, is of the worldly part, nourishes and pleases the worldly part in man, but pleases not the Father? Can that man who is not of the world, but truly of the Father, do anything that upholds the lust of the flesh, the lust of the eyes, or the pride of life, either in himself or others? Does not the Spirit of the Lord, where it is hearkened to, draw out of these, and out of all things which are of these? Therefore, consider well what it will cost, and how hard it is to follow Christ, so that you who desire to be the Lord's may receive help and strength from him to be faithful, that in his strength you may overcome all that stands between you and life.

Some Assertions Concerning the Seed and Way of Life

1. That it is a great and hard matter to come into a capacity of knowing and receiving the truth.

It is no hard matter to take up any religion that a man finds in the world. To read Scriptures and believe what is found related there (according to man's understanding of them); to believe that he has the light and help of the Spirit in his reading and understanding; to apply himself also to prac-tice and observe what he believes required; and to aim at holiness, etc.—this is no hard matter. Every man that is serious, and who seeks religion of any kind, may go this far. But all of this administers not the true capacity of knowing and receiving the truth, and he that desires to find it must go further than this.

2. *That which gives the true capacity is a seed of life from God, and there alone and nowhere else, can man meet with it and receive the truth.*

This seed is the seed of the kingdom, or heavenly leaven, with which the mind must be in some measure leavened, before it can come into a true capacity of understanding and receiving the truth. And in this leaven it must abide and grow up, if it is to abide and grow in the true knowledge.

3. *That from this seed, and in this seed, are all things given.*

Not only are the true light and knowledge of the Lord Jesus Christ given and received in this seed; but also the true faith, the true love, the true sanctification, the true justification, the true peace, the true joy, etc. And whatever of these is not received and held here, is not of the truth, but a garment of man's own forming, and not the covering of the Spirit.

4. *That the Spirit himself sows this seed, and is received in this seed.*

He that receives this seed, and is born of this seed, receives and is born of the Spirit. He that receives it not, nor is born of it, neither has received nor is born of the Spirit, but remains in imagination and self-conceit about the things of

God, and is not in the truth as it is in Jesus.

5. That in this seed the new covenant is made with the soul and entered into.

He that receives this seed from the hand of God, receives life, and enters into the covenant of life, and feels the pure fear wherein God cleanses the heart, and whereby he keeps the heart clean. Here the soul feels the laws of God daily written by the finger of God's Spirit, and feels the power and sense of the Spirit to teach and cause obedience. Thus the yoke, which is hard to the transgressing nature (being alienated from the life and power), is easy (and I may say natural) to him that is born of this nature. For being dead with Christ, and risen with Christ, and changed into the nature of Christ (by the seed which is of him), he can say as Christ did (by the same power and Spirit of Christ which works therein): "Lo, I come; it is my food and drink, yes, my great delight, to do your will, O God! Indeed, your law is written in the midst of my heart!"

6. Among those who are gathered into this seed, and abide in the sense, light, and life of this seed, there is great love and unity.

They are of one mind, of one heart, of one soul, of one spirit, of one life, gathered into one demonstration of truth. And there is no jarring, no doubting, no dissenting, etc. All this is out in the world, in the earthly wisdom, in the earthly professions and walkings; but it is excluded from the seed of truth, and from those that are gathered into and abide therein.

7. That all who are not gathered into, nor walk or live in this seed, they are yet in the darkness and err from the pure power of God.

These stand and walk in slippery places; and though their way may seem very right, and their estate and condition sure (with regard to God) in their own eyes and judgment, yet it is not really so; but they are in but a dream concerning the truth, and not in the truth itself. And however strange such an affirmation concerning them may seem to them at present, yet they shall certainly feel it to be so afterward, when the Lord by his powerful voice and bright appearance of his Spirit awakens them. For many things pass for truth now with men in the dark, which things will vanish like smoke before the light of the day. And then, only that which is truth indeed shall have the glory and praise of being accounted so. And what then will become of those who mistook the truth, and are not clothed with the pure wedding garment (the spotless life and righteousness of the Son)?

8. That to those who see in the light of this seed, the mountain of the Lord's house is discovered.

Those who abide and grow up in the mountain of the Lord's house know and experience it established above all mountains, and exalted above all hills—all earthly knowledge, earthly religions, earthly ways, earthly worships, earthly spirits and minds, etc. All of these, in their greatest exaltations and glory, are far beneath it. And on this mountain is the feast of fat things and wines well refined, even the fruit of the vine which makes glad and refreshes the very heart of God. For the Father, and the Son, and the Spirit are here revealed, in the holy house and tabernacle which are built here. And here they make their feast, bringing forth the riches of their nature, spirit, and precious life, on which they feed with the soul, and give unto the soul favor and ability to feed with them. For in this food there is the life, strength, righteousness, and joy of the kingdom given forth and received.

9. That it is this very seed in the heart which discovers iniq-uity, reproves it, witnesses against it, and strives with the mind to turn it from it, and to wait for life and power from on high.

In that seed is the divine nature, even the nature of God's Spirit, which was always against sin, and ever will be so. In all its appearances it testifies against it, and in love to the creature strives to convince it of that which is contrary to God, and to draw it to that strength and divine virtue which stops it, beats it back, and works it out of the mind and nature of the creature. For there is no salvation but by the cross and yoke of our Lord Jesus Christ. In that cross is the power to crucify the affections and lusts which lead into sin and death, and will not cease to tempt and lead aside till the soul be gathered into unity with that which is contrary to them. So that this is the main thing in religion: even to know Christ revealed in the soul as a standard against corruption, and to be gathered under his banner, which is the cross.

10. That the true and certain way of knowledge of the things of God is in the faith and obedience of this seed.

It is not by reasoning and considering things in the mind (after the manner of men) that a man comes to know spiritual things; but only as they are spiritually revealed by God,

and partake of these blessings from him?

Answer: In faith. This is what all his outward healings did signify, being dispensed according to faith. ("If you will believe, you shall see the glory of God. Your faith has made you whole. O woman, great is your faith! Be it unto you according to your faith, etc.") And in this same way all his inward healings are bestowed upon and received by the soul; that is, in the faith.

Question: But how did they come to have faith? Or how does any man have faith in the redeeming power?

Answer: It is bestowed upon them by God, in the sense which is from him. His Word goes forth from his mouth, and there is a witness of him in the heart. Now, in reaching to the witness, the Word immediately brings into a true sense,[1] and in that sense begets faith. And so this Word, being mixed with faith (which is of its own begetting) in them that hear it, begins the work of life and redemption in that heart where it is not yet begun, or carries it on in that heart wherein it is already begun. Thus faith has a work, a work from the begin - ning of the heart's turning to God even to the end. And he that abides in the faith till the end finds the work accom - plished.

Objection: But this faith is bestowed on only a few whom God has elected, and not on all men.

Answer: God has sent his gospel to be preached to every creature, and his Word is able to reach the witness, and work this sense or awareness in every creature. And in whomso-

---

[1] Or awareness, recognition, perception.

ever there is a sense wrought, as they listen to God in that sense, God works faith in them. And waiting on the Word, hearkening to the Word, and staying their minds there on the Lord, he will speak peace to them, and keep them in peace, daily removing them more and more out of the reach and power of that which troubles them.

Question: Does the new covenant lay all upon God, and require nothing of the creature? Or is there something required by God of the creature in the new covenant?

Answer: Consider well: In the new covenant, God requires of the creature what he also gives. Does he not require the faith, and the exercising of that faith, which he himself works and gives from the power and demonstration of his truth to the soul? The new covenant requires more of the creature than the old ever did; but it requires it not of the creature as he is weak in the fallen state, but as he is taught, strengthened, and enabled to walk with God in and by the power of the covenant. Indeed, all manner of holiness and righteousness of heart, life, and conduct is required in and by the new covenant. For even as the Lord works out of all things in the creature, so the creature works out all thereby in the Lord, according to that well known scripture, "work out your own salvation with fear and trembling: for it is God which works in you, both to will and to do of his good pleasure." And though the creature is able to do nothing that is good of itself, yet being grown up into the life and ability which is of God, he is able to do all things through Christ that strengthens him.

Question: But why is it said that Christ was anointed to preach the gospel to the poor, the meek, the broken-hearted, the captives, the bound in prison, and the mourners? Did not God give his Son in love to all? Was he not made a ransom and propitiation for all? Was he not anointed to preach the gospel to all? Why is it then here limited and restrained to some?

Answer: It is true, God has a general regard for all mankind in the gift and anointing of his Son. Even so, there are some who are in a better capacity to receive, that is, those already in a sense of the lack of him, and panting and longing after him. Indeed, there are some who are grievously sick in soul, and deeply wounded in spirit, who, in the sadness and misery of their condition, cry aloud for the help of the physician. Now the eye and heart of the Lord is more especially towards these; and so he bid his prophets to be instructing and comforting these concerning the salvation, the healing, the oil of gladness, and the Messiah to come. And when he came, he was sent up and down to seek these out, to keep company with these, to help and relieve these, having been given the tongue of the learned, to speak a word in season to these weary, distressed ones. These are not like the common, rough, unhewn, knotty, rugged earth, but are like earth prepared for the seed, and so they easily and naturally receive it.

The gospel is indeed preached to others at a distance; which, it is true, they may receive if they will hearken to it, and wait for it, and part with what must first be parted with. But such as these have a great distance to travel. However, the weak, desperate, mourning, captives, etc., these are near the kingdom, near that which opens and lets in life. These are quickly reached, melted, and brought into the sense in which (with joy) they receive the faith, and with the faith, the power also, which brings righteousness and salvation to their souls. Though the enemy is exceedingly busy with these also, to darken, disturb, and bow them down, that he might still keep them in the doubts, fears, chains and fetters, in the prison house, away from the liberty and healing which the word of the anointing brings.

Now mind: God is real towards all; he desires the life and salvation of all, and not the destruction of any one soul that he ever created. It is unnatural to him. And in the way that he holds forth his salvation, he stands ready to meet any man. Who is it that he does not draw? And who is it that may not come in the drawing? Is not his word a hammer? And who can it not break? Is it not fire? And whose corruption can it not burn up? Is it not water, wine, and blood? And who can it not wash and nourish? Therefore, let no man think to lay the blame upon God because of their perishing; for in this he will be deceived, and God will prove true. For God has said, "Man's destruction is of himself," and so every man is a liar who lays any blame on him for not giving further assistance with his power. Neither let man blame God for hardening him; for God hardens no man except for him who first refuses and grieves the power and love which would melt and soften him. It is true—we are the clay, and God the potter, and may not the potter make what vessels he will of his clay? This parable came from the Spirit of the Lord to Israel of old, but what use did the Lord make of it? Did he say to them, 'Do whatever you will; some of you I will cast off, and to others of you I will show mercy; for I have determined so?' No, not so! But rather, 'I have this power over you; therefore do not provoke me.' (Read Jer. 18.)

Was not God exceedingly tender to his outward people, in that outward covenant? Did he ever give them up to pain and sufferings without great provocations on their parts? "He does not afflict willingly, nor grieve the children of men."

And the Spirit of the Lord never failed to do what was his part, in turning them from iniquity towards the Lord in that covenant.

There is something that now springs up in my heart, which may perhaps open this thing further to the minds of some.

Cain was the first wicked man that we read of, and yet how tender was God towards him, even he that sacrificed not after the Spirit, but after the flesh, and slew his brother Abel! Now, can any man lay Cain's wickedness either upon the will, or upon the decree and counsel of God? Might he not have done well? Might he not have sacrificed to God in the faith, as well as his brother Abel? And if he had done well, and offered in the faith, would he not have found forgiveness and acceptance with the Lord? God accepts no man's person; God rejects no man's person. But there is a seed he has chosen, and to gather man into this seed is his delight and his work. And it is the delight, nature, and work of the other spirit to scatter men away from this seed.

Now, it is in this seed that he does accept, and not out of it. Yes, in this seed shall all the families of the earth be blessed, as they are gathered into and abide in it. And this seed is a word near in the mouth and heart, both of Jew and Gentile. And when it is hearkened to, this seed writes the law of the Spirit of life in the heart of both Jew and Gentile. And as they become sons, so the Spirit of the Father is poured out upon them, even the Spirit of adoption, which cries *Abba, Father*, in both Jew and Gentile.

Now, the Lord's mercy endures forever towards the seed of the righteous, and his justice and indignation forever towards the seed of the evil-doer. And man (simply considered) is not either of these; but only as he is gathered into, and brought forth in the root and spirit of either of these.

Now, every man has a day for the life of his soul; and power and mercy is near him, to help him to travel from death to life. Happy is he who is taught of God to make use of it.

Concerning Election and Reprobation

And let not men puzzle themselves about the mystery of *election and reprobation*, which cannot be understood by those who are outside of the thing wherein it is made manifest. Let me say only this at present: Pharaoh and Israel, Esau and Jacob, Ishmael and Isaac, etc., these were parables signifying something inward. What was Pharaoh? Was he not the oppressor of God's Israel? What was Esau? Was he not the first birth, which sold the birth-right and inheritance? What was Ishmael? Was he not the birth after the flesh? These are rejected, and cast off by God forever; and the spiritual Israel, the spiritual Jacob, the spiritual Isaac, are accepted.

Shall I speak of this thing yet more plainly? It is not the creature which is rejected by its Maker; but something in the creature, and the creature in that thing. Nor is it the creature (simply) which is elected; but something[2] in the creature, and the creature in that thing. Now, as any man comes into that thing, the election is begun in him; and as any man abides in that, he abides in the election; and as that thing is made sure to any man, his calling and election are made sure to him. But as any man departs from that, he departs from the election into the reprobation; and if he goes on in that, into the full impenitency and hardness, he will forever miss the election. Thus the reprobation, and a sealing up in condemnation, will be made sure to him. For God is no respecter of

---

[2] He means Christ, the chosen One.

persons; but everywhere, he that receives his holy seed, and therein works righteousness, is accepted of him. And he that receives the wicked seed, and therein works wickedness and unrighteousness, is with that seed rejected.

Objection: But I thought man and his works had been wholly excluded by the covenant of grace; but this seems to take both into consideration.

Answer: Man is wholly excluded from the covenant of grace as in himself, as he stands in himself, and in his own ability, apart from the newness of life and ability which is of the new covenant. But he is not excluded as he is renewed, and receives a new being, life, virtue, and ability, in the new covenant. Here much is required of him; and whatever he does in this new life is owned, acknowledged, and accepted by God. Here the true Jew has praise of God. Rom 2:29. He is commended for his faith, and for his obedience in the faith. He is commended for loving the Lord his God with all his heart, and his neighbor as himself, and for his washing his garments in the blood of the Lamb, and keeping them clean in the same blood, while others defile theirs. He is commended for his merciful nature and actions to Christ in his members, while others are rough and cruel, and for his watching against snares and temptations, while others are running into them. Yes, and for his denying and turning from all ungodliness and worldly lusts, even of the flesh, eyes, and pride of life; all of which are not of the Father, but of the spirit of the world. So that (mark well), though man is excluded in his corrupt nature and state, yet not the new man, not man in the regeneration. But man must be regener-ated, and thus must enter into the covenant of life, and abide and be found in the covenant of life, in the nature, in the righteousness, in the holiness, and in the power thereof, if ever God will own him.

Now, the difference in every man is by the grace, and not of himself; for he can do nothing that is good, as of himself, but only by the grace, which alone is able to work that which is good in him, and to cause him to work in it. Thus, as the grace reaches to him, draws him, giving life and causing him (in the virtue, life, and obedience that come from grace) to answer the grace; so does the work of grace go on in him. So there is condemnation to him who does not answer the grace; and there is justification and praise to him who does answer the grace. Yet this whole ability arises not from himself, but from the grace. And therefore, they who are justified, sanctified, and crowned by the grace, do rightly cast their crowns at the feet of the Lamb at the throne of grace, giving honor and glory to him who is worthy, and to his grace which has wrought all in them.

Now, if any man would know this thing truly and certainly, let him not run into disputes of the mind and brain, but come to a heart experience. Have you ever found the work of God's grace in your heart? Have you found your heart, at any time, believing and obeying in and through the strength of grace? Have you found your heart, at another time, negligent of or rebellious against the grace? When you were rebellious, were you not condemned? And when you did believe and obey, to whom did the honor belong—to you, or to the grace? Can you answer this? Well, as it is in you, so is the case between godly and wicked men. As there was a difference between when you obeyed the grace and when you disobeyed it, so is the difference between the unregenerate and regenerate man. When you did not obey, that which called for obedience condemned you; so it does them. When you obeyed, you did sensibly feel the praise was not yours, but rather belonged to the grace which wrought in you; so it is also in the regenerate man, in whom the Lord works by his grace, and who works out his salvation through him, making his calling and election sure. Leave your brain knowledge, and come to a true sense (where the mysteries of God are made manifest), and this will soon be easy and clear to you. But these things were never intended by God to be found out by man's disputing wisdom. For God, who gives the knowledge, hides them from that part, and gives them to the innocent, simple birth of his own Spirit.

Objection: But when the Father draws, can any man resist or hold off? Does not the power of the Lord make any man willing, towards whom he exercises his power?

Answer: The power of the Lord is great, and has dominion over all evil spirits that can tempt, and over all the corruption, backsliding, and withdrawing of the heart. But the Father does not save man by such an absolute act of his power. Rather, the power of the Lord works in and according to the way that he has appointed. And in this way the devil has liberty and power to tempt from, oppose, and resist the word of God. And they that hearken to him, and enter into the temptation and snare which he lays, let his power in upon them, and withdraw from the virtue, operation, and strength of the power of God. Yet for all this, the Lord not only begins his work in man, but also carries it on in the day of his power, giving not only to will, but also to do, what is right and pleasing in his eyes. But still, this is in and according to his own way and covenant.

Objection: If God put forth his power to save, and the devil interrupts and stops his work, then it seems that the devil is stronger than God. Is the devil stronger than God? If he is not, how can he resist and withstand him in the work of his power?

Answer: No, the devil is not stronger than God; though he is very strong. But if the heart lets in the enemy, grieves the Spirit, beats back his power in the way wherein it has appointed to work, then the devil may be more prevalent with him than the power of God. But in those that believe, and become obedient and subject to the power of God, his power is far stronger in them to defend and carry on his work, than the power of the devil is to work against and hinder it.

There are objections also relating to free-will, and falling from grace, which stick much in the spirits of many, and they cannot get over them. But it has pleased the Lord to clear up these things to us, and to satisfy our hearts concerning them, so that with us there is no difficulty or doubt about them.

With regard to free will: We know, from God, that man in his fallen state is spiritually dead, and has no free will to do good, but his understanding and will are both darkened and captivated by the enemy. However, in Christ there is freedom, and in his word there is power and life. And when this word reaches to the heart and loosens the chains of the enemy, it begets not only a freedom of mind towards good, but an inclination, desire, and breathing after it. Thus the Father draws, and thus the soul (feeling the drawing) answers in some measure; and the soul, coming to him in this way, is welcomed by Christ and accepted of the Father. But for all this, the enemy will tempt this soul, and the soul may hearken to, let in, and enter into the temptation, and so draw back from the plough to which it put its hand. "Now, if any man draws back, my soul shall have no pleasure in him," says the Lord. "And he that puts his hand to the plough and looks back, is not fit for the kingdom of heaven."

So concerning falling away: The Lord shows us what it is that is apt to fall, and what it is that cannot fall. Christ cannot fall; and that which is gathered into him, and stands and abides in him (so partaking of his preservation), cannot fall. There is no breaking in upon that power which preserves in the way that it has appointed. But there is a running and perishing out of the way. Outside the limits of the covenant, the preservation and power of the covenant is not witnessed. But in coming to Christ in the drawings of the Father, in the sense and faith which he begets, and abiding with the one that drew him, in the sense and faith which he daily and freshly begets anew (for he renews covenant and mercy daily, and keeps covenant and mercy forever) in this is the power and preservation felt. In this the Father's hand encompasses the soul, out of which none can pluck it. Now he that feels and experiences these things every day, that sees and feels daily how it is that he can fall, and how he cannot fall, how he meets with the preservation, and how he misses the preservation, how he abides in the pure power (which is the boundaries of this holy covenant), and how he wanders out of this power into the boundaries of another covenant, spirit, and power, this one knows these things indeed. But other men (who are not experienced in the thing itself) can only guess at them, striving to comprehend them in that part which God has shut out of them.

Now mind this parable with which I shall conclude. Though the natural and outwardly-visible sun be risen ever so high upon the earth, yet he that is naturally blind cannot see it, nor partake of its light. So also, though the spiritual Sun, the Sun of righteousness, the Sun of the inward world, be risen ever so high, and appear brightly in ever so many clouds, yet they that are spiritually blind cannot discern it, nor reap the benefits of his light, nor partake of the healing which is under his wings.

An Exhortation to the Desolate and Distressed

Now is the acceptable time; now is the day of salvation. Now is the life arisen, and now the light shines to guide out of the darkness and death, into the land of the living. Oh awake, you that sleep in the dust of the earth! Arise up from among the dead, and Christ shall give you light to walk along in the path of the living. Come to him whom the Father has sealed, to him who is life, and who gives life freely to all that come. Yes, he gives abundantly to those that wait upon him and walk faithfully in his covenant. Oh therefore, come into covenant with him! Mind the words of his lips, which beget a true sense, and in that sense his life stirs; and in the stirrings of his life the drawings of the Father are felt.

Hearken to the little movings and stirrings in you after that which is eternal. For he will not quench any desire which is truly after him (it is his nature to cherish it). And people, mind this (it is a true testimony): The door of life is now so opened by him who has the key and power, that whoever will, may enter. And as for you afflicted mourners who are seeking the way to Zion, bewailing the absence of your beloved in whose presence is life and redemption, resurrection from the dead, and victory over sin—what shall I say to you? Hear the joyful news: The apostasy is ended. Now, I do not say the apostasy is generally ended. No, no; there are many woes, plagues, judgments, and terrible thunders to come upon persons and nations before they feel it ended. But it is ended in some vessels which are upon the earth. The man of sin, that wicked one, the son of perdition, has been discovered by the Spirit of the Lord. He has been chased, consumed, and destroyed by the breath of his mouth, and by the brightness of his appearance in some. Yes, the church has come out of the wilderness, and the man-child is come along with her; for she is not come without her beloved, but rather leaning upon her beloved. And he is known to her as the one who rules with his golden scepter, and with his iron rod that batters down the corrupt, selfish, stubborn, earthly spirit, and raises up that which is meek, tender, lowly, bowed down and oppressed.

Now, as Christ said, when preaching in the days of his flesh, "This day is this scripture fulfilled in your ears." Luke 4:21. Was it not then fulfilled outwardly among the outward Jews? Were there any sick, or weak, or blind, or lame, or lepers, or possessed with devils, whom Christ was not ready to cure? And did he not go about doing good, and seeking them out to cure them? Even so it is now, in the Spirit and power of the Lord, among the spiritual Jews! "This day is this scripture spiritually fulfilled in your ears." Yes, what he did then outwardly is known in spirit to be done among you inwardly and spiritually. How many that were before blind do now see? How many that were before deaf do now hear? Those who were formerly lame do now walk, the leprous are now cleansed, the dead are now raised, the dumb do now speak. And the poor, the empty, the naked, are now clothed and filled with the riches and treasures of the everlasting kingdom. May it not be truly said, by many poor, distressed hearts, that the wilderness and solitary place is now glad? And that which once was parched with drought and barren-ness now feels the living springs, and the breaking forth of the pure, clear river of life, the streams of which make glad the city of God? Indeed, some may now say, "Where now is the envious, cruel, dragon-like nature?" Is there not a new creation? Is there not a new heaven and a new earth, and are not all things become new therein? Are not the old things of the night and of the darkness passed away, and all things become new in this day which the Lord has made in the hearts which have received and been subject to his light?

And now, what hinders you from lifting up your heads, and seeing the coming of the Son of man in the clouds wherein he comes, and partaking of the redemption, virtue, and power of his appearance? What are the clouds wherein he comes? Is his coming outward? Or are the clouds outward? Or is his coming inward and spiritual in ten thou-sands of his saints? Jude 1:14.[3] Did not Enoch see that he was to come in this way to judge the world? Does he not "come to be glorified in his saints"? 2 Thes. 1:10. Are not they to judge the world—they in him, he in them? Oh read aright; read with the Spirit and with his understanding! Then the truth of the letter will be manifest and shine in you. There is nothing that stands in your way but the lack of a spiritual eye to see his spiritual appearance in others (and so to wait for it in yourselves), even the eye of faith, which (as the Lord opens it) sees the invisible power and glory.

Now, this I have to say to you, in true sense and under-standing: Come down to the Gentile's light, come down to that which God has dispensed to the Gentile, as well as to the Jew—which is the word (or commandment) near in the mouth and heart. This word has been the lowest of all, despised by all, and yet it is in the heart of God to exalt over all, for it is above all. This is that which man ran from in the garden when the veil came over him. It is this which all the

---

[3] Most translations render this passage "Behold, the Lord comes *with* ten thousand of his saints." But the word in the original Greek is *in* and not *with*.

shadows of the law were to point out and signify. And as man is brought again to this, life springs in him, and the powerful redemption of the eternal word is witnessed by him. Yes, he that hears the voice of this, though he were ever so dead in trespasses and sins, shall feel life spring in him, and the covenant of life inwardly revealed. And this is the one truth, the one pure, eternal word and way to the Father, which was from the beginning, and remains the same unto the end. This is the only door, at which all have entered into life, at which all do still enter, and there is no other. Blessed forever is he who has made it so manifest and plain in this our day; and blessed are they that see it and enter into life at it!

A Visit of Tender and Upright Love

The main thing in true religion is to receive a seed of life from God, whereby the mind may be changed, and the heart made able to understand the mysteries of his kingdom, and to see and walk in the way of life. And this is the travail of the souls of the righteous—that they may abide, grow up, and walk with the Lord in this seed; and that others also, who breathe after him, may be gathered into, and feel the virtue of, the same seed.

But there is one that stands in the way to hinder this work of the Lord, who, with great subtlety, strives to keep souls in captivity, and to prejudice them against the precious living appearances of the redeeming power of the Lord.

One great way whereby he does this is by raising up in them a fear lest they should be deceived and betrayed, and then, instead of obtaining more, they lose the little of God which they have. With this fear I was exercised a long while. When life stirred in my heart, then this fear was raised in me, so that I dared not believe what I felt to be of God, even though it had a true touch of his quickening, warming, convincing, enlivening virtue in it.

Now, that this snare may be escaped by those who breathe after the Lord, oh let them wait, mourn, and cry to him, that he would write his pure fear in their hearts, and teach them when to fear, how to fear, and what to fear! And as this is brought forth in them, they shall see that they have more cause to fear their present state, than to fear that which (in the life-giving warmth and virtue of God) comes to make a change in their present state. Yes, then they shall see how the enemy now causes them to fear where there is nothing to fear, and keeps them from fearing that which all men should fear. And this indeed is the great thing that they should fear: that they should not hear the call of the Spirit of the Lord out of Babylon; and that they should not hear and mind the call of his Spirit unto Zion, the holy mount of God, towards which he leads his people in this day of the revelation and manifestation of his glorious love and power.

Oh therefore my friends, you that long after the Lord, you that desire to feel the power of his truth, wait for the seed of life from him to be revealed in you! Wait for the pure fear which is from the seed, that you may feel the Lord writing his fear, his pure, holy, preserving fear, in your hearts, so that you may know the way to him, and come and join to him in the seed, and never depart from him. The fear of the Lord arising from the seed of his life, will, without fail, effect this in you as you receive it from the Lord. But the other fear, the fear which the enemy begets, will not do it, but will be an obstacle in your way, till the Lord, by his holy power, removes it from you.

And now answer me one question uprightly, as in God's sight: Are you come to Zion, or are you at least traveling there rightly and truly? Have you ever known any of the travelers with whom you have been acquainted that could (in truth) say that they were come to Zion? The Christians, in the primitive times were come to Zion, and they were acquainted and dwelt with God and Christ there. These knew Jerusalem, the heavenly building, the city of the living God. Oh, where are you? Have you yet come out of Babylon? Do you yet know the wilderness, and the intricate passages therein, through which God alone can lead the soul? Oh, depart, depart from your present place (in the leadings of God's Spirit), unless you can say, in the true and unerring light, that you are at your rest, your soul's true rest, even the everlasting kingdom which cannot be shaken, which the primitive Christians received, and into which they found entrance.

And friends, let me tell you one thing further (for my heart is at this moment opened to you by the Lord). As the soul, in its travels, comes to Zion, the law of the Spirit of life in Christ Jesus is witnessed, which makes free from the law of sin and death. And then there is no more such a crying out because of the body of sin as there was before, but rather a blessing of him who has delivered, and daily does deliver from it. Yes, the body of sin is known and felt to be put off, and Christ put on in its stead. For, my friends, there are several states witnessed by the soul in its true and sensible travels towards the holy land. As for instance:

1. There is a state of Egyptian darkness and bondage, in which the power of death reigns and rules in the heart, subjecting it to sin and death. Here the soul is in the grave, and under death, captivity, and bondage, even in the midst of all its professions of religion and talk of God and Christ, and reading Scriptures, and observing ordinances and duties, etc.

2. There is a wilderness state, wherein the strength of captivity is somewhat broken, and the heart drawn to mind the leadings of life, and to follow after the Lord through the trials, through the preparations, through the several exercises, which the Lord sees good to exercise it with.

Here the mercy and goodness of the Lord is experienced, and also the deceitfulness and treachery of the heart. This is the place of humiliation and breaking, wherein the soul daily feels how unwilling and unaccustomed it is to the yoke, which must break the spirit, and subdue it to God. Here the Lord shows the soul what its heart is, that he might humble it, and do it good in the latter end. Here the very law of God appears weak, because of the strength of the flesh, which is not yet subdued. Now, here is mourning, and groaning, and crying to the Lord night and day, both because of the violence and multitude of the enemies, and because of the rebellion, distrust, and unbelief of the heart.

3. There is a state of rest, a state of peace, a state of life, a state of power, a state of grace, a state of dominion, in the life, and through the power of the Lord, wherein the law of life is manifested in dominion in the heart over the law of sin and death. There is an everlasting kingdom, wherein God and Christ reign, in which God treads Satan down under the feet of the soul, and makes the soul a king and a priest in the Son of his love; and the soul feels that it is one with, and accepted in, the beloved.

Now, friends, my earnest desires is that you may know this kingdom, travel faithfully towards it, feel and come into the reign of Christ in it, sit down in the heavenly places in Christ Jesus, and inherit substance. Oh that you would know the gathering to Christ in the name, and sit down in the name, where the enemy cannot touch you, but where you feel the preservation and powerful life and dominion of that seed which is over the enemy, and wherein and whereby the Lord scatters the enemy, bruising the serpent's head. And that you may know the precious and glorious building of life in the Spirit, even of the holy house and city of God, where the walls are salvation, and the gates, praise. For to this end it is in my heart from the Lord to write these things unto you; and may the Lord God of mercy open the door of entrance to you into these things. For there is but one door of life, and there is not another—which door is Christ, the seed. This seed is revealed within, there to break the wisdom, strength, and head of the serpent. And as far as he breaks it, there (and no further), true redemption and freedom are witnessed.

Oh that you might receive an understanding from the Lord, and be taught by him to deny and part with the understanding which is not of him, and that you might see things (from him, and in his light) which you have not yet seen! And oh that you knew (sensibly knew) what must live, and what must die in you, that you might feel the rising of your souls out of the grave, through the immortal seed of God, and the bringing of all your wisdom and knowledge (even of the things of God) into death!

Concerning Ordinances

Now, the great matter you seem to have against us with respect to ordinances is about the baptism of water, and breaking outward bread, and drinking outward wine. Concerning this I have two or three weighty inquiries to be seriously considered.

Inquiry 1: Were these things themselves the things of the

kingdom, or were these representations of something relating to the kingdom, as the shadows were under the law? And so, even though they might have had a use and service in the passing away from the law, yet should they have an absolute place in the gospel day? For as the day dawns and breaks, the shadows fly away. What should the shadow do when that which the shadow signified has come? What place is there for shadows in the substance, in the everlasting kingdom?

Now though the apostle Paul condescended so as to circumcise for the sake of the Jews, yet outward circumcision was not to abide. He condescended also as to John's baptism, that is, the baptism of water (for this was not Christ's baptism, his being that of the Holy Spirit and fire). Even so, the apostle blessed God that he did not make use of it, and said he was not sent to baptize. What was he not sent to baptize with? Why, *not with water*, not with John's baptism. But he was sent to baptize with Christ's baptism, that is, to baptize into the name, into the Spirit, into the power (and so were all the apostles), as well as to preach the gospel. Gal. 3:5. Matt. 28:19.

Then, as for the outward supper, was it not a shadow of the true, substantial supper of the Lord? Did it not outwardly signify the breaking of the true bread, and drinking of the true wine (the fruit of the vine of life) in the kingdom of God? Was not this kingdom at hand in John's time, and the disciples of Christ were to pray it might come? And did not the apostles witness it come (those who were in the power, life, righteousness, and joy eternal)? For mark: the promise was not only of a kingdom of glory hereafter, when the body is laid down, but rather they were to receive the kingdom, and feel an entrance (even an abundant entrance) into the everlasting kingdom ministered to them even then. They were to eat bread in the kingdom, and drink wine in the kingdom, even new bread, and new wine, fresh from the table of the Lord. Indeed, they were to eat with the Lord, in his presence, according to the promise that he would come and dwell in them, and walk in them, and sup with them, and they with him. And thus they in their day, and we in our day (blessed be the name of the Lord our God!) eat and drink of the heavenly bread and wine of the kingdom with Christ.

Inquiry 2: Have not these outward things been much abused, and the anti-Christian spirit appeared in them, and magnified them? And surely, when magnified by that spirit, they are neither of, nor for, Christ.

And consider well what that outward court was which God gave to the Gentiles, (see Rev. 11:2) and what the worship and ordinances of the outward court were. And so consider whether they are required by the Lord of the inward Jews, who are of the circumcision in the heart, and are come to inherit the substance.

Inquiry 3: Whether there is any virtue in these things in themselves, without God's requiring them? Can outward water wash the soul? Can outward bread and wine feed or refresh it? Indeed, if God requires a man to wash his body with water, he ought to be subject, and there will be profit to him in his subjection. But of itself it is only a bodily exercise, and without God's requiring it, it would be but will-worship,[4] and profit him nothing at all.

Now truly the Lord never did require this of us, but rather has shown us the true water with which our souls and bodies have need to be washed, and the bread and wine with which they are to be fed and refreshed. And in following the

---

[4] Will-worship is a term used to refer to any form of worship that comes from man's resources and is according to man's will.

Lord according as he has led us and required of us, we have found reconciliation, life, rest, peace, and joy with our Father, and pure refreshment from him.

Inquiry 4: With regard to duties, these are the two great duties we are taught: To love the Lord our God with all our heart, soul, and spirit; and to love our neighbor as ourselves. And these we learn by believing in him whom God sent, and receiving the seed of life from him. In the growth of this seed in us, we live and are made one with him, and are partakers of the ability which is of him. For not by working of ourselves do we attain to this, but by the working of his powerful life in us, through his mercy to us. He circumcises us, he cuts off the enmity, he brings under the old nature and spirit in us, and then the new springs up, and we are renewed in it. And in this we learn and are made able to love the Lord, and his children, and his creatures, yes, all that is of him. And this love constrains us to obey the Lord, and deny all for him, so that we can suffer anything through his strength (except for sin, corruption, unbelief, and disobedience to him). Yes, this makes us so tender towards him, that we would rather part with this entire world than lose the integrity and subjection of our spirits to him in the least thing that he requires of us. His truth (and our testimony thereto) in every respect is far dearer to us than our lives, and all the enjoyments and plea-sures of this present world.

From these two great duties flow many others towards God, such as: to fear him with the fear which is not taught by the precepts of men, but which he writes in our hearts; to wait upon him night and day in his temple, even in the holy place of his building; to call upon him in the motion, guid-ance, will, and help of his Spirit (for indeed when once we learn of God, we are taught to pray no more after the flesh, no more after the will, wisdom, or way of man); also to be sensible of his goodness, and give thanks to him in every condition.

And in this we feel his presence and acceptance, as the Lord is not forgotten by us. For when we eat and drink, walk abroad or stay at home, we feel him near, and our hearts acknowledge him, bow to him, wait upon him, bless him, and praise his name. We also speak words concerning him, or to him, with the outward voice, whenever he gives them and requires them of us. But truly we dare bring no sacrifices of our own, nor kindle any fire or sparks of our own, but rather wait for the holy breath, Spirit, and power of our God, to perform all in us and by us.

But now, because we do not pray at certain set times (as we formerly did), nor speak words before and after meals as formerly, you are offended with us and say we deny this duty. No, no; we do not deny to God the prayer which is from the immortal birth. But this we say and sensibly feel: prayer is a gift, and the ability thereof is in God's Spirit. For we do not know what to pray for as we ought, nor have we a power in us to pray when or as we will. But in the Holy Spirit, in his breathing in us, is our ability, and we are to wait on him for the moving and breathing of his Spirit. We are not to pray of ourselves, or in our own wills or times, but in the Father's. Indeed, it is a mighty thing to speak to God aright in prayer. Flesh must be silent before him, and be laid still and low in his presence so that the pure spring may open, the pure breath breathe, and the pure voice issue forth. For God does not hear sinners, but rather those that are born of him and do his will. Every soul must witness this according to its measure, as Christ witnessed it in fullness. And there is no serving God aright, or performing any duty or ordinance of worship to him aright, except in a measure of the same life and Spirit wherewith Christ served him.

Now, I do not only acknowledge the state of the Jews in their integrity, and of the primitive Christians in theirs, and of what the Lord has caused to break forth in this our day, but I also acknowledge all the appearances of God in the holy martyrs and witnesses which he raised up and enabled to bear testimony to his truth, and against the anti-christian practices of many, all throughout the night of the apostasy. And I also acknowledge all the work of God in my own heart, and in the hearts of others in former times. But the Lord has shown me that there is a great mixture in men's desires and endeavors after him; and that the evil spirit, by his subtlety, does often have his way in them, and turn the very zeal and earnestness of the mind (through prejudices and misapprehensions) against the Lord and his truth. Now, this is a very dangerous state, and there are some (though unaware) in this state, doing that against the Lord, and against his Christ, his truth, his people, which, if ever their eyes are opened, they will mourn bitterly over. And if their eyes are not opened, but they continue on in a wrong light (even by a light of their own gathering, imagining, and conceiving), where will it lead them, and what will be their end?

Oh that you could hear! Oh that you could fear aright! Oh that you could rightly consider! Oh that you could feel the life and power of the Lord near you, the Word of life near you, even as near as you have felt the enemy and his temptations. Then you might partake of, and witness with joy, the virtue and redemption of this Word! Oh that you could once rightly look upon him whom you have pierced, and still daily pierce, and cannot help but pierce, until the righteous judgments of the Lord be poured out on the head of the transgressor in you. Then the Lord will be waited upon, feared, and subjected to in the way of his judgments, and you will feel the refining work finished, the dross burned up, the temple prepared, the vessel brought out of the furnace! What then? Why, when the Lord has built up Zion, prepared his temple, cleansed his house, will he not appear there in his glory? Shall it not become a house of prayer, of pure prayer, and of pure praises? Shall there be any lame or blind sacrifices offered up there? Shall it not be the beauty of holiness indeed? Shall not the appearance of the Lord be more glorious than ever it was in the temple and ordinances under the law? Shall not every living stone in this building feel the God of life and power truly present, and feel not only the earth, but the very heavens melt before him and pass away, and nothing remain but the pure light and life of the Lamb?

Concerning the Gospel Rest, or Sabbath

What is the gospel rest? What is the gospel Sabbath? Is it a shadow, as that of the law was? Or is it the substance of that which the law shadowed out?

"The law was given by Moses." Moses, by the command of God, gave forth the shadows of the heavenly things under the law; "But grace and truth came by Jesus Christ." The true Sabbath, the true rest, the law of the Spirit of life, in and to the true Jews, comes by him. The law of Moses had the shadow of the good things to come; which good things themselves the gospel contains, bringing life and immortality to light, and the soul into the enjoyment and possession of the heavenly things themselves.

The apostle disputes the case about both these (Heb. 4), both about the seventh day of rest, and about the land of rest, showing that neither of them were the substance, but were the rests which were to pass away. He shows that besides

61

these, there was a rest remaining, a day of rest remaining, a land of rest remaining; of which these two (both the outward Sabbath of rest, and the land of rest under the law) were but figures.

Now, for whom did this rest remain? Why, it remained for the true Jews, for believers, for the spiritual circumcision in the times of the gospel. "And we (he says) who have believed, do enter into rest." The faith gives entrance, the Son's faith, the faith which stands in the power, the faith which is victory and gives victory over sin and the world, which removes the mountains and difficulties which stand in the way, and gives entrance into the gospel rest. Faith, which is from and of the power of the endless life, puts sin under, brings down self, gathers man into a new seed, brings man forth in a new seed, causes him to live and act in a new seed, etc. And as man comes here, and that life rises and has power in him, it causes him to rest from his own works, and to wait for and experience God, in and through Christ, to work all, and be all in him.

The apostle Peter also speaks of this rest, and declares how it is attained, even by suffering in the flesh, "He that has suffered in the flesh (he says) has ceased from sin." 1 Pet. 4:1. It is the fleshly part, the motions in the flesh, from whence sin arises.

"Lust, when it is conceived, brings forth sin." Now Christ has prepared and appointed a cross, a spiritual yoke, to bring down the flesh, which causes great suffering in the flesh to him that takes it upon him. To deny all ungodliness and every worldly lust, motion, desire, and delight of the fleshly mind and nature, is a sore suffering to the earthly part. But he that has taken up the cross wholly, and felt the thorough work of it, and suffered in the flesh the parting with and crucifying all that is of the flesh, that which would cause him to sin comes to be slain in him, and he ceases from sin. Then he is in the rest, and he keeps the rest fully. Then he knows the yoke and cross, which was once burdensome to him, to become easy and delightful, that part being worn out in him to which it was painful.

Now he that is in measure delivered, that has in measure suffered in this way, finds some rest, and may in some measure keep the Sabbath. Yes, in the faith, the weakest babe (abiding there) cannot help but keep the Sabbath, and offer up the sacrifices, and perform the services thereof to the Lord. For the worship of the new covenant relates not to outward times or days, but is in the Spirit, in the truth, in the name, power, and substance, on the day which the Lord has made, and makes, in the spirits of his people.

And here that scripture is experienced in those that are born of the Spirit, and live in the Spirit, and walk after the Spirit: "Sin shall not have dominion over you; for you are not under the law, but under grace." Who are not under the law, but under grace? Why, they that are gathered by the grace, that hear the voice of God in the grace, drawing and enabling them to follow. These are they whom the grace overshadows and protects from the power and dominion of sin; they are under it, they are sheltered, saved, and preserved by it.

He that is born of God does not sin, but obeys the grace; but he that commits sin is the servant of sin, and is not yet made free from it by the grace and power of the Son. Yes, the Son gives that freedom in his day from sin and the power of Satan. They that are outside of the light of his day cannot so much as believe; but they that are gathered into, and walk in the light of the day, these experience the law of the Spirit of life in Christ Jesus, making them free from the law of sin and death. Has not the one stronger than the strong man come, with his law and power of an endless life? Shall he not manifest his dominion in the heart, over the law of sin and death? Yes, as the law of life is received and let in, it works out, overcomes, bears down, and overruns the law of sin and death.

And if God, by the power and breath of his Holy Spirit, with its living and powerful law, kills sin and death in the heart, what shall make them alive again? No, no; then they are dead indeed, and the kingdom and reign of Christ is witnessed in that soul. Then the birth of life is witnessed. Then the man-child is witnessed, ruling with a rod of iron, dashing in pieces all motions and temptations to corruption, and all that would defile, so that they cannot enter the mind. And the mind is guarded in the pure peace, unspeakable joy, and rest of the Son continually. And there it is as truly experienced inwardly as ever it was at any time enjoyed or hoped for by the Jews outwardly, that the Lord's horn of salvation breaks all the horns of the oppressors. He gives rest to the soul from the enemies round about, so that, without fear of them anymore, it may serve the Lord in holiness and righteousness all the days of its life.

There are some good desires in many people, but there is also great error of judgment, and wandering up and down from the truth for lack of that which is able to stay the mind upon the Lord, and to guide it in the right way. Some run to this mountain, and sacrifice there; others to that hill, and offer there; but few know the true resting place, or the place of the true worship. Now in these errors, they can witness no acceptance with the Lord. Oh that they knew the acceptable thing, the acceptable way of worship, and might appear before the Lord there! Then they might begin in that which is substantial (in the gospel Spirit, life, and power), and come to inherit and sit down in that which is substantial and everlasting.

Chapter III

The Holy Truth and People Defended

The following is an answer to the chief passages of a letter, written to me, and replied to by me, before my imprisonment at Reading Jail (where I have been a prisoner above a year and a half, without any law broken, or cause given on my part). I am engaged in spirit to reply something to it, and to give forth to others what the Lord has given to me.

Objection: He objects in his letter that we deny redemption by the blood of Christ.

Answer: Oh how will he answer this charge to God? For none do so rightly and fully acknowledge redemption by the blood of Christ as the Lord has taught us to do! For indeed we acknowledge the blood of the Lord Jesus Christ both outwardly and inwardly; both as it was shed on the cross, and as it is sprinkled in our consciences. And we know the cleansing virtue of it in the everlasting covenant, and in the light which is eternal, outside of which light men have only a notion of it, but do not truly know nor own it.

Objection: He charges that justification is a single act of grace passed upon man by God freely, which act pronounces him to be righteous.

Answer: He that truly experiences salvation in Christ Jesus, witnesses it to be a continued act of grace. Grace appears to the soul, grace teaches, grace enables, grace makes a change from the ungraciousness of the heart and state. And then grace (or God by his grace in and through Jesus Christ) forgives the sins that were committed before. For though the Lord visit me with life, quicken me thereby, make a change in my heart and state, yet it is still his mercy to accept me, and to pass by (for his name's sake) my former debts and trespasses against him. Indeed, the new covenant is wholly a covenant of grace and mercy. The giving of Christ, the drawing of the mind to him, the accepting and justifying which are in him, etc., these are works of grace and mercy. So the spiritual Israel may rightly sing this song in the land of holiness and redemption, "O praise the Lord! For he is good, and his mercy endures forever."

Objection: He asks, do we think to satisfy the law by our obedience?

Answer: We do not look upon the law of Moses, which was given to the outward Jew, to be the dispensation of the new covenant, or to be the law of the Spirit of life in Christ Jesus. But indeed, the righteousness of the law is fulfilled in those who are in the new covenant, and who have God's law written in their hearts, and his fear put there (which preserves from departing from him), and his Spirit put within them to cause them to walk in his ways, and keep his statutes and judgments. These live in the Spirit, and walk not after the flesh, yet they do not magnify and claim their own obedience (nor call it their own righteousness), but rather acknowledge him from whom their obedience comes. For in the measure of his grace and living truth, the soul is one with him and all that he is, and all that he has done, is theirs. And it is he himself that is the righteousness of all that are in him; and they that abide in him partake of his righteousness from day to day, which flows in them like a stream.

He seems to pass by some things (which I spoke in tender love and weightiness of spirit to him) as the mere judgment of man in his day. But let him take heed, for when he comes to appear before God, he then will find it was the judgment of God's Spirit in the light of his day. This day is inward and spiritual, which believers are to hasten to, and which approaches in every heart, as the night is spent and passes away. And all true Christians and believers ought to wait for the passing away of the night, and the dawning of this day, and the arising of the day-star in their hearts.

And as for his remarks about the will of God done in heaven, are there not those here on earth who dwell in heaven? Are there not those whose citizenship is in heaven; even the witnesses of God's holy truth, who are ascended up above the spirit of this world, who dwell in God's holy Spirit, and walk in the light as God is in the light? Hell is not far from the wicked, nor is heaven far from those who are renewed in the spirit of their mind, and who witness the passing away of the old things, and the new creation in Christ. Oh that he could look and see how he has wrested those scriptures (Psa. 85:9-11, Isa. 4:2. and Ephes. 2:6) according to his own imaginations.

Objection: He charges that we account all religion and Christian profession in the world as below us and carnal.

Answer: Indeed we magnify the truth, the life, the anointing, the spiritual and inward appearance of our Lord Jesus Christ to which we have been turned. And all other knowledge, faith, profession, and religion which does not arise from this we cannot help but call carnal. For the enlightening Spirit of the Lord has given us this testimony to bear against all the dead, notional professors of this age, who build from the letter of Scripture (or rather their apprehensions of the letter) outside of the life. All of these celebrate Christ's name of "foundation" and "cornerstone," but they refuse, reject, deny, and turn from the cornerstone himself. They have neither the skill nor patience to try what he is, in this his pure, precious, living, powerful, and glorious appearance in the spiritual light of his inward day, after the long, thick darkness of the foregoing night. And woe would be unto us if we did not thus testify! For, it is for this cause that we were born and brought into the world, to testify to the present appear- ance of our God, and of his Christ, in this our day. Glory to him who has called and chosen us, and has (in a true and precious measure and degree of his own pure life) made us faithful therein.

Objection: He then objects as follows: "Instead of clapping us on the back, and ministering to us in our journey, you clog our march, and fall upon our rear. Instead of serving the kingdom of Christ, you deny the first principles of the gospel, and wholly disown the hope of Christ's second appearing and kingdom, acknowledging no other Savior, or no other kingdom, besides a seed or a light in yourselves."

Answer: "God is light, and in him is no darkness at all;" and this is the message of the gospel. 1 John 1:5. And Christ, who is one with the Father, he is one and the same light with him.

We confess we do not look for another besides him, nor for another kingdom besides the kingdom which is revealed in him; for the kingdom which is revealed and manifested in and by him is the spiritual, eternal, everlasting kingdom, and there is not another. We do not say that the fullness, or the full glory of the kingdom, is now revealed or enjoyed by us. No, we confess we have but the earnest in comparison, only a measure, a proportion. But this measure is the same in nature and kind with the fullness itself. And all that is of Christ, of his Spirit, of his nature, is saving. The least measure of his grace that appears in any heart brings salvation with it; the least touch of his finger has pure life and saving virtue in it. Nevertheless, this measure is not distinct or separate from the fullness, and so it is not another, though it is not the fullness.

And as for denying the first principles of the gospel, that belongs to yourselves. For do you not deny that light which is the foundation of all, and wherein and whereby all the mysteries of God's kingdom are seen? And without this light, do you not set up a notional, intellectual knowledge of your own conceiving, comprehending, and gathering from the letter (though no man can understand the letter except as he come into and abides in the light)? This we have experienced in ourselves formerly; for we were but guessing at and imagining things concerning the letter, until we were turned to the light of God's Spirit.

And as for disowning the hope of Christ's kingdom, the Lord knows that is far from us. For we ourselves do bless him for what of his kingdom has already appeared, and wait and hope for its further and fuller appearance. But this we confess: another Spirit, another Christ, another light, another life, another power, another kingdom, besides him who has already appeared, we do not expect. For Christ is our King and kingdom both, and the least proportion of his life and Spirit received (bought with the loss of all, and so purchased and possessed) is no less than a pearl of great price, and a heavenly kingdom to him that enjoys it.

Indeed, it is a great matter to know that throne which David's throne signified, and Christ sitting thereon. His kingdom, his throne, are not of this outward, worldly nature, but inward and spiritual; and his throne is in his kingdom and temple, where he reigns, and where he is worshiped. He that comes to know Satan overthrown and cast out, knows also Christ come in, and sitting on his throne. Oh that men did give over their dreaming about the heavenly glory, and come to this kingdom in the leadings of God's Spirit where it is revealed!

Objection: He says, Christ shall appear without sin unto salvation.

Answer: I grant it, but when, and how? Does he not inwardly appear without sin unto salvation to those who have waited for, hastened, and come to the inward day? Does not Christ appear without sin unto salvation inwardly in the day of his own Spirit? Is not the glorious salvation of the gospel brought forth in the gospel day?

Objection: He adds, "Is your attainment beyond Paul's, who found that in him (that is in his flesh) dwelt no good thing, and found his flesh lusting against the spirit so that he could not do the thing that he desired."

Answer: Paul did once experience such a state when he felt himself carnal, sold under sin. In this state he did not find how to perform that which was good, but rather did what he hated, the law of sin being strong (in his members) against the law of life in his mind. This state he calls a state of captivity to the law of sin in his members, and a wretched state. Rom. 7:23-24.

But did Paul never experience another state? Did he never witness the virtue and power of the new covenant, even the law of the Spirit of life, and the power thereof, freeing him from the strength and captivity of the law of sin in his members? There were young men whom John speaks of (read 1 John 2:13) who were strong, and had overcome the wicked one. Did Paul himself never attain to that state? He bid others be strong in the Lord and in the power of his might, and showed them how to resist in it, and so to overcome. Did he never experience and witness it himself? He said he had fought a good fight, and was more than a conqueror. Was he then a captive to the law of sin in his members? He said he could do all things through Christ that strengthened him. Was this not a different state from that wherein he found he could only will, but not do, the good he desired, but only the evil that he hated? And blessed be the Lord, there are many at this day who witness a further state of redemption and deliverance from sin than that state of captivity which Paul there expresses, under which he formerly groaned and complained. For indeed Paul was not in that state of captivity when he wrote the epistle to the church in Rome, but rather knew the dominion of grace over sin, and bid that church to be subject to the grace, and not give way to sin, but yield their members as servants to righteousness unto holiness, chap. 6.

And in that other place, where he speaks of the flesh lusting against the spirit, and the spirit against the flesh, Gal. 5:17, he does not there speak of himself, but of the Galatians, who were in a weak and low state, and fallen from the Spirit and power of the gospel, having let in that which was contrary to it. And so he strives to gather them into the Spirit again, and bids them live in the Spirit, and walk in the Spirit, and so they should not fulfill the lusts of the flesh. For in the new covenant, man is taught in the virtue and power of the covenant, so that he learns daily, and grows daily out of deceit into truth, until he come to be a true Israelite, in whom there is no guile. And so in this spiritual war, the house of Saul grows weaker and weaker, and the house of David stronger and stronger, until Saul's kingdom be at length over-turned and wholly destroyed, and the kingdom of David established in righteousness forever and ever. Then Jerusalem, the holy building, the city of the living people, the city of righteousness (the habitation of righteousness and mountain of holiness), is known, and Jerusalem is witnessed to be a quiet habitation, there being peace in all her borders. Then the mind is fully staid upon the Lord in all conditions, and he keeps it in perfect peace. Then the soul is anxious for nothing, but in everything makes its requests known to God by prayer and supplication, with thanksgiving. And the peace of God, which passes all understanding, keeps the heart and mind through Christ Jesus.

Surely the apostle had learned himself (when he taught others) to be content in every state. He knew how to be abased, and how to abound, etc. Oh glorious state! Oh pure state of pure life in the heart! And what if I should add, Oh perfect state! The apostle James says, "Let patience have its perfect work, that you may be perfect and entire, lacking nothing." James 1:4. When Paul had so learned Christ that abundance could not lift him up, nor any need deject him, or cause him to repine or distrust, what did he lack of this perfect state?

Objection: He claims, "Out of you have risen men that have more audaciously lifted up a standard against the sealed and experienced truths of the gospel than any other of which I have heard or read."

Answer: We are a people (many of us) who have gone through great distress for want of the Lord our God, and have exceedingly waited and longed for his living and powerful appearance. And as for my own part, this I can say, that had this appearance of the Lord not been in power, and in the evidence and demonstration of his Spirit to my soul (reaching to and answering that in me which was of him), I could never have acknowledged it, for I was so deeply jealous of it and prejudiced against it. But since my mind has been turned to the pure Word of life, even the Word which was in the beginning (I speak as in the Lord's presence), it has had singular effects on my heart. The light has so searched me as I never was searched before, under all my former professions of Christianity. And the Lord has given me a true and pure discerning of the things of his kingdom, in the light which is true and pure. And I have met with singular quickenings from his Spirit, and the faith which stands in his heavenly power and gives victory and dominion in him. And the love which he has given me is not notional, but arises from his circumcising of my heart, and corresponds to his nature which springs forth purely and naturally towards him, and towards those of his image, and all his creatures. Indeed, this love springs towards those who are enemies to me for his name's sake.

I might mention the patience also, and faithfulness to his truth, with the long-suffering spirit—which his Spirit testifies in me to be of a very particular nature (along with other things). And I am not alone in this, nor am I the chiefest; but

I have many equals; and indeed, there are those who far exceed me in the heavenly and divine image of my Father. The fruits are according to the root of life in us, and so they are acknowledged by all who look upon us with the true eye, the eye which God gives and opens.

Now, the same one that has worked inwardly in us, he has also required some outward behavior and expressions from us which are foolish and weak to the eye of man's wisdom, but are chosen of God to hide the glory of this life from the eye which cannot discern it, but rather despises the day of small things.[1] And though this is the least part of our religion (yet we submit to it because it is of God, whom we dare not disobey in the least), yet the spirit which is contrary to God belittles us, as if this were all, or at least the main thing in which we differ from others. But alas, it is in the main that we differ from you. For we hold our religion as we receive it from God—in the light and life of his Spirit. You, however, hold yours as you apprehend it from the letter. Christ is our rock and foundation as he is inwardly revealed; but he is yours only as he is outwardly conceived. We believe with the faith which is of the nature of him in whom we believe, which faith is mighty through God, and works over all the powers of darkness, giving victory over them all. But you believe with a faith which esteems victory impossible while in this world. And as our root differs, so too all that grows up in us differs from yours.

Now to close, I shall add a few words on that scripture, Phil. 3:3. "For we are the circumcision, which worship God in

---

[1] Penington here refers to some of the outward ways in which Quakers felt led to dress, speak, and live contrary to the proud and man-exalting customs and traditions of their day. Though these outward things played a small part in the Quaker's testimony against the man-centered religion of their time, they were by no means at the heart of their faith, nor the principle things that distinguished them from other professing Christians.

the Spirit, and rejoice in Christ Jesus, and have no confidence in the flesh." It is a precious thing to witness this scripture fulfilled in the heart, to experience that which inwardly circumcises and cuts off the foreskin of the heart. For this foreskin indeed lies over and veils the heart till it is cut off by the inward appearance of the life and power of the Lord Jesus Christ inwardly revealed. Then, when this is done, one can truly and sensibly say that he is an inward Jew. How so? How can that be proved? Why, he is inwardly circumcised! He has felt that knife within which circumcises the heart, and has borne its inward pain and cutting, and is circumcised by it. That which stood between him and the Lord is cut off, the veil is taken away, the stiff-neckedness and independence from God is removed, the wall of separation is inwardly broken down, and now he is in true unity of Spirit and communion with his God—even with the Father, and the Son, in that One Holy Spirit wherein they are One.

Now he can bow before the Father of our Lord Jesus Christ, and worship him in his own Spirit, even in the new and fresh life, day by day. Now his rejoicing is in Christ Jesus, whom the Father has sent, both outwardly in a body of flesh to fulfill the holy will, and also inwardly in his Spirit and power unto his heart, to destroy the works of the devil there. And he cannot help but rejoice both in what he did in his body of flesh for him, and in what he does by his Spirit and power in him.

Oh blessed be the Lord, I feel him near, his Spirit near, his life near, his power near, his pure virtue near, his holy wisdom near, his righteousness near, his redemption near; for he is my rock, and my strength, and my salvation, day by day. And I have no confidence in the flesh, in what I am, in what I can do after the flesh; but my confidence is in him who has weakened me, who has stripped me, who has impoverished me, who has brought me to nothing in myself, that I might be all in him, and that I might find him made all unto me. He is my peace, he is my life, he is my righteousness, he is my holiness, he is the image wherein I am renewed. In him is my acceptance with the Father. He is my Advocate, he is my hope and joy forever. He has destroyed that in me which was contrary to God, and keeps it down forever. He is my Shepherd, his arm has gathered me, and his arm encompasses me day by day. I rest under the shadow of his wings, from whence the healing virtue of his saving health drops upon my spirit day by day. Oh, I cannot tell any man what he is unto me! But, blessed be the Lord, I feel him near, his righteousness near, his salvation daily revealed before that eye which he has opened in me, in that true, living sense with which he has quickened me.

And now, you that have high notions, and rich, intellectual knowledge concerning these things, but not the thing itself, the life itself, the Spirit itself, the new and living covenant, and law of life itself, wherein alone Christ is livingly revealed,—oh, how poor, miserable, blind, and naked are you, in the midst of all your traditional knowledge and pretended experiences!

Come now, be quiet a while, and cease from bitterness of spirit, and reviling the work and people of the Lord. For the Lord knows, and will make manifest, both who are his and who are not his. All the living stones are his, but the great professors of the words of Scripture, who are without the Spirit and life of the Scriptures, are not his, nor ever were, nor ever will be owned by him.

Come now, learn to distinguish from God by his life, by his anointing, by the everlasting, infallible rule, and not by *words without life*. This is where the great error and mistake has been in all ages and generations. The great way of deceit has long been (and still is) by a form of godliness without power. Be sure you are not deceived in this way; for if you miss the power which saves, you cannot help but perish forever. And what if the appearance of the Spirit and power of our Lord Jesus Christ inwardly, which is that which saves, be as strange to your sense, understanding, and judgment, as his outward appearance was unto the people of the Jews? Take heed of their spirit, take heed of their judgment! For they judged according to the appearance of things to them, which they imagined and conceived from the Scriptures; but they judged not with the true and righteous judgment, which only the children of the true wisdom can.

The Dawning of the Spiritual Day

There are four or five very precious things which were generally witnessed in the days of the apostles among the true Christians, which are all mentioned together. Heb. 6:4-5.

First, they were truly enlightened.

The ministers of the gospel were sent by Christ to turn men from darkness to light, and from the power of Satan to God. Acts 26:18. 1 John 1:5. They were faithful in their ministry, and did turn men from the darkness and power of Satan to the light of God's Holy Spirit; and they were enlightened by it, and received power through it, and so came to be children of the light, and to walk in the light as God is in the light.

Secondly, they tasted of the heavenly gift.

What is the heavenly gift which Christ gives to those who

come unto him and become his sheep? He gives them life, eternal life. John 10:27-28. He brings them out of death, and gives them a savor and taste of the life which is eternal. This was what the apostles testified of, even of the life which was manifested in that body of flesh of our Lord Jesus Christ (1 John 1:2). They that turn from the darkness to his light, he gives them a taste of the same life.

Thirdly, they were made partakers of the Holy Spirit.

The gospel is a day of bringing forth the spiritual seed, and of pouring out the Holy Spirit upon them. The law state was a state of servants; the gospel, a state of sons! And because true believers in Christ are sons, God sent forth the Spirit of his Son into their hearts to cry, Abba, Father.

Fourthly, they tasted of the good Word of God.

That is, of that Word which was in the beginning of the world, which is ingrafted into the hearts of those that truly believe, which Word is able to save the soul.

Fifthly, they tasted of the powers of the world to come.

Of the power of the endless life, whereof Christ is the Minister, and according to which he ministers life in that holy, true, living, inward, spiritual temple, which he pitches and rears up for a habitation to God in his own Spirit.

Now, throughout the apostasy and night of darkness which has come over the Christian state, these things have been greatly lost. For there were none who were able to turn people to that light to which the apostles directed. None could tell men where the light is to shine, and where men were to expect it and wait for it. None were able to direct men to the seed of the kingdom within, to the Word of faith, the Word of the kingdom near in the heart and mouth. Much less were they able to instruct men how they might know and distinguish it from all other seeds, and the voice of the Shepherd from all other voices. Here it came to pass, that though at times God visited and opened men's hearts, warming them a little by the breath which came from himself, yet they knew not how to turn to the Lord and wait upon him for preservation in the gift and measure of his own grace. Thus the good seed was largely stolen away from them, and the building which was raised up in them was not a building of life according to the Spirit, but rather a building of wisdom or knowledge concerning the things of God according to the flesh. And so the building that was raised up in men's spirits has been Babylon, instead of Zion.

But the Lord has had a remnant all throughout the apostasy, who felt some true begetting of life, and had in measure some sense and taste of the heavenly things. These mourned after that state which was once enjoyed, and felt their lack of it, traveling from mountain to hill, seeking their resting place, about which none could rightly inform them.

But now, for the sake of these, God has at length appeared! "How has he appeared?" some may ask. Why thus: he who is light has appeared inwardly, causing his light to shine inwardly, causing his life to spring inwardly; so that he who is light, who is life, who is truth, is felt and known in his own inward visits, breakings-forth, and appearances. For God is a Spirit, and his appearance is spiritual, his day is spiritual, his kingdom is spiritual, his light is spiritual, his life is spiritual, his day-star is spiritual. And so his day dawns and his day-star arises in the heart.

In this way the day spring from on high did visit us, we who sat in darkness, and in the region of the shadow of death. And here we have met with what the apostles met with, the very same light of life, the very same enlightening Spirit and power, and we have been enlightened by it, and have tasted of the same gift.

The very same grace that appeared to them and taught them, has also appeared to us and taught us, and of it we have learned the same lessons, in the same covenant of life wherein they learned. And now we can set our seal to their testimony in the same Spirit wherein they gave it forth, and witness to the same eternal life, and the same holy oil and anointing, for our eyes have been opened and kept open by it. And though there are great disputes about our testimony in this our day (and the present professors rise up against us just as the former professors did against them), yet if any man come rightly to distinguish in himself between that which God begets in the heart and all other births, they will soon confess that our testimony is of God, and is given forth in the authority and by the commission of his own Spirit. True wisdom is justified by the children that are born of her, though the fleshly birth does not (nor can) acknowledge her. The fleshly birth can acknowledge former dispensations (according to the relation of them in the letter), but not the life and power of the present gift.

I have known the breaking down of much in me by the powerful hand of the Lord, and a parting with much (though not too much) for Christ's sake. The Lord has brought the day of distress and inward judgment over my heart. He has arisen to shake terribly the earthly part in me (yes, what if I should say that the powers of heaven have been shaken also), that he might make me capable to receive, and bring me into, that kingdom which cannot be shaken. And now, that which

God has shaken and removed in me, I see others building upon, and they think it shall never be shaken in them. But such know not the day of the Lord, nor the terrible searching of his pure light, nor the operation of his power, which will not spare in one what he has reproved, condemned, shaken, and overturned in another. He that knows the living stone within, and comes to him as to a living stone, and is built upon the revelation of his Spirit, life, and power (revealed inwardly against the power of darkness), is not deceived. All that build otherwise (I mean upon an outward knowledge concerning Christ, and not upon his inward life), their building will not be able to stand in the day of the Lord. I desire that they might have a sense of this in time, and that they might not perish forever, but rather experience the life and power of our Lord Jesus Christ, which redeems and preserves out of the perishing state forever and ever. Amen.

Chapter IV

Naked Truth

Given Forth by Way of Question and Answer

Question: What does this light do inwardly in the hearts of those that receive it, believe in it, and give up to it?

Answer: It does all that is required to be done, from the soul's coming out of spiritual Egypt into the land of rest; and all that is needful for its growth and preservation there.

First, it enlightens. It shows what is evil, and also what is good, according to the measure and proportion of it, and according to God's causing it to shine in the heart. It discovers the mystery of darkness, the mystery of ungodliness, the mystery of iniquity, the mystery of deceit in all its mysterious workings—for nothing is hid from the light of him with whom we have to do. And it also discovers the mystery of godliness, the mystery of holiness, the pure way and commandment of life; and gives all true believers the experience that "his commandment is life everlasting." There is nothing that the heart desires to know of God that this light does not make manifest in due season. It opens the very mystery of the Scriptures, gives the right understanding and application of the promises, and fulfills its prophecies in the heart.

Secondly, it does not only manifest the good and evil, but likewise inclines the mind to choose the good, and refuse the evil. It draws away from the evil, and towards the good; yes, and the soul is made willing in the day of him who is light, and who appears in the light, and reveals his power there. There is a way, a highway (spoken of in Isa. 35:8) called the way of holiness, which the unclean can neither discern nor pass over. But the light of the Lord Jesus Christ, the measure of grace and truth wherewith he enlightens men, so manifests and leads into this way, that they that are taught and guided by him, shall walk therein, and not err.

Thirdly, it scatters the darkness and breaks the power of the enemy, making the soul one with him who is all power, and who gives it abundantly. Indeed, power is given to the children of the light to become sons in the light; power is given to become kings and priests to God; power is given to reign in the dominion of his life, in the dominion of his truth, over sin, over death, over deceit, and to offer up the holy, living sacrifices to God.

What shall I say? The light is one with Christ; it is of his heavenly Spirit and nature. It makes way for him, it leads to him, it fills with him, it brings into unity and fellowship both with the Father and the Son, where the peace which passes understanding, and the joy unspeakable and full of glory, abound. This is the gospel message—that God is light. And they that are gathered into and abide in this light are gathered into and abide in unity and fellowship, both with the Father and the Son.

David had great sense and great experience of this light of God's Holy Spirit, and of his truth sent forth, manifested, and revealed in his inward parts, as is signified, Psa. 51:6, and again, in that vehement prayer of his in Psa. 43:3.

"Oh, send out your light and your truth; let them lead me, let them bring me unto your holy hill, and to your tabernacles! Then will I go unto the altar of God, unto God the gladness of my joy; yes, upon the harp will I praise you, O God, my God."

Indeed when the light shines, and the truth springs up in the heart, it leads to him that is true, it leads to the holy hill and mountain of the Lord. Indeed, it leads to the inward altar, where those who serve and worship at the outward altar have no right to eat. And here the harp is known upon which the Most High is praised, even that inward harp, whereof David's outward harp was but a figure. Therefore, they that come to the holy hill of God, to the mountain of the Lord's house, and to that holy building which was raised up, invite and encourage others to walk in that light which led them there, where communion with God, and oneness with each other, and the blessings of life and peace are enjoyed. Isa. 2:5.

But what should I speak of the sufficiency of the light and grace of the Spirit of our Lord Jesus Christ, or of what it is able to do? I shall only say this, that as the fullness was enough for Christ, to fit him for the work which he had to do; so the measure of grace and truth which he bestows is enough for every man. "My grace is sufficient for you," said God to Paul, and so it is for every man. There is no lack of sufficiency in the grace of God, in the seed of the kingdom, in the pearl of price, in the holy leaven, in the heavenly salt. Truly, the virtue and strength of it is greater than the enemy is able to withstand. And he that keeps to it, and departs not from it, shall feel life and power springing up from it to quicken him, and carry him through all that God requires of him. For the water which Christ gives is a well, springing up (in him to whom it is given) unto life eternal. This water is able to wash, able to nourish, able to fill the soul with living virtue, who waits for it and partakes of it. And all the nations of them that are saved are to walk in the light of God's Spirit. To this light men are to be turned, unto this they are to be gathered, into this they are to be translated (even from the kingdom of darkness, into the Son's marvelous light). And being changed by it (into its nature) they become light in the Lord, and ought to walk in the light, as God is in the light. 1 John 1:7.

Question: How does the mind come to be enlightened, and the candle of the Lord come to be set up in the soul?

Answer: By God's causing it to shine there, and the mind's being turned to it and given up to be exercised by it.

The power of the Lord reaches to his pure seed of life and light in the heart, in the seasons of his good pleasure. And as the mind is then turned to it, it becomes sensible of it, and willing to let it in, and become one with it (suffering with it, and bearing its cross). The seed then comes to grow there, and its light which was hid and overwhelmed under the earth (under the earthly wisdom, will, knowledge, desires, etc.) comes to shine there. Yes, then the life comes to be quickened more and more, and the holy leaven spreads more and more there. And this sensible plant of God's renown being thus cherished, and being not afterwards grieved, despised, quenched, or hurt, by the giving way to, and letting in of, that which is contrary to it, it shoots up into a kingdom of righteousness. Indeed, it grows into a tree of righteousness, under the shadow of which the soul sits down in peace and rest, and is defended and nourished with that which is pure and living, and full of pure sap and virtue. So it becomes strong in the Lord and in the power of his might, against the power and strength of darkness.

Now, all men may experience this (at first in some low measure and degree, and afterwards more and more) as they come to feel after, and have a sense of that which is of God, and come to join and give up to it. For then it will be working against, and purging out, all that is of a contrary nature, and it will overspread the heart with its own nature. Thus the seed which was the least will become the greatest; and that which was the lowest of all (and indeed trampled underfoot) will rise up into dominion and power over all, and bring all under. So that the lofty city, the lofty building of fleshly wisdom, and of sin and iniquity in the heart, will be laid low, and the feet of the seed shall tread it down.

Question: How is the light or candle of the Lord diminished, and at length extinguished or put out in some? How does this come about?

Answer: By their neglecting, despising, quenching it; by hearkening and giving way to the contrary spirit in its motions and temptations. For just as the good Spirit, when let in, stops and works out the evil; so too when evil is let in, it stops and works out the good. So the Philistine nature, when given way to, stops up the inward well which Jacob had dug and opened.

There is a time when life is a mystery, a fountain sealed; and there is a time when God unseals the fountain and opens the mystery in the heart. Oh, then great care must be had! The soul must lie very low in the pure fear, that it may continue in his goodness and walk worthy of his love, and so that the fountain may be kept open and the pure springs of the holy land flow, and not be sealed and shut up again. For there are some that rebel against the light, and they dwell in a dry land. There were some that did always resist and vex God's Spirit, and the Lord's Spirit ceased striving with them, and gave them up to a reprobate sense and judgment concerning the things of God. There are some that do not improve God's good talent, and from them that which was once given is taken away. Yes, the candle of the wicked shall one time or other be put out, and they shall be silent in darkness, and their mouth stopped from having anything to say against God, his truth, and his people for evermore.

Therefore, all men must take heed that they be not careless with the grace of God, or despise the day of their visitation by the holy light of God's Spirit. For if God takes away the talent, or if God puts out the inward candle, who can light it again? Oh, how did poor David, the man after God's own heart, suffer by letting the enemy's temptations in upon him! "Cast me not away from your presence," said he, "and take not your Holy Spirit from me." Indeed he did lose his condition at the present, and here he speaks as a man in danger of being quite undone. But afterwards he came to comfort and assurance that God would restore to him the joy of his salvation, and light his candle, and enlighten his darkness again.

I am not unaware of the doubts and disputes that are in men's minds about this testimony which we give (from certain knowledge and true experience) concerning the light wherewith God enlightens souls. At first, when the testimony first came forth, men would not acknowledge such a thing as a light from God in men which convinced of and reproved for sin. And now, though there are many who will assent to that, they still cannot believe it to be a measure of the grace and truth which comes by Jesus Christ, and that in it the sufficiency and power of God is revealed against the strength and power of Satan. But let such seriously consider the following:

First, who they are that have testified, and do testify of this light. They are persons who generally have been deeply exercised in religion, persons who have read the Scriptures very diligently, with much praying and waiting upon God, for the true, certain, and clear understanding of them. They are persons who (many of them) have had experience of most (if not all) separate persuasions and denominations, but could never meet with the answer of the cry of their souls, nor with satisfaction to that birth which breathed in them after the Lord night and day.

Secondly, consider what their testimony is, which is manifold. Such as, first, that they were by the Lord (even by his Holy Spirit, and the shining and springing of his precious seed in them) turned to this light, and shown it to be of God. Secondly, that in turning to it, they met with the presence, appearance, and power of the Lord working in their hearts. Thirdly, that it did not only discover sin to them, but also powerfully did resist it, fight against it, and bring it under, which no light and power besides the light and power of God's Spirit can do. Fourthly, that the life of the Son is manifested and revealed in it, and there they come to truly see, and taste, and handle the Word of eternal life. Fifthly, that in this light they come to witness cleansing by the blood of the Lamb, and the everlasting covenant made with them (even the sure mercies of David), and the holy, precious promises fulfilled in them, whereby they are made partakers of the divine nature, and come to witness an entrance into the holy city, and drink of the streams of the pure crystal river, which refreshes and makes glad the city of our God. Lastly, (not to mention more) the Lord has shown them how this same light had been formerly with them, even in the days of their former religious profession, and how God had worked by it in them in former times, though they then did not know it. But now they see that whatever ability they then had to understand anything of God aright, or to pray unto him, or reap any true benefit from the Scriptures, was through the stirring of this light in them, whereby God even then, in some measure, enlightened and quickened their minds.

Thirdly, again consider whether the light of Christ's Spirit, or the grace and truth which comes by Jesus Christ, has not this property of discovering, convincing, and reproving for sin. Doubtless, the law of the Spirit of life in Christ Jesus, in even the lowest ministration of it, is of that nature that it discovers and fights against the law of sin and death, wherever it finds it. And consider whether the Comforter, the Holy Spirit of truth, who leads out of all error and falsehood, and into all truth, is not also to be known by this, even by his convincing the world of sin, and inwardly reproving for sin, as well as by his comforting of the saints in their holy travels out of sin, and battles against sin.

Fourthly, consider whether anything can convince of sin besides the light of God's Holy Spirit shining in the heart? There may be an outward declaration of sin by the outward law, but it never reaches the heart and conscience except by the shining of the inward light. No, it cannot so much as reach to the understanding, except as God opens the heart and brings home the conviction by his light and power. This we have experience of in the Jews, who though the prophets came with certain evidence and demonstration from God's Spirit, yet they were not thereby convinced, but stood against them, and justified themselves against the voice and Word of the Lord. Indeed, their eyes were closed, their ears shut, and their hearts were hardened, as may be read in Jeremiah chap. 2. and diverse other places. And there is no wickedness so great that a hardened man will not plead for it, and defend and justify himself in it! Yes, and even if God opens men's understandings in some measure, so that they cannot help but confess certain things to be evil in general (as pride, covetousness, drunkenness, riotousness, lying, swearing, etc.), yet often they still cannot see or acknowledge these things to be in themselves. Rather, they produce all sorts of covers and excuses to hide behind, unless the inward light and Spirit of the Lord searches their hearts, and makes these things manifest to them.

Fifthly, consider the weight of the following two scriptures, and do not form for yourself another meaning, and so put off the meaning and intent of God's Holy Spirit in them. The first is that of the apostle, Ephes. 5:13-14. "But all things that are reproved are made manifest by the light; for whatsoever does make manifest, is light. Wherefore he says, 'Awake, you that sleep,'" etc. Every man is bid to awake, because every man has some proportion of that gift in him which (if hearkened to) will reprove, rouse up, and awaken him, and lead him out from among the dead, unto him who gives the light, and causes it to shine in him. The other scripture is that of Gal. 5:17, where the apostle speaks of the flesh lusting against the Spirit, and the Spirit against the flesh, and that these two are contrary. Did not God's Spirit strive with the old world (read Gen. 6:3), not only with the sons of God who had corrupted themselves, but with the rest also? And what is it that has striven with wicked men since, and that does strive with wicked men still? Is it not the same good Spirit? What is it also that inwardly resists and lusts against the will and strivings of God's Spirit? Is it not the flesh? So here are the two seeds (which are contrary to one another) near to man. For there is man the creature (which rightfully belongs to the Lord), into whom the destroyer has gained entrance, and in whom he rules by the law of sin and death. Now he who made man seeks after him, and finds his enemy in man, and gives forth a law against him inwardly in the heart. And, so far as any man gives ear to, believes, and receives it, there arises presently a fight and striving between these two contrary seeds in him, so that this man cannot do the things that he desires. Now, that which thus strives against sin in any man, and troubles him because of sin, reproving and condemning him for it, that is of another nature than the flesh (which harbors sin), and is contrary to it.

Sixthly, consider the great love of God to mankind, and the great care he has of them. First, with regard to their bodies; how does he provide for the bodies of all mankind! He desires to have none hurt, none destroyed, but rather feeds all, nourishes all, making plentiful provision, and giving fruitful seasons. He causes his sun to shine and his rain to descend on all. Then, as to their souls, he knows the preciousness of a soul, and what the loss of a soul is. Yes, he knows how eager the devourer is to destroy, and so sets himself against him. He is the Father of spirits, and his Son the Shepherd and Bishop of souls, whose nature it is to gather and save. And it is said expressly about God, by the testimony of the Spirit of truth, that he desires all to be saved, and come to the knowledge of the truth. And though it was said to the Jews that God was as a potter, and they as clay, and that he could make them vessels either of honor or dishonor at his pleasure, Jer. 18:6, yet this was said to this end—even to invite and encourage them to be subject to him, that they might be made vessels of honor by him, as appears in ver. 11.

Now consider, if God be as tender with respect to souls as he is the bodies of men, does he not make provision for the soul as well as for the body? Would he not desire the soul to live, and would he not desire the soul to be fed as well as the body? If so, then surely the light of his Holy Spirit does shine inwardly throughout all nations, and the saving grace and power is manifest everywhere, even in every heart, in some measure. And surely the flesh and blood of the Son of God (which is the soul's food) is offered to all. For truly, the Lord is not a hard master to any, as the unprofitable servant in every dispensation is ready to account of him. For God winked at, or passed over, the times of ignorance and darkness, being very tender towards men in that estate. Indeed, if man turns to and heeds even a little that is of him (according to the measure of understanding that God gives), it will be owned and accepted, even in the midst of a great deal of darkness and evil working against it.

Oh that men could die to themselves, even to their own wisdom and prudence, and not lean to their own understandings, nor idolize their own apprehensions and conceivings, but rather wait to receive understanding from God, who gives liberally of the true wisdom to those that ask and wait aright! And how does God give true wisdom and understanding? Is it not by the shining of his light in the heart? Oh that men were turned inwardly there, and were inwardly dead to that wisdom and prudence from which God forever hides things! He that will be truly wise must first become a fool, that he may be wise. He must not strive to learn in the comprehensive way of man's wisdom and prudence the things of God's kingdom, but rather feel the begetting of life in his heart, and in that receive something of the new and heavenly understanding. He must die to his own understanding, and no more know the things of God after the flesh. He must become a babe, a fool, and so receive and bow to that which his own wisdom will call foolishness, and will account weakness. But the other birth (which is begotten and born of

God), will know, and daily experience this to be the wisdom and power of God unto salvation.

A Few Clarifications by Way of Question and Answer

True knowledge and true experience, especially concerning necessary things, is of great concern to the soul, such as: to know the true foundation, the cornerstone, which God lays in his spiritual Zion; and the heavenly Jerusalem, which is the mother of all that are born of God; and to be gathered out of the spirit of this world (with its vanity and falsehood) into God's Spirit, which is truth and no lie; and the building up of the holy temple, in which God appears, and is worshiped; and the heavenly communion with the Father and Son, in the one pure light which shines from them into the heart; and the one faith, the one circumcision, the one baptism, the one water of life, the one bread, the one cup of salvation, etc.

Now the things of the kingdom are all at the disposal of the king. Therefore, whoever will understand aright, must receive understanding from him; and whoever will repent aright, must receive repentance from him; and whoever will believe aright, must receive faith from him; and whoever will hear and see aright, must receive an ear and eye from him; and whoever will come unto him, and receive him, must witness that new heart being formed in him, wherewith and whereby he is received. Men greatly mistake and err about the gospel knowledge and religion by beginning in it without the gospel spirit and power.

Therefore the man that desires not to be deceived and lose his soul forever, let him take heed how he begins, how he stands, and how he proceeds in his religion. The Jews stood in the revelation of God's Spirit and power outwardly. The state of the Christians, the new covenant state, stands in the revelation of God's Spirit and power inwardly. For none can beget a new birth to God inwardly except his own Spirit and power working inwardly in the heart. Therefore, you that desire to live with God forever and not perish from the presence and glory of his power, mind these three things:

First, mind God's inward visiting you, and making a real change in you. I do not mean a change in your mind from one notion to another, but a change in your heart from one nature and spirit to another. This is the great work, which nothing but the mighty power of God (which raised Jesus from the dead), can effect in the hearts of the children of men.

Now, that this may be wrought out in you, wait for the appearing and working of that power which does effect it daily more and more in those that unite to it, and give up to its operations. Oh wait to feel the power begetting something of its own nature in you, leavening you into its nature by the pure, heavenly leaven wherewith God desires to leaven your heart! In this way, feel your beginning from the true root, from the holy seed, from the seed of the kingdom. And then wait to feel that seed grow up in you, so that even as the beginning is pure, so the growth may be pure also. For after God has visited you, and begotten something in you, and leavened you in some measure so that there is true life, true sense, true hunger, true breathings, then (secondly) mind and wait to learn of the true teacher how to come to the true waters, that you may drink thereof, and of no dirty puddle of your own or any other's forming.

Now, lastly, after God has made his covenant with you, and spoken peace to you, and given you of the power, righteousness, and joy of the kingdom, and set the holy hedge of his power and wall of salvation about you, you must take heed of going forth after any lust, after any desire of the flesh, after any temptation of the enemy. You must keep within the holy limits, and not touch any dead or unclean thing, lest you be defiled, and so in degrees be separated from him who is pure.

Question: Are the illuminating and sanctifying Spirit one and the same Spirit or no?

Answer: The Spirit which illuminates and the Spirit which sanctifies, is one and the same Spirit, and the illumination of the Spirit is unto sanctification. The same light which discovers the darkness also chases away the darkness. According as this light is received and subjected to, so it purifies the mind. For the light has not only a property of enlightening, but also of cleansing and sanctifying. And the reason why men are not changed, justified, and sanctified, in and by the light, is because they do not love it, nor bring their hearts and deeds to it. Thus the light remains only their reprover and condemner, and not their justifier and sanctifier.

Question: How does God write his law in the heart?

Answer: By his Spirit and power working there, whereby he both creates a new heart and writes the new law, even the law of the Spirit of life in Christ Jesus. It is written, "The isles shall wait for his law." Whose law? The law of the Messiah, the law of grace, which gives dominion, the law of the anointing, the law of the new birth, the law of the holy seed. "His seed remains in him." 1 John 3:9. In that seed is the new nature, and the new law both. Now consider—what is the law of sin? What is the law of death? How is it written in the heart? How does the enemy write it there, except by his corrupt spirit and nature? And does not God, by his holy Spirit and nature, write the new law, the law of life, in the hearts of those that are renewed and made tender to the impressions of his holy, quickening power? Every motion and drawing of His Spirit is then a law to them who are born of the Spirit, and taught of God to see and walk after the quickening Spirit.

Question: What is the true gospel church?

Answer: It is a company of true believers in the Spirit and power of the Lord Jesus Christ. It is a company of true Jews, inward Jews, Jews in Spirit, of the true circumcision, whom the Father has sought out, and made true inward worshipers. It is such as are gathered to the name, and gathered together in the name of the Lord Jesus, to offer up spiritual sacrifices to God through him. It is a company of living stones, who have received life from him, the foundation stone, and who meet together to wait upon and worship the Father in the light and Spirit which they have received from him. This is the holy church, or living assembly of the New Testament, and blessed are they that are of it! For they that are added by God's Spirit and power to this church, and abide in it, shall certainly be saved.

Question: Which is the certain and infallible way to salvation?

Answer: It is a new and living way; it is such a way as none but the living can walk in. It is a holy way, which none but the cleansed, the ransomed, the redeemed of the Lord, can set one step in. The way, the life, and the truth are all one; blessed are they that find it, and walk in it! In plain and express terms, it is the Lord Jesus, the light of the Lord Jesus, the life of the Lord Jesus, the Spirit of the Lord Jesus, the truth as it is in him, his wisdom, his power, he himself, the covenant or holy limit between God and the soul. He that comes into him, comes into the way; he that abides in him, abides in the way; he that walks in him, walks in the way.

Question: How does Christ save the soul?

Answer: By visiting inwardly, knocking inwardly, appearing inwardly, causing the light of life to shine inwardly, and so enlightening and quickening inwardly, breaking the strength of the enemy inwardly, and bringing out of the region and shadow of darkness inwardly, into the region and path of light. It is by the light and power of his Spirit he begets a child of light. This child of light he brings out of Egypt, the dark land, out of Sodom, the filthy, unclean land, out of Babylon, the land and city of confusion, and brings him into the light, where he and his Father dwell. And this child of light is not of the nature of darkness, but of light in the Lord, and he walks in the light, as he is in the light. And by the further shining and working of the light and life in him, he preserves and saves him daily more and more.

Question: What is regeneration, or the new birth?

Answer: It is an inward change, by the Spirit and power of the living God, into his own nature. It is a being begotten of his Spirit, born of his Spirit, begotten into and born of the very nature of his Spirit. ("That which is born of the Spirit, is Spirit, "John 3.) It is a change which God, by the very same power wherewith he raised our Lord Jesus Christ from the grave, makes in the hearts of those whom he visits, who are sensible of, receive, and are subject to his inward life, light, and power.

Question: What is true holiness?

Answer: It is that holy nature, and those holy actions, which arise from the holy root; all else are but imitations of holiness, and not the true holiness. The tree must be made good first, and then the fruit will be good also. There are many likenesses of true holiness throughout the world in several professions of religion; but there is no real holiness to be found (nor righteousness either) except in the trees of God's planting, in the branches which are ingrafted by him into the true vine and olive tree, whose strength of virtue and holiness lies in the sap, which they daily receive from him.

Question: Which are greater, the works which Christ did outwardly on the bodies of men in the days of his flesh, or that which he does inwardly in men's minds and spirits by the powerful appearance and operation of his Spirit? For Christ said that the works he did, those that believed on him should do, and greater also, because he went to the Father. John 14:12.

Answer: Without question, to reach to the soul, and quicken the soul, and raise the soul out of the grave of death, and cure the blindness, deafness, hardness, and disease of the soul, is greater than the outward, and indeed this was signified by the outward.

Question: What is the yoke or cross of Christ?

Answer: It is inward, for that which is to be crucified is chiefly inward. It is that gift of God, that light of his Spirit which is contrary to the darkness, contrary to all that is corrupt, which wills and wars against it. And being received, subjected to, and borne patiently, the cross takes away the life of the flesh, the will and wisdom of the flesh, and all the subtle reasonings and devices of the fleshly part. So it is that the flesh comes to languish and die, and God's plant within is eased of its burden. The soul then, abiding under this cross, comes into the true, pure, and perfect liberty, where it has freedom unto holiness and righteousness, and yet is bound and chained from all liberty to the flesh, and from all unholiness and unrighteousness of every kind.

Question: How may a man "make his calling and election sure?" 2 Pet. 1:10.

Answer: By making the gift of God sure to him; that is, by making that seed sure to him, in whom is the calling and election. For God's choice is of the seed, the holy seed, the inward seed, the seed of God's Spirit, and of the creature as he is joined to the seed. God desires none to perish, but would have all come to the knowledge of Christ, the truth, who is the seed, in whom the election stands. And his holy advice to men is, "to make their calling and election sure." So the way of making the calling and election sure is to make the gift sure, the seed sure, the leaven sure, the pearl sure, which God will never reject, nor any that are found in true union with it, and in the love and obedience of it. Therefore, as God visits with power (with his powerful gift), give up to the truth in the inward parts, come into it, dwell in it, that you may feel its virtue and delivering nature from every enslaving thing, and then stand fast in the liberty wherewith Christ the Lord sets you free. Here you will experience your calling and your election day by day, and will find them sealed and sure to you in that truth, in that heavenly light, in that holy seed, which came from God and is of him, and which he delights to own, and will never reject.

Question: What is true prayer?

Answer: Prayer is the breathings which arise from the true birth, from the living sense which God gives to the true birth. There is a Spirit of prayer and supplication given by God to his children to wrestle and prevail with him. All prayer that arises from, and is given by, that Spirit, is true prayer. All other prayer is not right and true, but is at best an imitation of the true. "We know not what to pray for as we ought; but the Spirit makes intercession for us with groanings which cannot be uttered."

Question: What is true repentance?

Answer: It is the repentance which Christ gives, whom God has exalted to be the prince and Savior, and to give repentance and forgiveness of sins. Acts 5:31. It is not in man's power to repent, for his heart is hard and impenitent. It is God's power which melts, tenderizes, and changes the heart. So there is a great difference between the sense and sorrow of man's nature, and the sense and sorrow which God gives to the heart that he renews and changes. The one is of an earthly nature, the other of a heavenly nature. The one is like the early dew, or morning cloud, that soon passes away; the other is written in the new heart, and abides. In true repentance there is a real sorrow and mourning over the corrupt nature, and all the dead works of the flesh, and a turning from them, and meddling no more with them. This is the repentance which is the gift of the Lord Jesus Christ.

Question: What is the true faith?

Answer: The Scripture speaks of a new creation in Christ. Indeed all true believers are so; and they have the ability, the faculty, the power of believing that comes from him who creates them anew. There is that which is called faith in unregenerate men, but that is not the faith of which I am now speaking. I speak of that faith which is the gift of God to his own birth, to his own begotten. "To you it is given not only to believe," etc. Phil. 1:29. Notice: It is *given* to believe. Oh, this holy gift! This faith of the new birth is the faith which pleases God, prevails with him, purifies the heart, gives access to God and interest in his power and promises, and victory over the worldly nature, and over all the soul's enemies. Blessed be the Lord for bestowing and increasing this faith in the hearts of his children.

Question: What is obedience?

Answer: True obedience is that which flows from the true understanding of God's will, and from the holy nature which he begets in the heart. It is the obedience which flows from a true sense, a true understanding, and a true faith. There is no birth that can believe aright except one; nor is there any birth that can obey aright, except the one that believes aright. The true believing is from the quickening virtue of God's Spirit (all other faith is but dead faith); and the true obedience is in the newness of the Spirit. Rom. 6:4 and 7:6. Man may strive to understand and obey all his days, but he can do neither, except as he is quickened, taught, and enabled of the

Lord. "Teach me, O Lord, the way of your statutes." Psa. 119:33.

There is a mystical path of life. The way of wisdom, the way of holiness, the holy skill of obeying the truth, is hid from all living, from all mankind, except those who are begotten and brought up by him in the holy skill and mystery of subjection to the Lord. "Your people shall be a willing people in the day of your power." It is the power of God that works the will in the heart, and the same power works to do also. No one can learn either to will or to do aright, except as they come to be acquainted with that power, are joined to that power, and feel that power working in them. And here, in the birth from above, true faith and obedience become as natural as unbelief and disobedience are to the birth of the flesh.

Question: What are good works?

Answer: Good works are those that flow from God's good Spirit, the works that are wrought in God. The works of the new birth, of the new creature, are good works; whereas all the works of the flesh are bad, though they be ever so finely painted. All its thoughts, imaginations, reasonings, willing, running, hunting to discover God and heavenly things, with all its sacrifices, all are corrupt and evil, having the bad leaven of the bad nature in them. Make the tree good, or its fruit can never be good. Therefore, good works are only those that flow from the good tree, from the good root. And here all the works of the flesh, though ever so glorious and appealing to man's eye, are shut out by God's measure, by God's plumb line of righteousness and true judgment. And every work of God's Spirit, the smallest work of faith, the least labor of true love, the least shining of life in the heart, and the giving up thereto, is owned by God as coming from him, and wrought in him, who works both to will and to do, of his own good pleasure.

He that is gathered to the light with which God has enlightened him, this one has received the light, dwells in the light, and walks in the light. The Spirit of the living God is near him, and dwells with him, and works in him, and brings his deeds to the light, where it is manifest that they are wrought in God. But he that is outside of the inward light of God's Holy Spirit, his works are not wrought in God. And though they can make a fair show in the flesh (to the fleshly eye), they are not good in God's sight. The erring man's way and works are often right in his own eyes, but blessed is he whose way and works are good and right in the eye of the Lord, in the judgment of his searching, unerring light and Spirit.

Question: Which is the true love?

Answer: The love which arises from the nature which God begets, and from his circumcising the heart from the other nature. Love is greatly commended and admired, and there are many pretenders to it; but none have the true love except those that are born of God and circumcised by him. "The Lord your God will circumcise your heart, and the heart of your seed, to love the Lord your God with all your heart, and with all your soul, that you may live." Deut. 30:6. Note: the true love arises from the true circumcision; and the more a man comes to have his heart circumcised from the fleshly nature, and to grow up in the pure and heavenly nature, the more he loves. God is love; and the nearer anyone comes to him, and the more he partakes of him, the more he becomes love in the Lord, and the more he is taught of God to love the Lord his God, and his brethren in the Spirit, and all mankind, who are of his blood (for of one blood God made all mankind) according to the flesh, or according to a natural consideration.

Question: What is the knowledge of the new covenant?

Answer: It is the knowledge which is given by God to the new birth; for to it the new covenant belongs, and the knowledge of it. For the knowledge of the kingdom of God is given to the truly begotten of God, the true disciples of Christ; but to others it is not given. For in the case of the outward Jew (the first birth, the birth after the flesh), the priest's lips were to preserve knowledge, and man was to seek the law at his mouth. Under this covenant, God sent prophets to speak to them, and he taught them by his prophets. But concerning the inward Jews, the children of the new covenant, the children of the Jerusalem which is above, concerning her seed it was prophesied that they all should be taught by the Lord. These all should hear and know the voice of the Shepherd himself; they should all be gathered to the Shepherd and Bishop of the soul, and be taught by him. So that in this new, holy, living covenant, God himself is the Shepherd, God himself is the Teacher, not only of the greatest, but also of the very least. Heb. 8. These are taught to know the Lord, and to know his Son, and to come to his Son, and to love their Father and one another. So the one that is taught of God, he has the true knowledge, the living knowledge, the substantial knowledge, the knowledge of the thing itself, of the life eternal itself. All that are not taught in this way (but learn only from a literal description and relation of things) have not the knowledge of the new covenant, the knowledge of the thing itself; but only an outward knowledge, such as the first birth may lay hold of and comprehend.

Question: What is the fear of the new covenant?

Answer: It is the fear which God puts in the hearts of his children, which cleanses their hearts, and keeps them from departing from their God. There is a great deal of difference between the fear which may be learned from precepts from without, and the fear which God puts in the hearts of his children from a root of life within. This fear is of a heavenly nature, and is the free gift of God to his own heavenly birth, and to no one else. For no man can possibly attain this fear by any thoughts or reasonings of his own, but only by the springing up of life from God. And he that would have this fear, must know the place of wisdom, and wait there for it; and when he has it, this fear will soon begin to make him wise towards salvation, and teach him to depart from evil, which is the cause of destruction. Job 28:28.

Question: What is the true hope?

Answer: It is the stay of the mind upon the Lord, the stay of the heavenly birth upon its Father. Now, we must distinguish between hope and hope. There is the hope of the hypocrite, or false birth, which hope shall perish. And there is the hope of the true birth, which hope shall never fail nor make ashamed, for this birth is taught of God to hope aright.

Now, concerning hope, there is both the ground of it, and the hope itself. The ground of the hope is God's love, God's truth, God's faithfulness, God's grace, his seed, his Christ felt within. There is the truth of being of him, being united to him, in him, and he in me. This is the ground of my assurance of the everlasting glory and inheritance, which is sure to the seed, and to all that are of and in the seed. So knowing Christ within me, feeling Christ within me, living in him, and he in me, I have an anchor sure and steadfast within the veil, which no storms, tempests, trials, or temptations, present or to come, have power over.

Then there is the hope, or hoping itself; that is, the staying of the mind upon the Lord, the leaning upon the Lord, the retiring beyond all thoughts or reasonings or looking out, to the inward life; to feel something spring from it, for the soul to hope or trust in, beyond all outward appearance. This hope never deceives nor makes ashamed those who are taught of God thus to stay their minds upon him. No, though the state be darkness, and no light is seen, yet beneath the darkness there is something to stay the mind of the child and servant of the Lord till he appear, and cause light to break out of obscurity. For light is sown for the righteous, and joy for the upright, even in their darkest, saddest, and most distressed conditions, in all of which the Lord is near, and there is still ground to hope in him.

Question: Which is the true joy?

Answer: It is the joy which flows from God's presence, and the work of his power in the heart, and the assured expectation which he gives of the full inheritance and glory of life everlasting. When the bridegroom is present, when the soul is gathered home to him, married to him, in union with him, in the holy, living fellowship, then there is joy. Indeed, when he appears against the enemies of the soul, rising up against them, breaking and scattering them, and giving good things, filling with life, filling with love, filling with virtue, feasting the soul in the presence of the Father; oh, what fullness of joy is there then in the heart! "In your presence is fullness of joy, and at your right hand are pleasures for evermore," said the psalmist. Ps. 16:11.

Christ said to his disciples, that because of his going away they should have sorrow; but he would see them again, and their heart should rejoice, and their joy no man should take from them. John 16:22. How or when was this fulfilled? For what reason were they grieved? Was it not for the loss of his outward presence, which had been so sweet and comfortable to them? How would he come to them again? Was it not by the Comforter? Was it not by his inward and spiritual presence? So that he that was with them should now be in them? Before they knew Christ with them; now they should know Christ in them, and the Father in them, and they in him. This is Immanuel, the gospel state, God with us, dwelling with us, tabernacling in us, living in us, walking in us, and we living and walking in him. When the apostles came to this state, then they came to witness the joy in the Holy Spirit, even the joy unspeakable and full of glory. And so it is that the gospel state is a state of joy and rejoicing in the Lord, even in his glorious, living presence, and in the glory of his power. For now the true light shines inwardly in the heart, and the life is manifested; and they that come into the manifestation of it, come into the holy union, the holy fellowship with the Father and Son, where the joy is, and where the joy is full.

Question: What is the right poverty of spirit, and the true humility?

Answer: True poverty of spirit and humility is that which springs from the same root from which the faith, love, peace, joy, and the other heavenly things arise; and it is of the same nature.

Now, there is a voluntary humility, and a voluntary poverty (even of spirit), which a man can cast himself into, and form in himself by his own working and reasonings. This is not the true, but rather a false image, a counterfeit of the true. But then there is a poverty which arises from God's emptying the creature, from God's stripping the creature; and there is a humility which arises from a new heart and nature. This is the right kind, and it is lasting, and remains even in the midst of the riches and glory of the kingdom. For just as Christ was poor in spirit before his Father, and lowly in heart in the midst of all the fullness which he received from him, so it is with those who are of the same birth and nature with Christ. They are filled with humility, and clothed with humility, in the midst of all the graces and heavenly riches with which God fills them and adorns them. If they keep in the faith, keep in the truth, keep in the light and power, it excludes all boasting in or after the flesh, and keeps the mind in true humility and poverty of spirit. And so the Lord of life is alone exalted, and the creature is kept abased before him and low forever, and he is nothing except as the Lord is pleased to fill him.

The Conclusion

He that desires to witness, know, experience, and enjoy these things, must mind that seed in which they are all wrapped up, and out from which they spring and shoot forth. The kingdom is in the seed, the throne in the seed, the power in the seed. And he that is united to the seed, and abides in the seed, receives power from the seed, and overcomes. He shall inherit all things, and "I will be his God, and he shall be my son." Rev. 21:7. But he must not be fearful or unbelieving of overcoming sin, or of his soul's enemies, but must depend upon the almighty and all-sufficient power of God. For the seed will give him victory over sin, and teach him to touch no unclean thing, that he may be holy, as the Lord his God is holy. Truly it is good for the heavenly children to partake of the divine life and heavenly nature of their Father, and become like him.

Chapter V

The Experiences

A Preface

The Father, in his love, has brought us to the Son, and the Son in the same love, has brought us back to the Father; and now the love flows from the Father most naturally and abundantly in and through the Son. And wherever the heart is circumcised, there the love returns back to him most truly and naturally, so that the Lord our God is loved with all the heart, and with all the soul, and nothing is thought too good to sacrifice to him, nor anything too much to suffer for him. Oh, the pure love that springs and flows between the heavenly Father and the spiritual child! The best love that is found in this world (among men of this world) is not worthy to be a shadow of it.

Now, from this Fountain issue forth not only springs and streams of life to refresh our own hearts, but also testimonies concerning the life which we feel and partake of, and concerning our travels from the dark land, through the valley of tears, towards our resting place. Many times these spring up in us for the sake of others, and the following things are of that nature. For it is not for my own sake that these did spring up in me at this time, but to signify to others the mercy the Lord has shown me, and the way wherein he has led me, and what he has given me to taste of and experience in the way. And having received them from the Lord for this very end—to hold them forth to others in love and tenderness of spirit—my heart is freely given up to him therein. I aim at nothing in this but his glory singly, and the good of such souls to whom he shall be pleased to extend favor and show mercy, in opening the heavenly mystery of life and salvation to them.

Indeed, my wound was deep and seemed incurable. But blessed be the Lord who has made known to me the physician of value, for whom no disease is too hard. Surely he is able to cure every sickness, and relieve and rescue all that are captive and oppressed by the devil, who come unto him and wait upon him in the way of his righteous judgments and most tender mercies. For after all my religion and deep exercises, and inward experiences and knowledge, I came to such a loss of what I once had, that I sensibly felt I knew not the Lord, and I lay continually groaning and mourning after him. Oh, the pure light, and precious life, and sweet presence of my God that my soul lacked, insomuch that my moisture was turned into the drought of summer, and my bones grew dry and withered! But at length, the Lord, in his goodness, breathed upon the dry bones, and I felt life enter from him into me, and the days of deep sorrow and distress were at length forgotten, because a man-child was conceived and brought forth. And now where is the sackcloth? Where are the ashes? Oh, there is beauty in life, instead of the ashes in the lifeless state; there is a garment of praise instead of the spirit of heaviness! Oh glory, glory to him who binds up the bruised and brokenhearted. Glory to the Redeemer of the captives, to the repairer of the breaches, to the builder of the wasted and desolate ones!

I. Concerning the Seed of the Kingdom

Concerning the seed of the kingdom, this I have experienced: that it consists not in words or notions of the mind, but is an inward thing—an inward, spiritual substance in the heart, as real inwardly in its kind as other seeds are outwardly in their kind. And being received by faith, this seed takes root in man (his heart, his earth, being plowed up and prepared for it), it grows up inwardly, and brings forth fruit inwardly, as truly and really as any outward seed does outwardly. This seed is known by its opposition to, and enmity against, the seed of the serpent, and against all the seeds of evil in the hearts of men. It discovers them, turns the mind from them, wars against them, and bruises and overcomes them in all that receive it. It also lets in its own holy nature, which, as a holy leaven or salt, works out that which is unholy and unrighteous, dark and dead, and seasons the soul with light, with life, with grace, with the holiness and righteousness of truth.

II. Concerning the Soul's Food

The soul's food is that which nourishes it, which is the same as that which gives it life. Every word proceeding out of the mouth of God, every motion, every quickening, every operation of his Spirit, is living, and nourishes the soul (which receives and feeds upon it) with life. The spiritual manna, the spiritual water, from the holy well or fountain, the milk of the word, the flesh and blood of the Son of the living God, his words, which are spirit and life, nourish up the living birth unto life everlasting. How does a man come to live at first, but by hearing the voice of him that gives life? And how does a man come to live afterwards, and to increase in life, but by hearing the same voice? "Incline your ear, and come unto me; hear, and your soul shall live," etc. Isa. 55:3. This I have also experienced to give me life, to nourish up and strengthen me in life, even fresh life communicated from the living Fountain. And so my life is not in myself, not in anything I can comprehend concerning Christ, but in being joined to him, in being ingrafted into him who is the holy root, the true olive tree, into his Spirit. And so by the sap that springs up into me from him, my life is maintained and increased in me daily. Glory to his name forever.

III. *Concerning God's Power*

Concerning God's power, this I have experienced: that it is the power of God which does the work in the soul. It begets to God, it brings out of the land of darkness, it leads through all entanglements, and preserves in the midst of them all. It breaks down the old building of sin and iniquity (both inwardly and outwardly, both in the heart, and also in life and conduct), and raises the new and holy building. It makes willing, it makes obedient, it gives ability to believe and to suffer. Oh, blessed be the Lord for the day of his power which has inwardly broken forth! Oh, blessed are they that know the ministration of the life inwardly, the power of life inwardly! For in life, in the seed of life, is the holy power which manifests, appears, and works as it gains ground in the creature, exercising in it the virtue and strength which it daily receives from its Father.

IV. *Concerning Temptations*

Concerning temptations, this I have experienced: that the strength and hurt of them, as to the soul, lies in the soul's looking at them. For the strength of God is revealed in his children against the tempter, which being patiently waited for, and trusted in, will never fail them. The Lord does not desire that even the least babe let in temptation and sin, but rather watch in that, and keep joined to that which will preserve out of all temptation and sin. "Look unto me and be saved, all you ends of the earth." This is universally true. Look unto me, trust in me; look not at yourselves, trust not in yourselves; look not at the enemy, fear not the enemy; I will save you from every snare, every temptation, as your eye is steadfast upon me. What if the enemy comes in like a flood? If the Spirit of the Lord lifts up a standard against him, can he prevail? What if he casts fiery darts? Will not the shield of faith quench them all? Will not the whole armor of God defend and keep safe from them all? If the enemy is resisted rightly (that is, in true faith in the power which is engaged for the soul against him), does not the power of the Lord arise and scatter him, and strengthen and establish the soul in grace and truth? Oh look not at the enemy! Let not in the reasonings of the mind, but keep in the patience, keep in the pure fear, and in the holy, living sense. Be only what you are in the seed, in the new birth, in the life which God has begotten in you; for then are you safe, then are you in the name of the Lord, which is the strong tower. The enemy indeed may make a noise about you with his lusts, with his temptations, with his floods, with his storms, with his fiery darts; but he cannot enter your habitation. The Spirit of darkness, the prince of darkness, is shut out of the land of the living. Abide there. Dwell in the light, and walk in the light, as God is in the light, and he shall never have power over you.

V. *Concerning Prayer*

I have experienced prayer to be the breathing of that birth which God begets, unto the Father of life which begat it; who by his Spirit makes known its condition and needs, and gives sensible cries unto him for them. For as it is not in man to beget himself to God, no more can he pray to God in his own will or time, but only as God pours out the Spirit of prayer and supplication upon him, and by his Spirit teaches and helps him to pray as he ought. "Because you are sons, God has sent forth the Spirit of his Son into your hearts, crying, Abba, Father."

I have had a sense of the natural man, and of the spiritual man, and of the cries and prayers of each. And this I have been taught and learned of God—that the gospel prayer is the prayer of that birth which is begotten by the Spirit and power of the gospel, and which prays in the Spirit, and in the springing up of the holy life and power. In this way, prayer rightly wrestles and prevails with God, obtaining the mercies and blessings which it wrestles with him for. For to this child there is access to God in the faith, through that Holy Spirit of life which makes way for it to obtain grace and mercy in the time of need. And through this Spirit it prays to God, and prevails with him on behalf of others also. For the prayers of the righteous avail much, as it is written.

VI. *Concerning Justification and Sanctification*

Some things which it has pleased the Lord, in his tender mercy, to give me to experience:

First, that it is the same Christ, the same Spirit, the same life, the same wisdom, the same power, the same goodness, love, and mercy, the same water, the same blood, which both justifies and sanctifies.

Secondly, that justification and sanctification are both of and through grace. It is so in the beginning, and it is so all along. "By grace you are saved," says the apostle. The whole work of salvation is begun and carried on through grace. It is through that grace that God visits and reaches to the soul with his quickening virtue and power. He regenerates by grace, and through it he justifies, sanctifies, etc. So that as the work goes on, "grace, grace," is to be cried unto him that does the work, from his laying the foundation and fastening the soul thereupon, to his laying of the top stone.

Thirdly, that faith and obedience are of the same nature, and always go together, so that wherever there is faith, there is likewise obedience; and wherever there is obedience, there is faith. Obedience flows from faith, and cannot be without it; for the very nature and virtue of faith is in it. And faith is obedience. For this is the command of God, that the soul believe on him (and in his appearances) whom he has sent to save. Indeed, this believing is obedience unto him that commands it. And this faith, and this obedience, is holy and just in God's sight; and through it (but not without it) the soul is both justified and sanctified.

Fourthly, that the works of faith, the works of the new life, are not the works of the law (or works of the old covenant); nor are they excluded from justification, as the works of the old covenant are. For I have found that the Lord, who has condemned and excluded all my doings which-ever I have been able to do of myself, still justifies and accepts that which his Spirit and holy power does in me. These are not of the same nature as the works of the law, nor are they so accounted in the eye of the Lord. For the Lord distinguishes between root and root. Whatever springs from the holy root, he justifies as holy; whatever arises from the unholy root, he condemns as unholy.

Fifthly, that by the law of faith all boasting is excluded in the whole work, both in justification and sanctification. For what is the law of faith? Is not this its law—to fetch all from the Son, and to do all in the Son? Is it not to quit self and its own ability, and to perform all things in the newness of the Spirit, in the ability which God gives and continues supplying in and through his grace and mercy, to the soul that is in the Lord Jesus Christ? All the veins of life, all the streams of the new covenant run here. Here there is no boasting for the creature, nor can there be, for all man's ability and strength is shut out, and that which is given of God is all and does all. Yet every inward Jew here "has praise of God." Rom. 2:29. His faith is commended, his love is commended, his faithfulness is commended, his zeal for the Lord, his obedience to the Lord, his patience in suffering, is commended, etc. But the praise and honor of all rebounds not to his flesh, but to the Spirit and grace of God in him. So that here flesh is laid low and kept in the dust forever, and God alone is exalted in this day of his pure power in the heart.

He that truly believes enters into rest. How into rest? From what does he rest? Why, from his own works, from the works of the flesh. Yes, he rests from the works of the old covenant, from the works that arise from his own ability, from the works wherein he can never be justified with the gospel justification. But does he cease from the works of faith? Does he cease from the labor of love? Does he cease from obedience to anything that God requires? No, but rather he begins to work and labor in the vineyard, and his labor is not in vain in the Lord.

VII. Concerning Faith

Several things I have experienced concerning the nature, virtue, and operations of faith; some of which (as I feel them spring up livingly in my heart) I may mention at this time.

First, this I have often experienced—that it is a hard thing to truly and rightly believe. It is an easy matter to believe notions concerning God and Christ, but to believe in God, to believe in Christ, to believe in him that raised up Jesus, to believe in the light, life, and power which flows from Jesus, this indeed is hard because of the great darkness and ignorance which man is fallen into through transgression.

Secondly, I have experienced this also—that faith is God's gift, and that it flows from the power of his life. There is first a quickening, first a touching of the heart by the holy, pure power of the Lord. Then, only when a man is touched and quickened in and by and through that virtue which flows into him, he can believe in that which touches and quickens him.

Thirdly, that faith never stands in a man's own power, but always in the virtue and power of the life of the Son, so that he that will believe aright must wait to feel the life of the Son revealed in him, and faith flowing from him. For the true belief springs from the life of the holy root, and it is from the flowing up and springing up of that life that faith receives its nourishment and daily virtue.

Fourthly, I have observed this in my travels—that the earthly wisdom and its notions, when gotten into the mind and held in the mind out of the sense of life, are a great obstacle to faith. For these strengthen and nourish that in man which must be weakened and die if the true birth of life will ever reign in the heart. Man is to die; man is to be ceased from; his understanding, his wisdom is to be brought to nothing. But after it has had a stroke and wound from God's Holy Spirit and power (even the very wound which tends to death), yet it will be seeking life again (getting its deadly wound healed), and nourishing its life by those very notions which came from the life and power, which in measure slew it. In this way, the outward Jew finds his life in the outward knowledge, in the outward law, in the letter which kills. For indeed, the descriptions and outward knowledge of things kills and deadens more and more, unless man comes into the inward life and virtue. "If you live in the Spirit, walk in the Spirit," said the apostle. A man cannot live in an outward knowledge concerning the Spirit and power of the endless life. He that would truly live must live in the Spirit itself, and he that would rightly walk on in his way, must walk in that Spirit wherein he received life.

Fifthly, this I have also observed—that all notional faith without the living virtue (as concerning Christ, his sufferings, death, resurrection, ascension, intercession, justification by him, etc.) the enemy will let the soul alone with, and let him enjoy peace in. But he will desperately war against the true faith, against faith in the true power, against faith in the light of life. Oh, how many sore and sharp assaults does he make against the faith which receives its virtue from God, and causes the soul to live to God! And how painful it is in the soul, when faith is weak, and the enemy comes against it with the strength of his assaults and temptations. "Lord, increase our faith," said the sensible disciples.

Sixthly, that it is in the pure fear (not that which is taught by the precepts of men, but which God puts into the heart) that faith has its strength, and exercises its strength. Oh, who knows the preciousness of this fear! The power of faith, the power of life, the power of salvation and everlasting preservation is revealed in it. Therefore, when the Lord speaks of providing for his children a new covenant, he says, "I will put my fear in their hearts, and they shall not depart from me."

Now it behooves everyone to deeply consider of what nature his faith is, and what virtue is in it. What can it do in and through the power of the Lord for him? Does it indeed fetch the true, living nourishment every day? Does it deliver the soul and give it victory over that which faith was appointed to deliver from? For he, who through faith over-comes that which is contrary to God, shall receive the inheritance; and he that fights the good fight of faith shall overcome. But he that does not overcome his enemies which stand in his way, shall be sure to be hindered by them from reaching his journey's end.

VIII. *Concerning Obedience*

First, true obedience, gospel obedience, flows from life, flows from the living faith. If I could obey in all things that God requires of me, it would not satisfy me unless I felt my obedience flow from the birth of his life in me. "My Father does all in me," said Christ. This was Christ's comfort. And to feel Christ do all in the soul is the comfort of everyone that truly believes in him.

Secondly, true obedience, gospel obedience, is natural to the birth which is born of God. It is unnatural to the flesh, to man's wisdom, to deny himself and take up the cross, but it is natural to the birth which is born of God's Spirit. "That which is born of the Spirit, is Spirit," and it is natural to it to be acquainted with, and exercised about, that which is spiritual.

Thirdly, that honoring, pleasing, and answering the will of the Lord is the proper aim of the truly obedient. Oh, how do they delight to do the will of God! "I have food," says

Christ, "that you know not of." To do the will was his food and drink, and it is food and drink to all that are of his nature and Spirit. If I should never have any reward other than the pleasure of obedience, still I could not help but testify that in answering the law of the pure life, in keeping the holy statutes and commandments of God's Spirit, there is great reward. Yet there is a crown also, and a reaping after this life of everything that is sown to the Spirit.

Oh, blessed is he who meets with the power of life which enables him to obey, and blessed is he who is obedient and subject to that power! For he that truly believes in Christ is turned by him to his light, and to the power of his Father, and all peace, growth, joy, blessedness, etc. is witnessed in subjection thereto.

IX. Concerning the Cross of Christ

This I have experienced concerning the cross of our Lord Jesus Christ—that it is an inward and spiritual thing, producing inward and spiritual effects in the mind. For it is the cross of Christ which slays the enmity in the mind, and crucifies to the world and the affections thereof. "God forbid," said the apostle, "that I should glory, save in the cross of our Lord Jesus Christ, whereby the world is crucified unto me, and I unto the world." Now note: that which is contrary to the world, and crucifies to the world, that is the cross. The cross alone has this power and nothing else, so there is nothing else in which to glory. "The flesh lusts against the Spirit, and the Spirit against the flesh; and these are contrary one to the other." Here is the cross: the Spirit which is contrary to the flesh, which mortifies the flesh, in the obedience of which the flesh is crucified. "If you, through the Spirit, mortify the deeds of the body, you shall live."

Whatsoever is of and in the Spirit is contrary to the flesh. The light of the Spirit is contrary to the darkness of the flesh. The holiness of the Spirit is contrary to the unholiness of the corrupt heart. The life of the Spirit is contrary to the life (or rather death) that is in sin. The power of the Spirit is contrary to the power that is in Satan and his kingdom. The wisdom of God is contrary, and a foolish thing, to the wisdom of man. Yes, the new creature, which springs from God's Holy Spirit, is contrary and death to the old. Now he that comes here, out of his own wisdom, will, thoughts, and reasonings, and comes to a discerning of God's Spirit, and to the feeling of his begetting of life in the heart, and waits here, and receives counsel here, such a one is taught to deny himself, and to join to and take up that by which Christ daily crosses and subdues in him whatever is contrary to God.

Here is the fight of faith and the true journey under the cross, whereby the enemies (which rise up to oppose in the way) are vanquished and overcome. For here (in the cross) is the power revealed, the preserving power, the leading power, the conquering power of him who rides on conquering and to conquer his spiritual enemies in the hearts of his children. These know his voice and are subject to him, and daily deny themselves, taking up his cross and following him. Woe to them that are at ease in Zion with anything that is contrary to God. But blessings are upon those whose dwelling is under the cross, and who know no ease except what it allows. It will make truth, life, holiness, righteousness, faith, obedience, meekness, patience, love, separation from sin, communion with the Lord, and all the fruits of the Spirit, as natural to them in the renewed state, as ever sin was in the corrupt state. For Paul, who once complained of his captivity, and that he did what he hated, yet after he had known the power of the cross, and was crucified with Christ, he could then do nothing against the truth, but only for the truth. Yes, then being a conqueror, having overcome the enemies which stood in his way, he could do all things through Christ that strengthened him.

The cause of so many complaints, and so much mourning because of the prevailing of the enemy (through temptations, sin, and corruption), is because the cross of Christ, which is the power of God, is either not known, or not taken up. And this is the reason that many who make a fair show for a while, yet afterward come to nothing (but are like untimely figs, or like corn upon the housetops, which hastily spring up, but soon wither) because they never rightly learn or keep to the cross. For the cross alone has power from God to bring down and keep down that which is contrary to him. But out from under the cross of Christ, there is no witnessing salvation or preservation from the Lord. Outside the limits of the cross, the enemy has power to recover and bring back under his dominion again. And whosoever in his travels leaves the cross behind him, draws back unto perdition, and cannot travel on in the living faith, and the newness of obedience, towards the salvation of the soul.

X. Concerning the Mystery of Life, and the Mystery of the Fellowship which is Therein.

God is hid from man so long as he lies in his sinful and fallen state; and no man can find or know him, except as he is pleased to reveal himself by his own blessed Spirit. When Christ appeared in the days of his flesh, flesh and blood could not reveal him, but only the Father. And he is the same today as he was yesterday. He is not to be known now, except in the same Spirit, in his own grace and truth, in a measure of his own life. The dead cannot know him, but only those who are his sheep, who are quickened and made alive by him.

Now this life is a mystery; none can understand it except they that partake of it. Can a man that is naturally dead know what the life of nature means? No more can a man that is spiritually dead know what the life of the Spirit means. The natural man may get the words that came from life, and claim and commend them, and speak great words about the fame of wisdom, but the thing itself is hid from them all. Oh, it is a narrow gate through which the birth enters, and through which none else can enter! The wise and prudent learners and searchers according to the flesh (even of the Scriptures, as they can put meanings upon them and compre-hend them) are shut out in every age. But there is a babe born of naked truth (born of the pure simplicity) who is admitted by God.

The fellowship of the saints is in the life and in the light, which is a mystery. The fellowship is not outward, but inward. All they that meet together in the outward place are not in the fellowship, but only they that meet together in the inward life and Spirit. "They that worship the Father, must worship him in Spirit and truth." There is the worship; there are the worshipers. They that are in the Spirit, in the truth, meet in the Spirit, in the truth, they meet together in the one spiritual place, as I may call it. And so we know no man after the flesh, no man according to the appearance, but only in the righteous judgment of the Spirit, those only who are of the Spirit. Indeed, we are tender where there is the least beginning of the work of God in any heart, indeed, where there is only so much as a conviction of the understanding. But they are not truly one of us, who acknowledge our princi-ples in words or outward appearance, but only those who are inwardly changed thereby in the heart.

XI. Concerning the Increase of the Kingdom

Was it not the great doctrine of Christ to preach the kingdom? And how did he preach it? Did he not preach it as a seed, as a grain of mustard seed? Did he not liken this spiritual seed to leaven, to a precious pearl, to treasure hidden in a field, to a piece of silver lost, etc.? Oh how happy is he who knows and enjoys the thing itself which Christ preached! All the prophets prophesied concerning him, and when he came, this was his doctrine—that men should mind this precious seed, look after it, purchase it, possess it, feel it planted and growing up in them, and themselves ingrafted into and growing up in it.

Now, there are many sorts of talkers concerning the thing, but there are few travelers into it. Only the one who is a true traveler into it, and who finds his rest there, can certainly know and truly witness what is to be found there. And this is the reason that so many (who seem to be wise and learned) cannot receive our testimony—because they know neither the seed nor its voice, concerning which and by which we testify. But wisdom is justified by her children, and they that know the voice of the Shepherd know his present appearance in this our day, which is contrary to the wisdom and knowledge of all other seeds and births whatsoever. "He that has an ear to hear, let him hear." But he that has not the true ear cannot hear the true testimony, though it should be ever so often declared unto him. But blessed is he that knows and stumbles not at the appearances of the seed and power of life in his own heart, but rather is turned from the darkness to the light there, and from the power of Satan to the manifestation of God's Spirit there. For the end of words (even of Christ's own directions in the days of his flesh) is to turn men to the holy life and power from whence the words came.

Unto this is the soul's true travel, waiting on the Lord in the way of his judgments and tender mercies, to witness a translation from darkness to light, and from the kingdom of Satan into the kingdom of the dear Son, which kingdom is at first but as a grain of mustard seed.

And now let every serious heart examine concerning himself. Do you know the kingdom? Is the seed grown in you? Does it overspread you? Are you in it as in a kingdom? Do you feel it overshadowing you? Are you in unity with it? Does it speak peace to you from the Lord? Is the wall of partition broken down in you? Is there of the two made one new man? Do you feel that which is contrary to Christ subdued in you by his power? Do you feel his holy nature, life, and Spirit, reigning over it? Do you experience that scripture, "If you through the Spirit mortify the deeds of the body, you shall live"?

Ah, how much do men talk of Christ, the power of God, and yet miss the effect and work of his power in them! Faith is a powerful thing, it gives victory (true faith gives victory). It scatters that which stands between, and gives real access to God, and lets in his pure, fresh, living virtue, upon the heart.

Love is a powerful thing, it constrains unto obedience, and the heart that is circumcised to love the Lord God, oh how does life flow from him into it!

Oh, away with empty notions, and come to the ministration of the Spirit, where the knowledge is living, the faith victorious, the love pure and undefiled, the worship truly spiritual, even flowing from, and comprehended in, the life and virtue of the Spirit! Oh that all that truly breathe after the Lord might be gathered here, found here, and dwell here! Amen.

A Few Words Concerning the True Christ

Question: How may the inward and spiritual appearance of Christ be known?

Answer: The inward appearance is to be known in the same way, and by the same means, as was his outward appearance, which was by the revealing of the Father. For "none knows the Son but the Father, and he to whom the Father reveals him." And when Simon Peter confessed him to be Christ, the Son of the living God, he said, "Blessed are you, Simon Bar-Jona, for flesh and blood has not revealed it unto you, but my Father which is in heaven." Matt. 16:16-17. Now, if none could know Christ in his appearance in the flesh (despite so many manifest and express prophecies concerning him), but only such to whom the Father revealed him, how shall any know his inward and spiritual appearance, unless they be taught of the Father, and hear and learn of him?

The true Christ is known by the manifestation of his life within, by the fullness of the grace and truth which dwells in him, and puts itself forth, so as to be discerned by the inward and spiritual eye in man. He is known by his voice and knocks. His sheep know His voice. He speaks in his Father's authority (not as the scribes, not as earthly-wise, learned men); he speaks in the evidence and demonstration of God's Spirit. The words which he speaks are Spirit and life, and they that hear his voice live. Oh, the beatings of his hand upon the tender and sensible hearts and consciences! Oh, his secret reproofs, his secret instructions, his secret quickening and enlightening!

He is known by his baptism, or by his baptizing into his own Spirit and power. While people were in expectation, and mused in their hearts about John, whether he were the Christ or not, John answers the case, and tells them how they might discern and know the true Christ. It is not I, who baptize only with water; but he that baptizes "with the Holy Spirit, and with fire; whose fan is in his hand," etc. Luke 3:15-17. He that knows him who inwardly and spiritually baptizes, who has the fan, and who inwardly fans and purges the floor, gathering in the wheat and burning up the chaff, does he not inwardly, truly, and spiritually know Christ? He that knows the word which is quick and powerful, and sharper than any two-edged sword, piercing even to the dividing asunder of soul and spirit, and of the joints and marrow, and is a discerner of the thoughts and intents of the heart, does he not know "the word which was in the beginning, which was with God"?

He is known by his mighty works. "The works which the Father has given me to finish, the same works that I do, bear witness of me, that the Father has sent me." John 5:36. And when John sent two of his disciples to Jesus with this question: "Are you he that should come, or should we look for another?" Christ bids them go and tell John what things they had seen and heard: "How that the blind see, the lame walk, the lepers are cleansed, the deaf hear, the dead are raised, to the poor the gospel is preached; and blessed is he whosoever shall not be offended in me." Luke 7:22-23. "Why, herein is a marvelous thing" said the blind man "that you know not where he is from, and yet he has opened my eyes." John 9:30. He who has the power, and shows forth the power inwardly— who opens the inward eye, the inward ear, looses the inward tongue, causes the inward feet to walk in the way of life, and the inward hands to work the works of God—this one is the Messiah, the Savior, the Word of life, the Son of the living God. They that believe in him, in his Spirit, in his power, in his inward appearance, have the witness in themselves, the living testimony, which none can put out, or take away from them. Oh, he has opened my eyes, he has opened my heart, he has raised me out of the grave, he has given me eternal life! He has changed me inwardly, created me inwardly, by the working of his mighty power! And now I daily live, and am preserved, and grow by the same power. I feel his life, his virtue, his power, his presence day by day. He is with me, he lives in me, and I live not of myself, but by feeling him to live in me, finding life spring up from him into me, and through me. Herein lies all my ability and strength forevermore.

Chapter VI

A Brief Account Concerning
the People Called Quakers

We are a people of God's gathering, who (many of us) had long waited for his appearance, and had undergone great distress for lack thereof.

Question: But some ask, "What appearance of the great God and Savior did you lack?"

Answer: We lacked the presence and power of his Spirit to be inwardly manifested in our spirits. We had (as I may say) what we could gather from the letter, and endeavored to practice what we could read in the letter; but we lacked the power from on high; we lacked life; we lacked the presence and fellowship of our beloved; we lacked the knowledge of the heavenly seed and kingdom, and an entrance into it, and the holy dominion and reign of the Lord of life over the flesh, sin, and death in us.

Question: How did God appear to you?

Answer: The Sun of righteousness did arise in us, the dayspring from on high, the morning star did visit us, insomuch that we did really see and feel the light and brightness of the inward day in our spirits, as ever we had felt the darkness of the inward night.

Question: How did God gather you?

Answer: By the voice of his Son, by the arm of his Son, by the virtue of his Son's light and life inwardly revealed and working in our hearts. This loosed us inwardly from the darkness, from the bonds of sin and iniquity, from the power of the captor and destroyer, and turned our minds inwardly towards our Lord and Savior, to mind his inward appearance, his inward shinings, his inward quickenings, all of which were fresh from God and full of virtue. And as we came to be sensible of them, join to them, receive and give up to them, we came thereby to partake of their virtue, and to witness the rescuing and redeeming of our souls. So that by hearing the Son's voice, and following him, we found him to be the way to the Father, and we came to be gathered home by him to the Father's house, where there is bread enough, and places of rest and peace for all the children of the Most High.

Now with respect to the blessed seed of truth, which we have had experience of, and testify to (for how could we conceal so rich a treasure and still be faithful to God?), it is no new thing in itself, though of late it is more clearly revealed, and the minds of men are more clearly directed and guided to it than in former ages. It is no other than that which Christ himself abundantly preached, who preached the kingdom, who preached the truth which makes free, using many parables and resemblances. Sometimes he spoke of a little seed, sometimes of a pearl or hidden treasure, sometimes of a leaven or salt, sometimes of a lost piece of silver, etc. Now what is all this, and where is this to be found?

What is this which is like a little seed, a pearl, etc., and where is it to be found? What is the field? Is it not the world, and is not the world set in man's heart? What is the house which is to be swept, and the candle lighted in? Is it not that house, or heart, where the many enemies are? A man's enemies, says Christ, are those of his own house.

Indeed, the testimony concerning all this was precious to us; but finding and experiencing the thing testified of was much more precious. And this we say in perfect truth of heart, and in most tender love to the souls of people—that whoever tries shall find this little thing, this little seed of the kingdom, to be a kingdom, to be a pearl, to be heavenly treasure, to be the leaven of life, leavening the heart with life, and with the most precious oil and ointment of healing and salvation. So we testify to no new thing, but to the truth and grace which was from the beginning, which was always in Jesus Christ our Lord and Savior, and was dispensed by him in all ages and generations. For it was he who quickened, renewed, and changed the heart of the true believers in his inward and spiritual appearance, and thereby destroyed the enemies of their own house, and saved them from them. For indeed there is no saving the creature, without destroying that in the creature which brings spiritual death and destruction upon it. Israel of old was saved by the destroying of their outward enemies; and Israel now (the new Israel, the inward Israel) is saved by the destruction of their inward enemies. Oh, that people could come out of their own wisdom, and wait for God's wisdom, that in it they might come to see the glory, the excellency, the exceedingly rich virtue and treasures of life that are wrapped up in this seed of life! Then they would receive it, give up to it, and come to partake of it.

And with respect to doctrines, we have no new doctrines to hold forth. The doctrines held forth in the holy Scriptures are the doctrines that we believe. And this does further seal to us our belief of this seed, because we find it to be the key by which God opens the Scriptures to us, and gives us the living sense and evidence of them in our hearts. We can see and have felt to whom the curse and wrath belong, and also to whom the love, mercy, peace, blessings, and precious promises belong. And we have been led by God's Holy Spirit and power through the judgments to the mercy, and to the partaking of the precious promises. So then, why would we publish any new faith, or any new doctrines? Indeed we have none to publish, but our only aim is to bring men to the ancient seed of truth, and to the right understanding and practice of the ancient, apostolic doctrine and holy faith once delivered to the saints. Head notions cause only disputes; but heart knowledge, heart experience, real sense of the living power of God inwardly, and evidence and demonstration of his Spirit in the inward parts, this puts an end to disputes, and sets men upon the inward travel and exercise of spirit by that which is new and living.

Now, many are offended at us because we do not preach more doctrinal points, or touch more upon the history of Christ with regard to his death, resurrection, ascension, etc. For indeed, our declaration and testimony is chiefly concerning a seed, and our desire is to direct and guide men's minds thereto. Therefore, in order to give a plain account of this thing (as it pleases the Lord to open my heart at this time in love and good will), and to satisfy and remove prejudices wherever they may be, this I will say in brief:

First, that which God has given us the experience of (after our great loss in the literal knowledge of things), and that which he has given us to testify of is the mystery, the hidden life, the inward and spiritual appearance of our Lord and Savior Jesus Christ, revealing his power inwardly, destroying enemies inwardly, and doing his work inwardly in the heart. Oh, this was a joyful sound to our souls, even the tidings of the arising of that inward life and power which could do this! Now this spiritual appearance of his was after his appearance in the flesh, and is the standing and lasting dispensation of the gospel, even the appearance of Christ in his Spirit and power inwardly in the hearts of his. So that in minding this, and being faithful in this respect, we mind our distinct work and are faithful in that which God has distinctly called us to and required of us.

Secondly, there is not as great a need of publishing the other as there formerly was. The historical relation concerning Christ is generally believed and received by all sorts that profess Christianity. His death, his miracles, his rising, his ascending, his interceding, etc., are generally believed by all people. But the mystery they miss, the hidden life they are not acquainted with, and they are alienated from the life of God in the midst of their literal accepting and acknowledging of these things.

Thirdly, the knowledge of these (doctrine, history, etc.), without the knowledge of the mystery, is not sufficient to bring them to God. For many set up what they gather and comprehend from a relation concerning the thing, instead of the thing itself, and so they never come to a sense of their true need, or how to rightly seek after it. And so many are builders, and many are built up very high in religion, in a way of notion and practice, but they are without acquaintance with the rock of ages, without the true knowledge and under-standing of the foundation and cornerstone. My meaning is, they have a notion of Christ to be the rock, a notion of him to be the foundation stone, but they never come livingly to feel him to be the rock, to experience him as the foundation stone inwardly laid in their hearts, and to know themselves made living stones in him, and built upon him. Where is this to be felt but within? And they that feel this within, do they not feel Christ within? And can any that feel him within deny him to be the strength of life and the hope of glory? Well, it is true once again (spiritually now, as well as literally then) that "the stone which the builders refused" (Christ within, whom the builders of this age refuse) "is become the chief cornerstone." It is he who knits together his sanctified body, his living body, the church, in this our day, more gloriously than in the former ages and generations. Blessed be the name of our God.

Fourthly, the mystery, the hidden life, the appearance of Christ in Spirit, comprehends the outward knowledge, so that it is not lost or denied but rather found, discerned, and acknowledged more clearly and abundantly. For the inward was to be after the outward, and so comprehends that which went before it. Paul did not lose anything of the excellent knowledge of Christ when he said, "Therefore, from now on, we know no one according to the flesh. Even though we have known Christ according to the flesh, yet now we know Him thus no longer." If he did not know Christ after the flesh, how did he know him? Why, as the Father inwardly revealed him. He knew him in his Spirit and power. He knew his death inwardly; he knew his resurrection inwardly; he knew the Spirit, virtue, and power of it inwardly; he knew the thing in the mystery in his own heart. Oh, precious knowledge! Oh, the excellency of this knowledge of my Lord and Savior Jesus Christ! What is the most exact, literal, outward knowledge without this?

What then? Do I now deny or slight the outward? No, but I have it here in the inward. For by the inward life and teachings of God's Spirit, I am taught and made able to value that glorious outward appearance and manifestation of the life and power of God in that heavenly flesh (as in my heart I have often called it), for the life so dwelt in it, that it was even one with it. Yet still it was a veil, and the mystery was behind it; and the eye of life looks through the veil into the mystery, and passes through it (as I may say), that it may behold its glory in the inward.

The Way of Peace

"The way of peace they have not known." Rom. 3:17.

There is a way of peace, of true peace with God, who is an adversary to all that is unholy and unrighteous. Those who have been unholy and unrighteous, who have been awakened, troubled, and could find no rest (but found rather the severe and righteous judgments and wrath of the Lord lying upon their spirits night and day), having at length had their ears opened by him, and being led by him out of the unholy and unrighteous way, into the holy and righteous way, have found both life and peace therein.

Now, there are two sorts of people (or two states) which the apostle here mentions, who have not known, nor can know, the way of peace with God. For the Lord is an adversary to them both, and will one day speak trouble to them both, when their souls and consciences come to be searched and judged by him.

The one state is the profane, or the Gentile state, which is without the sense of God, not heeding any appearance of his, or any inward voice of his Spirit, or the writing of his law upon their heart. These never knew the way in which the heart is inwardly and spiritually circumcised and renewed, sin forgiven, and peace obtained.

The other is the professing or outward Jew's state, who may study the letter, and apply themselves to conform outwardly to the letter, but are not acquainted with the inward Spirit and power. These greatly differ from the Gentile or profane state, both in outward appearance and in their own estimation, but they are on the same ground with the Gentiles, and know no more of the way of peace than the other does.

Question: But what is the way of peace, which neither the profane, nor any sort of professors outside of the life and power, ever knew or can know?

Answer: It is an inward way, a way for the inward Jews, for the inwardly renewed and circumcised to walk in. It is a holy or sanctified way for the sanctified ones to walk in. It is a living way, which none but the living can find. It is a new way, which none but those to whom God has given the new eye can see. It is a way that God prepares and sets up, and leads men's spirits into (who hearken unto him), and in which he guides the feet of his saints. It is a straight and narrow way, which no lust of the flesh, nor wisdom of the flesh, can find out or enter into. Oh, how little, how low, how poor, how empty, how naked, must he be, that enters into this way, and walks therein! Many may seek after it, and may think to find it and walk in it, but few shall be able, even as our Lord has said. Here the outward circumcision avails nothing, and lack of that circumcision does not hinder. Here bodily exercise profits little. Here there is a new creature, and the cross of Christ is all, the power of God is all; and he that walks according to this rule, peace is upon him, and upon the whole Israel of God. But he that does not know this rule, nor walk according to this rule, peace is not upon him, nor is he one of the inward Israel of God, who receive power to become sons, who receive the law of the Spirit of life in Christ Jesus, which is the inward rule of the inward Israel.

This was the way of peace from the beginning; this is the way of peace still, and there is not another. To be new created in Christ Jesus, to be ingrafted into him, to abide in him, to have the circumcision of the flesh (the body of the sins of the flesh cut off) by the circumcision of Christ (made inwardly in the heart without hands), and to walk not after the flesh but after the Spirit, even in the newness of the Spirit, here is life and peace, rest and joy forevermore. May the Lord in his tender mercy give men a sense of it, and lead men into it more and more. Amen.

The Conclusion of the Whole

There is a birth which is born, not of blood, nor of the will of the flesh, nor of the will of man, but of God. John 1:13. And this birth, which is born of the Spirit, is spirit. John 3:6. Now this birth, which is born of the Spirit, and is spirit, has a life and way of knowledge suitable to its nature and being, which is very far above man. Its life is in the Spirit, and its walking is in the Spirit, and its knowledge is after the way of the Spirit, very far above man's way of conceiving or comprehending. The birth itself is a mystery to man, and its way of knowing is a way altogether hidden from man. For this knowing is the evidence and demonstration of God's Spirit by the shining of his light in the heart: "In your light shall we see light." The true birth knows what this means.

Now, there is a wise and prudent part in man from which God hides the sight of his kingdom, and the heavenly glory thereof. But there is also a babe to whom God reveals his mysteries. Flesh and blood cannot reveal, but the Father can and does to his children, for he is the teacher of them all, from the least to the greatest, in the new and living covenant. There is man's day, and there is God's day. There is man's day of gathering knowledge according to his fleshly manner of comprehending; and there is God's day of giving knowledge, by the shinings of the light of his own eternal Spirit. In man's day, how does wise and prudent man beat his brains and labor in the fire for mere vanity! But in God's day, how does the knowledge of the Lord cover the earth even as the waters cover the sea! When the dayspring from on high visits inwardly, when the Lord lights the candle inwardly, oh, how clear is the knowledge of the Lord, and how does it then abound! Oh what a difference there is between man's apprehensions and conceivings concerning Christ, and God's revealing him inwardly! What a difference there is between man's coming to Christ according to his own apprehensions, and his coming to Christ in the heavenly drawings and teachings of the Father! John 6:45.

Oh that the birth of life were felt in men's hearts, that in it men might know the day of God, and the kingdom of God, and the treasures of wisdom which are hid in Christ, and will ever be so, except as Christ is inwardly revealed and formed in the heart! Many may have notions of Christ being formed in them, but oh to feel it inwardly! There is the sweetness, the assurance, the life, the peace, the righteousness of the Lord Jesus Christ, and there is the joy of the true Christian forever. Come now, all sorts of tender professors, come out of yourselves and into God's Spirit, into God's truth, that you may know what it is to be in the Spirit, and in the truth, and what it is to live there, and to know things there, and to worship there, and to have fellowship with the Father and Son there. It is the poor who receive the gospel; the poor receive the kingdom; the poor receive the power; the poor receive the righteousness and salvation of our Lord Jesus Christ. You are too rich in your comprehensions and gathered knowledge from your own literal concepts to learn to wait aright, to receive of him his gold, his raiment, and his eye salve. What pleasure is it to us to testify against you? Were it not for obedience to our God, and love to your souls, we would never do it. We are content and satisfied to be of the little, despised flock, which the Shepherd feeds, giving to everyone his proportion of daily nourishment, life, peace, righteousness, and joy. It is our love to you that we would not have you lay out your money for that which is not bread, and your labor for that which will not satisfy the truly hungry and awakened soul. We desire that you might come to feed on substance, on the life itself, on the sweetness and fatness of God's house, where nothing that any of his children can need or long after is lacking. Oh that you had the sense of our love! If you had the true understanding and sense of God's love, you could not help but have a sense of our love also, for it comes from him, and it flows towards you in his will and tender movings.

Do you love God? Are your hearts circumcised to love God? If not, you do not truly love. And if you loved him that begets, you would love them that are begotten by him. Your love is to your own notions and apprehensions of God, not to his nature; for if you loved his nature (that holy, heavenly, spiritual nature as it is in him), you could not help but love it in his children also. Well, our God is love, and he has taught us to love even our enemies, and to wrestle with our God for them, that if it be possible, the Lord may remove the scales from their eyes and give them repentance to the acknowledgment of the truth as it is in Jesus. Here they will know truth to be living and powerful, more effectual and operative (inwardly purifying, sanctifying, yes, and justifying also), than any can know except those only that are born of God, and kept alive by him.

The Doings and Sufferings of the Despised People Called Quakers

First, their doings are looked upon by many to be from a natural principle, and according to the covenant of works, and not from the free grace and gift of God's Spirit.

Now concerning this I can speak somewhat faithfully, as having been long experienced in the principle, and as having had experience of the grace and tender mercy of the Lord from my childhood. Indeed, it has been this way with me from my childhood—that whatever has been done in me, or by me, that was good, I have felt it to be from God's grace and mercy to me, and I have cried "grace, grace, mercy, mercy," to the Lord continually for it. And then, when I was turned to his truth in the inward parts, I found it was God's grace and tender love both to turn me and to keep me turned, causing truth to spring in me day by day, and give me ability through it. But oh, none knows (besides those who have had experience) how we have been weakened in the natural part, how poor we have been made, that we might receive the gospel. Oh how poor in ourselves we are kept that we might enjoy the riches and inheritance of the kingdom. And this we daily experience, that it is not by the works of righteousness which we have done, but according to his mercy that he saved us, and does daily save us, by the washing of regeneration, and the renewing of the Holy Spirit. Yes, it is God who has written his law in our hearts, and placed his fear there, and put his Spirit within us to enlighten and quicken, and cause us to walk in his ways, and to keep his statutes and judgments, and to do them. And all the mortifying of sin, and denying of the lusts of the flesh, and performing that which is holy and acceptable in the eyes of the Lord (as all that proceeds from his own Holy Spirit is),—all this is of the new covenant, and performed by the working thereof. It is not by the working of the natural part in itself, but by the working of the Spirit of life in the new birth, and only through the natural part as his instrument. So let none reproach the works that God brings forth in us, who has created us anew in Christ Jesus unto good works, lest thereby he reproach the Holy Spirit and power of the living God in which they are wrought, and by which they are brought forth.

Then as for our sufferings, indeed they are gifts we receive from God, so that we can truly say it is given us by the Lord our God not only to believe in his Son, but to suffer for his sake. And it is only in good conscience to God, and by the assistance of the Lord, that we suffer, so that the patience and meekness with which we suffer is not of ourselves, but of him. Whenever the Lord permits afflictions or sufferings to come upon us, our eye is unto him, and we enter into them in his fear, knowing our own inability to go through them, and looking up to him for strength. And when we are in them, while they continue, we daily look up to him for strength, and have been, many times, very weak in ourselves, when immediately or very soon after, we have felt great strength in the Lord. Also, after our sufferings, when the Lord has been with us all along and brought us through our sufferings in the peace and joy of his Spirit, we do not look back boastingly, as if we had been anything or done anything of ourselves. Rather, we bow before the Lord, and bless the Lord, in consideration of how he has been with us, and how he has upheld us by the right hand of his righteousness.

Therefore let none reproach, misrepresent, or vilify our sufferings, which our God has helped us through, and for which we, in humility of heart, give him thanks. For we cannot help but do so all our days, because the thankful remembrance and sense of them is written by the finger of his Spirit upon our hearts. Oh all sorts of people, whom we love and travail for, know the inward appearance and visits of the Shepherd and Savior of the soul! Turn to him (looking in true faith unto him), and be saved! I say unto you, in tenderness of spirit, oh do not repay us so wrongly for our love and truth of heart towards you. Truly our love is from the God of love. We could not so love you as we do, if our God had not taught us. Nor could we seek after you as we do, in tenderness of heart, if we were not instruments in the hand of the Shepherd of Israel. And the light we testify of, which we feel shine in us, it is no less than the true, sure light of the Sun of righteousness, which God has caused to shine in our hearts, who also loves mankind, and causes it to shine into the darkest corners of the earth. And the life by which we are quickened and raised out of sin and transgression, and the power we have received to become sons of God—it is from him who is the fountain of life, and has all power in heaven and earth. Oh that you could receive the blessed report! Oh that the arm of the Lord might be revealed in you! Oh that you could feel and witness the Savior working out your salvation in you, binding the strong man in you, casting him out of you, together with all his goods. And oh that the place of the wicked one might no more be found in you, nor any of his lusts or vain thoughts be lodged in your hearts, but you might witness and experience the new heart, the clean heart, the pure heart, in which God dwells, and the eye that sees him who is invisible.

An Exhortation to True Christianity

It is easy to profess Christ, but to be a true Christian is very precious, and many tribulations and deep afflictions are to be passed through before it is attained.

Now everlasting happiness and salvation depends upon true Christianity. It does not depend upon having the name of a Christian only, or professing such and such Christian doctrines, but upon having the nature of Christianity, upon being renewed by the Spirit of Christ, receiving the Spirit, walking in the Spirit, and bringing forth the fruits of the Spirit. Oh, here is the Christian indeed, and it should be everyone's care not to fall short of this. Now, because there is a contention about Christianity (as to who is the right Christian), it behooves every man to take care concerning himself to receive from God, and to be made by him, that which none but a true Christian can be. And having had some experience of this thing, and understanding what the Christian state is, and what accompanies it, I will set down the following things which the true Christian inwardly knows, witnesses, and enjoys.

First, he that is a new creature is without doubt a true Christian. He that is regenerated, is renewed in the spirit of his mind by Christ Jesus, is newly created in the holy and heavenly image, has felt the power of God's Spirit begetting him anew, forming him anew, out of the old nature and image of the first Adam, into the nature and image of the second Adam (who is the life-giving Spirit), this one is a Christian indeed.

Secondly, he that is in the new covenant is a true Christian. He that has thirsted after the living waters, has heard the call to the waters of life, has heard the voice of him who gives life, and has received life from him (taking up his cross to follow him), such a man is without doubt one of Christ's sheep, whom the Shepherd owns and cares for.

Thirdly, he that is inwardly circumcised with the circumcision made without hands, he is an inward Jew, an inward Christian (in the sight of God). This one has felt the Spirit and power of the Lord, and rejoices in Christ Jesus, and is one of those worshipers whom God has sought out, and has taught to worship him in the life and Spirit of his Son.

Fourthly, he that is inwardly washed with clean water, with the inward water, he is the inward Jew, the inward Christian. God promised to pour out clean water upon his Israel and they should be clean. He who has the clean water inwardly poured upon him, which inwardly washes and cleanses, he is without controversy one of God's inward Israel.

Fifthly, he that feeds on the bread of life within, and drinks the water of life out of his own well or cistern, he is without doubt living. He that is invited to the marriage supper of the Lamb, and comes and sups with the Lamb, he is one of the same nature and spirit with him. He with whom Christ sups, who has heard Christ knocking at his door, has opened to him and received him in to purify his heart, and to dwell in him, and sup with him, so that he eats bread in the kingdom, and drinks wine in the kingdom, and partakes of the feast of fat things, which God makes for his Israel in his holy mountain, this one is without doubt one of Christ's, and partakes of all this in and through him.

Sixthly, he that lives the Christian life, who walks not after the flesh, but after the Spirit, who does not fulfill the lusts of the flesh, but has the law of God written in his heart, and his fear put within him, is indeed a Christian. He who has been given the Holy Spirit to instruct him and guide him to answer the holy law written in his heart (which the carnal mind is not subject to, nor can be subject to), without a doubt, such a one is spiritual; he is a true Christian.

Seventhly, he that lives by faith, who knows the faith which is the gift of God, has received it, and lives by it, this one is a true Christian. Such a man can do nothing of himself, but only by faith in that holy power which does all in him, so that he lives, and believes, and obeys from the holy root of life, which causes life to spring up in him, and love to spring up in him, and the Lamb's meekness and patience to spring up in him, and all grace to spring up in him. The man that lives in this way is without a doubt ingrafted into the true vine, into the true olive tree. The true root supports him and ministers sap unto him, and he is a true, fresh, green, living branch of the true vine, of the holy olive tree.

Many more things might be mentioned, as they are experientially known and felt among those who are true Christians, but these are mentioned to give a taste. He that knows and feels these things may also know and feel the rest; he that does not know or feel these would not know or feel the rest even if ever so many more should be mentioned. Now the way to feel these, and to become a true Christian (and to grow up in the Christian life), is to feel the seed of the kingdom (which is the beginning of the kingdom, the beginning of true Christianity), and then to feel the seed abiding. Here is the constant seal of Christianity in my heart. Here are true and certain evidences, day by day, of the Christian nature and spirit manifesting themselves inwardly and undeniably.

And now, having the witness in myself, testifying to his own work and to his own birth, of what value are any testimonies of men against this? Christianity is a mystery, and the true Christian is he who has the inward eye opened, and with that inward eye is taught of God to pierce into that wherein Christianity consists. There have been many Christians of men's making, and others who are of God's and Christ's making. Oh let men have a care that when God comes to distinguish between cattle and cattle (between Christian and Christian), they are found to be such as God will own as the sheep of his fold. Oh that we be made able to bear the trial of his searching judgment, his pure, impartial eye, and not such as are still found to be workers of iniquity, not created anew in Christ Jesus unto good works, and therefore not truly of him.

Chapter VII

To the Jews According to the Flesh
and According to the Spirit

First: To the Seed of Abraham After the Flesh

Oh, the glory of your outward state, you who were the people whom God once chose and loved, and manifested his power and presence among above all people! Your land was the glory of all lands, to which God brought you out of Egypt by an outstretched arm, through a dreadful wilderness, wherein you were tempted, tried, and exercised. Oh, what laws and statutes, and righteous judgments did God give you, such as no other nations had! What a temple you had in which to appear before God, and the ark of the covenant, and holy priests, kings, and prophets! And how near was God to you, to be inquired of by you, and how ready he was to hear your prayers, in all that you called upon him for! The eternal God was your refuge, and underneath were the everlasting arms (the Lord was your rock, and you were built upon him). He did thrust out the enemy before you, and when the arm of the Lord destroyed them, you dwelt in safety, and the Lord was a fountain of living waters to you, and his heavens did drop down fatness upon you. Happy you were, O Israel! Who was like you, O people saved by the Lord! And indeed, it might have still been so with you, had you not been unmindful of the rock that begat you, and forgotten the God that formed you. For your glory should not have been taken from you, but rather swallowed up in a higher glory, wherein you might have had the first and chiefest share, had you not (by your almost constant rebellion and unbelief), provoked the Lord against you. For he was moved not only to afflict, but at last to utterly cast you off from being a people, and to choose a people in your stead, who should bring forth better fruits to the Lord of the vineyard, than you in your day had done.

Yet when your state was glorious, it was not a state of the truly substantial, lasting glory, but rather a shadowy state or representation thereof. Your day of glory was not the day of the Messiah, the day of everlasting inward light, in which the Lord alone is exalted inwardly in the hearts of all, where he breaks down all that is contrary to the light of his day. Your day was but the day of the outward shadows of heavenly substance; and when that day (the day of the inward substance and glory) shined, your shadows or shadowy state was meant to fly away and be swallowed up in the pure substance and spiritual kingdom of the Messiah.

Your birth from Abraham after the flesh was not the birth which was to inherit the promise in the kingdom of the Messiah. There is, however, an inward birth of the Spirit, born after Abraham in his faith, who travels inwardly, as Abraham did outwardly, and seeks an inward country and city, whose builder and maker is God. It is to these that the spiritual kingdom and promises belong.

Your circumcision was but the outward circumcision, the circumcision of the flesh; it was not the circumcision of the heart. The circumcision of the heart is for the inward Jew, which indeed the Scripture required of you (because there was something near you which would have so circumcised you, had you hearkened and given up to it, see Deut. 30:14). But you, as a people, were not so circumcised, but were a stiff-necked people (as Moses and the prophets complained of you), uncircumcised in heart and ears, resisting God's Spirit in your own hearts and in the prophets, until the Lord was provoked to take away both vision and prophet from you.

The Egypt where your fathers were in bondage, and the Pharaoh who oppressed them, was but the outward Egypt and outward Pharaoh. There is an inward Egypt, wherein the spiritual seed in the inward man, the soul, is in bondage. There is a spiritual Pharaoh that oppresses the spiritual seed, in spiritual Egypt. And there is a stretching out the arm of the Almighty inwardly, to break the strength of the inward Pharaoh, to pierce Leviathan the crooked serpent, and to deliver the soul from under his captivity.

The wilderness also, that your fathers were led through, was but the outward wilderness, where they were tempted and tried by the Lord many ways, that he might do them good in the latter end. But the inward Israel, after they are led out of the inward Egypt, are tried in the inward wilderness. Here they are judged after the flesh, and that which is not to enter into and inherit the good land is wasted in them. Here they are tried in the furnace of affliction, and their filth is purged away by the spirit of judgment and burning. Then the righteous nation, which has received the holy inward law, and keeps the truth, may enter into the good land, city, and kingdom of the Messiah, and inherit the blessed promises of life and salvation there.

Moses, your great prophet, was a type of the great, lasting, standing prophet, whom God would raise up like unto Moses, who was to give his inward law as Moses did the outward, and to lead all spiritual Israel as Moses did outward Israel. His word was to be heard and stand in all things whatsoever that he shall say to his people, and whosoever will not hear and obey this prophet shall be cut off from among the holy, spiritual, and inwardly living people. Deut. 18:15.

Joshua, who succeeded Moses, led into the figurative rest; he was but a figure of him that inwardly leads into the inward and spiritual rest, which the true Jews (who are inwardly created and formed by God, and made a willing people in the day of his power), enter into.

The pillar of cloud and pillar of fire in the wilderness were but figures of the spiritual pillar of cloud and fire, by which the spiritual Israel are led and defended in the glorious gospel day of God's Spirit and power. Read Isaiah, chap. 4, which speaks of the gospel day, and the pillar and cloud of fire to be created therein, and of the defense which is to be on all the inward and spiritual glory.

The land of Canaan, the outward land and kingdom of Israel, was but a figure of the inward land and kingdom of the inward Israel in the days of the Messiah. This is the land of Judah in which the song is sung because of the strong inward city where God appoints salvation for walls and bulwarks. Into this city enters the righteous nation which keeps the truth. Isaiah 26.

The outward kings in that land, and particularly David, were but types of the spiritual king, the spiritual David, whom God would raise up to the spiritual people who seek the Lord their God, and David their king. He shall be their spiritual shepherd and ruler, whom God has appointed to feed them in the integrity of his heart, and to guide them by the skillfulness of his hands, who is King of righteousness and peace inwardly, and who ministers righteousness and peace to the sheep and lambs of his pastures.

The outward priests (even their high priests) were but a representation of the great high priest of God, who was to be a priest forever according to the order of Melchizedek. Psa. 110:4.

The outward covenant (made with them from the outward mount Sinai, upon the giving of the law, and holy statutes and ordinances, by which they were to live and enjoy God in their outward state) was but a shadow of the inward and spiritual covenant, the new and everlasting covenant, which God makes with his inward and spiritual people in the latter days.

Their outward law, as written and engraved in tables of stone, was but a shadow of the inward law, which God puts into the children of the new covenant, insomuch that they need not seek outwardly to learn the knowledge of God, or his will or law. Rather, the inward Israel finds the law written within, and the islands who wait for the law of the Spirit of life, for the law of the Messiah, receive the ministration of the law (in the Spirit and power of the Messiah) which they wait for.

The outward Mount Zion, on which the outward temple was built by Solomon (that wise, righteous, peaceable king), was a figure of the inward mountain, whereupon the inward house is built in the days of the gospel, in the days of the Messiah; and to this mountain the spiritual people come up and worship. And this is the Zion and Jerusalem (even inward and spiritual Zion) from which the law and word of the Lord go forth in the days of the Messiah. Here the spiritual house of Jacob agree together to walk in the light of the Lord, who sends forth his light and truth, and leads them to his holy hill, and to his tabernacles.

Their outward tabernacle and temple, sanctified by God for him to dwell and appear in, was a shadow of God's inward dwelling place in man; "I will tabernacle in them." God dwells not in houses or temples made with hands; that is not the place of his rest, as says the prophet Isaiah. Rather, the high and lofty One that inhabits eternity, whose throne is in heaven, and the earth his footstool, he dwells also with him that is of a humble and contrite spirit, to revive the spirit of the humble, and to revive the heart of the contrite ones.

The outward sabbaths were not the lasting Sabbath or rest of the gospel, but were given for a sign. For the day of redemption from sin, the day of resting from sin, the day of ceasing from the works of the flesh, the day wherein God is all and does all by his Spirit and power inwardly, and wherein he alone is exalted,—this is the day of rest which the Lord has made for the spiritual Israel, in which they are glad and rejoice.

So their incense and sacrifices were not the lasting incense and sacrifices, but shadows thereof. For the prayers of the saints, when God pours out the spirit of prayer and supplication upon them, and they pray to him therein, that is the incense. "Let my prayer be directed before you as incense, and the lifting up of my hands as the evening sacrifice." And this was the incense and pure offering, which in every place was to be offered up to God's name among the Gentiles, when his name should be great among them, as Malachi foretells. And what said David of old, when God's Spirit and the holy vision was upon him? "Sacrifice and offering you did not desire; my ears you have opened; burnt offering and sin offering have you not required. Then said I, lo I come; in the volume of the book it is written of me. I delight to do your will, O my God. Yes, your law is in my heart. The sacrifices of God are a broken spirit (rend your hearts, and not your garments, and turn to the Lord your God). A broken and a contrite heart, O God, you will not despise." The offering of praise to God from a sincere heart, and the ordering of the life aright, these are the sacrifices well-pleasing to God. For sacrifices were not the thing which God chiefly required of outward Israel, but this: "OBEY MY VOICE." For obedience is more acceptable than all other sacrifices, and to heed than the fat of the choicest rams.

Moreover, those outward sacrifices could not remove or take away sin from the conscience, but he that came to do the will of God, and to put an end to those sacrifices and oblations (which were but outward and imperfect), he does both wash and take away sins from within, and also brings in everlasting righteousness where his light shines, and his pure life springs inwardly in the heart.

Now this is the substance of all the shadows—even the eternal light, the eternal word, the Son of the living God (who is light as the Father is light), the word near in the mouth and heart, the word of the new covenant to which Moses directed your fathers, Deut. 30, and by which the Lord speaks, and has spoken throughout the world, Psa. 50:1. And it is by this word that God teaches every man that hearkens to his voice to do justly, love mercy, and walk humbly with his God, as it is expressed by the prophet Micah.

Now to you Jews of the outward line of Abraham (whose return to the Lord my soul most earnestly desires after, and for which I have most vehemently prayed to the Lord), here are a few weighty inquiries upon my heart:

Inquiry 1: How did David come to pant after the living God, like the deer after the water brooks? Was it not from the quickening virtue of this inward word, which Moses, the man of God, had directed the mind to? Read Psa. 119, and see how he breathed for quickenings from this word upon which all depends. And now, if you come to experience this word, and the quickening virtue of it, and follow the Lord therein, you will soon come to know the day of the Messiah, and the glory of his kingdom, which is not outward, transitory, and of a perishing nature, but inward, spiritual, and everlasting (as David well knew, and spoke sensibly of, see Psa. 145 and else-where).

Inquiry 2: What are the waters which every thirsty soul is invited to? Isa. 55. Are they not the waters of the Messiah? Are they not waters that flow out of the wells of salvation? Isaiah 12. Is not the spiritual Israel to draw spiritual water out of the wells of the Savior in the days of the Messiah? What is it to come to these waters? Oh that you experien-tially knew! But this I will tell you from true and certain experience, that if you come to take notice of this word of life, which God has placed near in your mouths and hearts, and incline your ear to it, and come away from that which it reproves in you, as it draws to itself, then your souls shall soon come to live. And he that gives you life will make an everlasting covenant with you, even the sure mercies of David. But you must be still and mind him as a witness, and leader, and commander, inwardly in your hearts, that you may be preserved in the covenant, and enjoy the blessings of it; see Isaiah 55.

Inquiry 3: Did not the Messiah come at the set time, at the time set by the Holy Spirit of prophecy? Did he not come in the prepared body to do the will of God? And did he not do his will? And after his obedience to his Father, was he not cut off, though not for himself? Dan. 9:26. And after his cutting off, were not you (natural Israel) made desolate? Why were you made desolate? Why did such a stroke come upon you as never before? Oh, consider it! Read Dan. 9:24

to the end of the chapter, and let him that reads understand.

Inquiry 4: What was that curse, and upon whom did it fall? "Let their table become a snare to them," etc. Psa. 69. Was it not on those that gave gall and vinegar to the Messiah to drink, of whom David was a figure, and concerning whom he spoke in the Spirit? Whose eyes are always darkened? Does not the veil lie still on your whole nation? Do you know the inward mountain, where the veil of the covering is destroyed in the inward day and light of the Messiah? To what purpose is it for you to read Moses and the prophets when the veil is still upon you, that you cannot see what is to be abolished, and is abolished, by the dawning of the glorious day of the Messiah? Here there is a Judaism, there is a circumcision, there is a Sabbath, there is a rest, etc., for the inward and spiritual people, which is to remain, and never to be abolished.

Inquiry 5: What was that people and nation with which God would provoke you to jealousy? Deut. 32. Was it not the spiritual people, the holy inward nation, the true Jews, whom God took from among the Gentiles? Was it not those in whom he appeared and was a God and a Father to, when he cast off and forsook the outward Jews, and left them to be a desolation?

Inquiry 6: Who are those that shall be hungry when God's servants shall eat, and thirsty when God's servants shall drink, and ashamed when his servants shall rejoice? Are not your souls hungry and parched for lack of the spiritual suste-nance with which the living God satisfies his servants on his inward holy mountain? And are not you ashamed of your expectations of the Messiah, even while the servants of the

Lord rejoice in him, their Prince and Savior, and witness him daily a leader and commander to them? What is the people whom the Lord has slain and made desolate? (Are not you a slain people to God, alienated from his life, Spirit, and power, dead in your literal notions and observations?) And what are the servants of the Lord, whom the Lord has called by another name, even a name that you never knew? See Isa. 66. And consider, how all your day God spread out his hands to you, and you were rebellious, and would not hear. But now night has come upon you, and your visitation, as a people, has been long ended. See Luk. 19:44

Inquiry 7: Now that the inward people, and the inward covenant, the new covenant, are brought forth, shall you ever be owned or regarded again as an outward people, according to your outward covenant? Will not all such expectations fail you forever? You have looked from generation to generation for the coming and appearing of the Messiah outwardly, after an outward manner, but now his coming and appearance is inward. For he sets up his kingdom, his everlasting kingdom, in his saints, and in their hearts he rules inwardly; and it is there that the Messiah, the seed of the woman, bruises the head of the serpent.

Oh that you knew the substance! Oh that you knew the word of life in the heart, and were turned to it, and daily faithful and obedient! Then you would feel it crushing and dashing the power of sin and corruption in your hearts. This is the consolation, hope, and joy of the inward and spiritual Israel. Oh that you might be made partakers of it, and that your long outward captivity and desolation might at length end in inward freedom and redemption! Amen.

Second: To the Spiritual Seed of Abraham

"The scepter shall not depart from Judah, nor a lawgiver from between his feet, until Shiloh come; and unto him shall the gathering of the people be."—Gen. 49:10.

Old Jacob, in the spirit of prophecy, saw that Judah was to have the scepter, the kingly power, and it was not to depart from him, it was to be his right, and the lawgiver was to be his until Shiloh[1] came. Then the right was Shiloh's to reign, and to give laws to his people, whom he would gather out of the kingdom of darkness, and from Satan's power, into his own inward, spiritual, and everlasting kingdom. This was the true king, God's king, whom he would set upon the holy hill of spiritual Zion, and all the holy, inward, spiritual gatherings of all people must be unto him.

"I will overturn, overturn, overturn it, and it shall be no more, until he comes whose right it is, and I will give it to him." Ezek 21:27. And his dominion shall not pass away, or the scepter and lawgiving power shall not pass away from him, as it did from Judah, nor shall his kingdom ever be destroyed, Dan. 7:14. For God will give to him the throne of his father David, and he shall reign over the house of Jacob forever; and of his kingdom there shall be no end.

Question: But who are the people that shall be gathered to him?

Answer: The people that shall hear his voice, and come at his call, that shall receive the instruction of wisdom, and feel

---

[1] The term "Shiloh" in Genesis 49:10 comes from an obscure Hebrew word that is variously interpreted to mean "the sent one," "the seed," or "the peaceable and prosperous one." Whatever the correct translation, the word is universally accepted to be a reference to the Messiah.

the drawing power and virtue of the Father in the day of his power. It is written in the prophets, "All your children shall be taught of the Lord." And everyone that is taught and learns of the Father comes to the Son, comes to the Messiah, comes to Shiloh, to the Word eternal, to the Word of life in the heart.

Question: Were the Jews then excluded from this gathering?

Answer: No, they were to be gathered to Shiloh, as well as others. Indeed, the Lord had a special regard to them, for the gospel was first preached to them. They had the first offer, or the first call to the spiritual glory. They were the children of the prophets, and of the covenant of God made with their fathers. And unto them God, having raised up his Son Jesus, sent him to bless them, in turning away every one of them from their iniquities. And the whole nation, turning from their iniquities, should have been gathered by him, and should have enjoyed the blessing of his day and kingdom. For truly, the first gathering was from among them, and the first glorious gospel church was at Jerusalem, where the Spirit and power of the Lord Jesus did most eminently and wonderfully break forth, and great grace was upon them all. But the nation at large was not gathered to Shiloh, nor did it come under his scepter and government, but only a remnant of the nation. And so, these being gathered, the rest were cast off, and the banner was carried among the Gentiles, and the great gathering was there among them.

Question: How is it manifest that the great gathering unto Shiloh was to be from among the Gentiles?

Answer: By many express prophecies of Scripture, and

promises to the Messiah, that he should have the Gentiles for his inheritance and possession. When God established his king, the Messiah, upon the holy hill of spiritual Zion (notwithstanding all the heathen's rage against him, and the people of the Jews imagining a vain thing, thinking to keep his body in the grave, who was the resurrection and the life), what says the Lord to him? "Ask of me, and I will give you the nations for your inheritance, and the uttermost parts of the earth for your possession." Psa. 2:8. The Lord said in another place: "It is a light thing that you may be my servant, to raise up the tribes of Jacob, and to restore the preserved of Israel; I will also give you for a light to the Gentiles, that you may be my salvation unto the ends of the earth." Isa. 49:6. Again the Lord says further: "From the rising of the sun, even unto the going down of the same, my name shall be great among the Gentiles, and in every place incense shall be offered unto my name, and a pure offering. For my name shall be great among the nations, says the Lord of hosts." Mal. 1:11. "Sing, O barren, you that didst not bear! Break forth into singing, and cry aloud, you that did not travail with child. For more are the children of the desolate than the children of the married wife, says the Lord." Isa. 54:1. Who was the married wife? Who was the mother in the days of the first covenant? Was it not the Jerusalem below? And who was then the desolate and barren one? Was it not another Jerusalem which is free, and the mother of all the spiritual children? Why was she now to rejoice and sing, but because she was to break forth on the right hand and on the left, and her seed was to inherit the Gentiles, and make the desolate cities to be inhabited? ver. 3. For indeed, the covenant of Mount Sinai did bring forth a great people, whereof Jerusalem below was the mother. And the covenant made afterwards was as yet barren, and did not bring forth a people to the Lord. But this second covenant, and the Jerusalem above, was to have a time wherein her seed would inherit the Gentiles, and the Maker, the Husband, should be called the God of the whole earth. ver.5.

Read also Gal. 4, and see how the apostle of the Gentiles expounds the mystery, showing which is the free woman with her free children, and which is the bondwoman with her children of bondage. For the children of bondage are cast out in the day of God, and in the shining of his heavenly inward light, and cannot inherit the glorious kingdom of the gospel with the children of the free woman.

Now consider: Who were the people in the time of the first covenant who obtained mercy? Were they not the Jews? And who was it that were not a people, and did not obtain mercy, but were left out of the love and mercy of the first covenant? Were they not the Gentiles? And did not the Lord promise that he would "have mercy on them that had not obtained mercy"? Did he not promise to say to them that were not his people, "you are my people;" and they would say, "my God"? (See Hos. 2:23. compared with Rom. 9:26.) Was not this once gloriously fulfilled? And is it not again gloriously fulfilled by now visiting them again with the fresh sound of the everlasting gospel, as was promised, Rev. 14:7.

But why should I mention any more scriptures unto you concerning this thing, when you have so large, full, certain, and daily experience of it, in that which is pure and living? For you (spiritual Israel) are begotten by his Spirit into his own image and nature, and have received the Spirit of adoption, wherein you cry, "Abba, Father," to the Father of spirits. He found you indeed in a strange land, under great captivity and alienation from him. You have been in Egypt, in Sodom, in Babylon, spiritually; but the mercy of the Lord has followed you there, and the arm of the Lord has reached to you there, and has wounded the Dragon. Yes, he whom the Lord has given for a light to the Gentiles has shined to you there, in the midst of your darkness. For God sent among you the prophet like unto Moses, Deut. 18:15 (though far above Moses), and hearing him, he led you out of Egypt, and by the rod of his power he did signs and wonders and valiant acts to break that power which held you captive and oppressed you. And you have known the travel, trials, and temptations in the spiritual wilderness, and the falling of the carcasses which were to fall there, and the holy leading by the pillar of cloud and fire through all the entanglements and dangers. And truly, the faithful among you, the tried and prepared among you, have passed over Jordan, the river of pure judgment, into the good land. You have come to witness David and Solomon (who are one in Spirit) your King, who rules in righteousness, and ministers to you peace everlasting. And you have a High-priest there, not after the order of Aaron, but after the order of Melchizedek, who is made the everlasting High Priest of God, not after the law of a carnal commandment, but after the power of an endless life. And now his lips preserve the knowledge of the law for you, in that endless power of life, and he ministers for you and to you in that endless power, and intercedes with power and efficacy, and sprinkles the blood of the covenant upon you, which takes away sin from your hearts and consciences. So that you know the inward Jew's state, the inward holy land and kingdom, the inward circumcision, before you enter into that land. You know the inward Lamb, the inward Passover, the inward Mount Zion and Jerusalem, the inward sacrifices and incense, the inward tabernacle, temple, and ark of the covenant, the inward shewbread, the inward manna, the inward rod that budded, the inward candlestick and lamps which are never to go out in God's temple. And what more should I say? All that that people were to be outwardly, in an outward way and state, God has made you inwardly in the substance. And what God would have been to them outwardly (had they only obeyed his voice and kept his statutes and judgments), that he is to you inwardly, who are the called and chosen and faithful followers of the Lamb. Oh, you are the enjoyers of their blessings and promises inwardly! Oh, the glory of your state to the eye that is opened to see it!

Now, something does remain on my heart unto you. Oh, remember what a great covenant God has prepared to make with you, as you incline your ears to him, and are led by him into this holy agreement! For it is a covenant which is not weak, as the old covenant was, but rather full of virtue and power, to enable you to do whatever God requires of you. Mark what it contains: putting God's fear into you—not the fear which is taught by man's precepts, which man may get into his carnal mind, but that which God places as the treasury of life in the heart, as it is written, "The fear of the Lord and his treasure." Isa. 33:6. And oh, who knows the preciousness of his treasure! How it does cleanse the heart, and keep it clean, and will not allow the mind that is seasoned with it, and kept to it, to depart from the living God! It protects from unbelief, from disobedience, and will not permit the soul so much as to meddle with any appearance of evil. Oh, precious, glorious, blessed treasure! Happy is the man that fears always with this fear!

Another precious thing this covenant contains is this— the law written in the heart. For this law shall be as near, yes even nearer, than sin is, in the heart that is made tender, and has the law of the Spirit of life written in it. Who knows what it is to have the law of love, the law of life, the law of the Spirit, the law of faith, the law of new obedience, livingly written by God in his heart? Surely none can know but those in whom God writes it! And such cannot help but desire to have it written in their hearts by his blessed finger daily more and more. But this covenant contains yet more—even the putting of his own Spirit within, to be a fountain of life there, a fountain of strength and wisdom there, to make them more and more willing in the day of his power. And this Spirit will cause them to walk in his ways, and keep his statues and judgments, and do them, so that the Lord their God may bless them and delight in them.

Oh, who would not long after, and take up the cross and shame, in order to enjoy the glory of this state? Oh, what has God done for a poor despised remnant among the Gentiles! Oh, who would not desire to keep this blessed covenant with the Lord, that he might fully enjoy the Lord, that the marriage with the Maker might be witnessed in his loving kindness and everlasting righteousness, and all unrighteous- ness and uncleanness might be put away, removed, and separated from the heart forever! Ah, the virgin spirit which the Lamb loves and delights to marry! "He that is joined to the Lord is one Spirit." And he that would be joined to the Lord and be one Spirit with him must part with all that is old, evil, unclean, and corrupt in him.

Oh, who would lose the precious fear of the covenant, which is clean and endures forever, and keeps clean and chaste to the Lord forever! Who would miss even one law which God has to write in the hearts of his children, when every law is a law of life, and changes the mind into the nature of the lawgiver! And who would grieve God's Spirit, which is our Comforter, or quench that which kindles the pure flame of love and life in our hearts! Or how could one of his dear and tender children be willing to vex him, by mani- fest carelessness and disobedience towards the one who gives us to drink of the river of his pleasure.

A Few Words to England, My Native Country

O Land of my Nativity! O my dear Countrymen! The pure power of the Lord is upon me, and the springs of life are opened in me, and among many other things, I am melted in love and desires after your welfare. And this is in my heart to say to you: If I now testify to you in truth of a pearl, a heavenly pearl, an everlasting pearl, will you not hear me? If I tell you your heart is the field, or earth, wherein it is hid, will you not consider it? If the everlasting gospel is preached again, which contains true tidings of redemption from sin, will you not listen to it? If the kingdom of God, and righteousness of Christ, is to be revealed within, would you not willingly learn to wait for it there, and beg of God that the eye may be opened in you which alone can see it when it does appear?

Indeed, God's visitation is upon this nation in a special manner; his light and power is breaking forth in it against the darkness and power of the spirit of Satan, which has captivated and still captivates many. You desire outward liberty, and the enjoyment of your outward rights; but would you not be free inwardly? Do you not desire to be free from the base, earthly, selfish nature and spirit, which man (fallen from God, and the glory wherein he created him) is degenerated into? Oh, is not the power of God and the life of Christ able to restore man? He that created man at first so glorious, in his own image, is he not able to create him anew? Oh listen, my dear countrymen! The power is revealed which creates anew; and they that receive it (and are as clay in the hands of the great Potter, given up to be formed by it), are daily created anew into a holy, heavenly, innocent, living, tender, righteous frame, day by day. They are made willing, daily more and more, to be the Lord's, in this day of his power; and to receive power to become sons, and strength against their soul's enemies. For the glorious work of redemption which God has begun in them, is carried on in them by the arm of his strength, to their comfort and his everlasting praise.

There is a spiritual Egypt and Sodom, just as well as there was an outward. There is a spiritual wilderness, and a Canaan also; and the arm of God's power inwardly and spiri- tually has been revealed in this spiritual Egypt, wilderness, and Canaan, as truly as ever it was in the outward. Do you not read of an inward Jew, and an inward circumcision, and the inward leaven, and keeping the feast of unleavened bread, even of bread that is not leavened with sin? And he that eats of the unleavened bread, it unleavens him of sin, and leavens him with life and holiness; for it is a holy bread, and a living bread. This is the bread which comes down from heaven, which they that feed upon live, and they that live do feed upon. And though they be many, yet feeding upon this bread, they become one bread, one living body, consisting of a living head, and living members. For the same life and pure heavenly nature which is in the head, is communicated by him to the members.

But how shall we find this, some may ask. I will tell you how we found it, and how none can miss it, who sweep the house and make a diligent and faithful search after it. That in the heart of man which turns against sin, discovers sin, draws away from sin, and wherein God ministers help against sin,— that is it. That is the pearl hid; that is the kingdom hid; in that is the righteousness of God revealed from faith to faith, in all that receive and give up to this holy leaven. This seed is of the nature of God and Christ. This is a measure of his light, of his pure life. This is the law and everlasting commandment, which God writes in the hearts of his spiritual Israel. For the inward Jew has inward tablets where the inward law is written, for the inward eye to read.

Oh, how near is God inwardly to the inward people in this our day! Oh the pure glory has broken forth! But alas, men are in their several sorts of dreams, and take no notice of it. What shall the Lord do to awaken this nation? In what way shall his power appear, to bring down unrighteousness, and to bring up righteousness in the spirits of people? Do you not think the Lord has been at work? Oh, take notice of the handiwork of the Lord, you children of men, and wait to feel truth near. Oh, partake of the living virtue and power of it, that you may feel your hearts created anew, and the old heavens and earth inwardly passing away, wherein dwells unrighteousness, and the new heavens and the new earth inwardly being witnessed, wherein dwells righteousness. Oh that everyone might be sensible of his presence, power, kingdom, and righteous government inwardly in the heart, from the king that sits on the throne, to the beggar on the dunghill! Surely man was not made for himself! Surely he was not made such a creature as he now is, but rather in the holy image of God, with love in his heart to God above all, and to his neighbor as to himself. Oh, what good are the religions and professions of those where this love is not found? The Lord is restoring his image, and bringing forth the true, pure religion again. The pearl, the truth, contains and comprehends it. Oh, buy the pearl! Oh, buy the precious truth! Sell all that is contrary to it for it! Take up the cross to all that is evil in you, as the light in you makes it manifest! Then you shall have the free possession of it in your heart, and feel it to be a root of life, a treasure of life, a well of life, out of which the living water will be daily springing up in you unto life everlasting. Amen.

The True Church and Ministry Under the Gospel

Question: What is the true church, or the gospel church, or the church according to the new covenant? (For there was an old covenant, and a church according to that, under the law; and there is a new covenant, and a church according to that, under the gospel.)

Answer: To answer this, let us inquire and consider what the new covenant is, and then it will more easily appear what the church according to the new covenant is.

The new covenant, according to plain scripture, and according to manifest experience in this blessed day of the shining of the gospel light in men's hearts, is this: God putting his law in the inward parts of his people, writing it in their hearts, becoming their God and making them his people, and teaching them all to know him (inwardly and experientially) from the least to the greatest, being merciful to their unrighteousness and remembering their sins and iniquities no more. Jer. 31:33-34, Heb. 8:10-12.

Now if this is the new covenant (the covenant of the gospel church), then they are the church who are the people of God according to this covenant. These have the law put by God into their inward parts and written in their hearts, and so according to this law and covenant, they have God to be their God, and they are his people, and are taught by him to know him (as it is written, "All my people shall be taught of the Lord," Isa. 54:13. and John 6:45). To these God has been merciful, and their sins and iniquities he remembers no more, having been washed away from their consciences by the blood of the everlasting covenant (which the blood of bulls and goats could never do). So that this is the New

Testament church (or gospel church)—a church of inward Jews, even as the law church was a church of outward Jews. It is a church of inward worshipers, of worshipers in Spirit and in truth, John 4:23, even as the law church was a church of outward worshipers. It is a church of inwardly circumcised ones, even as the law church was a church of outwardly circumcised ones. Rom. 2:29. It is a church of such as are inwardly holy, even as the law church was to be a church of such as were outwardly holy. It is a church of such as offer inward incense and sacrifices, even as the law church was a church of such as offered outward incense and sacrifices. It is a church of inwardly redeemed ones from the inward Egypt, from the inward darkness and power of Satan, even as the law church was a church of such as were redeemed from the outward Egypt, and the power of outward Pharaoh. It is a church that has the inward ark (Rev. 11:19), the inward presence, the inward manna, etc., even as the outward church of the Jews had these things outwardly.

Question: What is the true gospel ministry, and who are the true gospel ministers?

Answer: Those whom Christ sends forth in the Spirit and power of his Father to gather and build up this new covenant church. Christ had all power in heaven and earth given him, even to this very end—to gather, defend, and build up his church. He bid his apostles to wait for the same power, and even now sends forth his ministers in the same power, that they may be able ministers of the gospel, which is not words but power, even the power of God unto salvation. Rom. 1:16. The new covenant stands not in the letter, but in Spirit and power. Those who are the ministers of it must receive life, Spirit, and power from Christ, or they cannot nourish and build up his members. They must preach and minister to the world in this power, Spirit, and life, or they are not able to gather others out of the world into it.

Christ, the Lord of his church, the foundation of life in his church, the everlasting rock, is a living stone, and his church is built of living stones. How can anyone minister life unto them, or build them up in the life, Spirit, and power, besides those who are in the life, Spirit, and power, and who receive from the Head to further quicken and build up the living members? The milk which nourishes the living babe is living, and must come pure from the breast of life, and not be mixed with man's wisdom or brain inventions. What then must the bread and wine and water of the kingdom be, upon which the children and heirs of the kingdom must feed and be satisfied? The ministers of the gospel are stewards of this heavenly life, this heavenly Spirit, this heavenly power, this heavenly treasure, which they have in earthen vessels, and which God enables them to bring forth for the feeding of his lambs and sheep. Christ said unto Peter, "Do you love me more than these?" Peter answered him, "Yes, Lord, you know that I love you." If it be so, "feed my lambs, feed my sheep," said Christ to him. But how should he feed them? With what should he feed them? All power, says Christ, is given me in heaven and in earth, and I am to ascend to my Father to receive the fullness of his Spirit. If you wait, you shall receive abundantly of the same Spirit and power, and then in that Spirit and power you shall be able to feed my lambs and sheep that are begotten and gathered to me. But apart from this Spirit and power, none is able to feed and build them up, for this alone is the thing with which they are to be fed, and in which they are to be built.

Indeed, a man may be a minister of the letter, a minister of the law, without the Spirit and power. But such a one

cannot possibly minister the gospel, for it consists not in
letter, but in Spirit, 2 Cor. 3. And the faith that is to be
begotten in the gospel is not to stand in the wisdom of man,
but in the power of God. The gospel state, the gospel church,
the gospel building, begins in the power, is carried on in the
power, and is finished or perfected in the power. The whole
ministry of the gospel is to partake of this power, and
minister in it, otherwise they can do nothing in this work.
Christ Jesus our Lord began it in this power, and none can
carry it on without this power. The Lord God of glory laid the
foundation—"Behold, I lay in Zion for a foundation." etc. Isa.
28:16, 1 Pet. 2:4-6. And the quickening Spirit alone is able to
make living and spiritual stones. The Lord alone is able to
build them up by the operation of this Spirit and power, and
they that are the true ministers of the gospel are to wait for it
daily from God, so that they may minister in it.

Question: What is the maintenance of the ministers of Christ,
or what is to be the maintenance of the true ministers under
the gospel?

Answer: Christ, who has sent them forth to minister in his
name, has provided for them; and they that are his true
ministers are satisfied with what he has provided for them,
Matt. 10:10. These are careful not to make the gospel, which
is to be an inward blessing, outwardly chargeable to any. The
mind of the true minister is concerned with the service of
Christ—how he may be faithful to him, gather souls to him,
feed others with the bread of life from him. He is not
concerned with what he shall have from men for so doing, for
such ministers covet no man's gold or silver, etc.

The Everlasting Gospel

The blessed message which the apostles (who were sent by Christ to preach the gospel) heard of Christ, and were to declare to others was this: "That God is light, and in him is no darkness at all." 1 John 1:5. The goal of Christ's sending them with this message was that thereby (preaching it in the evidence and demonstration of God's Spirit) they might "open men's eyes, and turn them from darkness to light, and from the power of Satan to God, that they might receive forgiveness of sins, and an inheritance among them that are sanctified by faith that is in him." Acts 26:18.

Now, as the eye of the mind is opened, and the mind is turned from the darkness within to the light within, and from Satan's power to the power of God (which is revealed in the light), the soul in the light comes to see (over the darkness, and over Satan who darkened it) the things of God and his kingdom.

First, it sees him who is the rock, the holy foundation of God, the holy foundation of life in the soul, the living stone, by which all the other living stones are made alive. These are taught of God to come to him as to a living stone, and so are built upon him, and become God's building, and new creation in him. 1 Pet. 2:5, 2 Cor. 5:17. And here, in this light, none can miss the true coming, hearing the voice of the Father, and being drawn and taught by him to come to the Son. John 6:44-45.

Second, here the true Jew's state, the state of the inward Jew, and the inward circumcision, and the true worship (even the worship of the Father in Spirit and truth) is known. For the inward Jew is a child of light, begotten in the light, redeemed out of darkness, who dwells and walks in the light, as God is in the light. 1 John 1:7. And the circumcision is not a fleshly act, but rather the cutting off of that which is fleshly from the mind by the Spirit and power of Christ. And the gospel worship, or the worship of the inward Jew, is the worshiping of God in the newness of the life of his Son.

Third, here is the true repentance from the dead nature and dead works, which no man can attain to of himself, but is God's gift through his Son. For God has appointed Christ to be a Prince and a Savior, to give repentance and forgiveness of sins. Acts. 5:31. It is here that repentance is known, waited for, and received. For it is not to men who are in the darkness, loving the darkness, that the true repentance is given, but to those who are turned to the light—to them is repentance given unto life. Acts 11:18, compared with chap. 26:17-18.

Fourth, here the true faith, the precious gift of faith, is received, whereby men believe in him who gives life, and receive life from him. And this is the faith which gives access to God, and gives victory over the world and all that is contrary to God. Indeed, the faith which is given in the light does so, but the faith which men hold in the darkness does not do so.

Fifth, here is the cross of Christ known, which is an inward, living, spiritual thing, effectually crucifying the man that takes it up and daily bears it, to all that is earthly and sinful. Then the pure seed and life of Christ springs up in his earth, rising over the world and every worldly thing. Gal. 6:14.

Sixth, here the pure love springs in the heart, both to him that begets, and to him that is begotten. In the light there is nothing but love, but in the darkness there is no true love to be found; and even the love that is found there is of the nature of enmity. It is the light of truth that purifies the heart to unfeigned love. 1 Pet. 1:22, Deut. 30:6.

Seventh, here the Lamb's patience and meekness is experienced, and the soul is adorned with it. The Lamb is the light of the world, and they that are made lambs by him partake of his sweet and meek nature, learning of him to be meek and lowly in heart, and so have that patience and meekness from him which no other can attain to. Matt. 11:29.

Eighth, in the light, the precious promises are fulfilled and experienced, which make those who partake of them (in whom they are fulfilled) partakers of the divine nature. For the divine nature is not partaken of in the darkness, but rather in him who is light. Man (who is darkness) cannot partake of the promises which belong to the children of light. But when, by the operation of God's power, his state and nature are changed, and he is now no more darkness, but light in the Lord, then he has his share in the promises which were made to the children of light. Eph. 5:8, 2 Pet., 1:4.

Ninth, in the light, the holy anointing is received, the voice of Christ is heard, and the new everlasting covenant (even the sure mercies of David) is made with the soul. Isa. 55:3. The law of the new covenant (even the law of the Spirit of life in Christ Jesus) is written in the mind, and the holy fear of the new covenant, which cleanses and keeps clean, is put in the heart. The blessed Spirit of the Father is given and received, which gives power (in those who receive it) to become the sons of God, causing them to walk in his ways, and to keep his statutes and judgments, and to do them. Oh that the sons of men would hear and understand this precious lovingkindness of the Lord, and put their trust under the shadow of his wings, and know what it is to be satisfied with the fatness of his spiritual gospel house, and to drink of the river of his pleasures, and in his light to see light! Psa. 36:7-9.

Tenth, in this light the true church, the gospel church,

the New Testament church, is known. This is the church of the children of light, a building built in the light, which church is in God the Father, and in the Lord Jesus Christ, 2 Thess. 1:1, in whom they are built together for a habitation of God through the Spirit. Eph. 2:22. Yes, in him all the building, fitly framed together, grows into a holy temple in the Lord, ver. 21. And all that are here gathered out of the darkness into the light, who walk in the light, and abide in the light, are built upon the foundation of the apostles and prophets, Jesus Christ himself being the chief cornerstone, ver. 20, and are no more strangers and foreigners, but fellow-citizens with the saints, and of the household of God, ver. 19.

The gospel church is the spiritual house of Jacob, which walks in the light of the Lord, Isa. 2:5. These go up to the mountain of the Lord (to that which is revealed to be the mountain of God in the last days, even spiritual Mount Zion, Heb. 12:22), to the house of the God of Jacob, where he teaches his spiritual people, the inward Jews, his ways, and they learn to walk in his paths. For out of this Zion shall go forth the law of the Spirit of life in Christ Jesus (in the days of the gospel), and the word of the Lord shall proceed from this Jerusalem, Isa. 2:3. For the Jerusalem above is free, which is the mother of all the children which are born of God's Spirit. Gal. 4:26, John 3:6. And she being the mother of them all, nourishes them all with the Word of life, which goes forth from her, and all her children know her. Matt. 11:19. Oh that all, both Catholics and Protestants, knew this true mother church, this mother of all the living, who nourishes the living with the law and Word of eternal life!

Chapter VIII
A Testimony to Truth

Concerning the True Church and Ministry

There is a great noise in the world about church and ministry. Many are affirming what it is, and many are doubtful and inquiring about it. And some are truly and rightly satisfied, having received the knowledge of the thing from God, who is not deceived about it, nor deceives any, but gives the true understanding of these and other things to them that wait upon him aright (that is, in his fear, and in the silence of the fleshly-wise part). Now, I have a testimony to give concerning these things, which that ear which is of God can hear; and to that ear I desire to speak.

The true church is the spiritual body of Christ. The church is Christ's spouse, and he is the husband. The head is living, and so are all the members of the body. The head is anointed, and the oil with which the head is anointed runs down from the head upon all the body; and that upon which the oil does not run is not part of the body. Now, no outward thing can make one a member of this body; much less can any outward thing, way, profession, or practice make a church. The church under the law was made so by outward things, by an outward gathering, an outward circumcision, an outward law, an outward worship, etc. But the gospel is a state of substance, a state of the invisible things, of persons invisibly gathered by the Spirit into the life and power of God, inwardly circumcised, inwardly baptized with the Holy Spirit and with fire, inwardly worshipping in Spirit and truth, bowing at every sound and name of the Lord Jesus. And whatever is of an outward state here under the gospel, is brought forth and preserved by the power of the inward appearing, and by dwelling in it. Therefore, this is the church now—a people gathered by the life and Spirit of the Lord. It is a people gathered by the power from on high, abiding in the power, acting in the power, worshipping in the power, keeping in the holy order and government of life by the power (both inwardly in their own hearts, and outwardly in their assemblies and lives).

Christ was made a king, priest, and prophet, not after the law of a carnal commandment, but after the power of an endless life. It is in this power that he gathers, governs, and preserves his church, and ministers from and by his Spirit and power in it. Now, find this power of the endless life, find a people anywhere gathered by this power, and in this power, and there is the church, there is the living body, there is Christ the head, whose dominion and strength is over all, against whom the gates of hell cannot prevail.

It is the same for the ministers of this church. I mean, the same thing that manifests the church manifests the ministers thereof. For these also are of God, called by him, receiving power from him, and abiding and ministering in that power. So that there are three things requisite to a true ministry, without which they cannot be right, or execute their office rightly.

1. They must be called by God. The ministry under the law was warranted by its call and appointment by God. Christ himself took not the honor to himself, but he was called of God to this priesthood, even as Aaron was to his. So too the apostles and ministers, in their declaration of the gospel, were called and appointed by Christ.

2. They must receive ability and power from God. The elders that were to help Moses were to receive of his Spirit. Under the law, the priests were to be anointed with the outward, literal oil, and the ministers of the gospel are to be anointed with the inward, spiritual oil. Their work is spiritual; and how can they perform it except by the anointing, by that presence, guidance, life, virtue, and power of the Spirit putting itself forth in them? The apostles themselves, who had been taught by Christ, who knew his manner of life and his doctrine, who were eye-witnesses of what they were to declare, and had received an authority and commission from him, yet were not to go forth merely upon this call and commission, but to wait for power from on high. Only when they had received the Spirit and power, then they were made able ministers of the new covenant, not of the letter, but of the Spirit and power.

3. They must abide in the power, keep in the power, feel the motion, virtue, and assistance of the power in all their work and service. They must neither pull down, nor build up, nor watch over, or oversee the flock in their own wisdom, in their own spirit, in their own wills; but only in the anointing, in the light and guidance of the Lord. This gathering, this building, this work of the Lord begins without flesh, apart from man, and flesh must be kept out of the whole carrying on of it.

Indeed, unless the ministers of the gospel are in the Spirit, in the life, in the power, how can they minister to the nature, to the spirit, to the life in the body (even so much as to the least member)? They may minister outward knowledge to man's wisdom and understanding, but that is not the food that is to be ministered to the church, nor is it the part in man which is to be fed by the true minister. Rather, they are to minister life (living food) from the living fountain, from the head, from the Spirit of Christ in them, to the particular members under their charge. Thus they are to be good stewards and shepherds to the flock, giving everyone their proper portion in due season.

Now consider: it was no small matter to be a minister under the law. It was easy to err, and to minister amiss. It was easy erring from the letter, unless great care and circumspection was used to keep strictly to it. But it is a much more weighty thing to minister under the gospel, to receive the power, to minister in the power to that which is begotten and born of the power.

This ministry is precious, and is of God, wherever it is found. But only they that are of God can hear and receive this ministry, 1 John 4:6. The uncircumcised ear cannot hear, nor the wise and knowing according to the flesh. For the wisdom of God is foolishness to man, and the mysteries of his kingdom (the mystery of his life, and the true godliness) are riddles and madness to the eye of his wisdom. Indeed, man is degenerated from God, and held down with chains of darkness and corruption. And he that would know the true church, or be of it, and hear the voice of God in his true ministry, must first take up the cross to that part in him which is not of God, and receive from God the eye which sees, and the ear which hears.

Objection: It is objected against us, that this which we testify to, hold forth, and practice, is a new way, having sprung up of late, never known or heard of in the world till some few years ago.

Answer: The light eternal, when it shines out of the darkness, is new indeed to those that were overwhelmed and buried in the darkness of the night, and so never saw or heard of it before. However, it is not new in itself, but is the same that was from the beginning.

This seed of life, this seed of blessing, is the same that was promised at first to bruise the serpent's head. It is the same which was promised to Abraham, when the gospel was preached to him. It is the same that saved all (who believed in it) under the law; for it was not the types and shadows and outward ordinances which saved the soul then, but the seed, who was the Savior from the beginning, and is the Savior all along, even to the end. For the apostles preached the seed also, the word of faith, Christ the way, Christ the power. Yes, and all along the times of the apostasy, this was the thing that preserved the witnesses, saving them from being swallowed up in the darkness, and keeping them alive in their testimony. And there is no other thing held forth now by those who are in the truth, and raised up by the power of God in it to give testimony to it. This is the seed from which life has sprung in any that have felt life, in all ages and generations. This is the root and offspring of David, the bright and the morning star. This is the desire of all nations (oh that they knew their desire!) And, O you, whosoever has felt anything of God at any time, either in reading the Scriptures, or hearing a ministry, or in private breathings, etc., this was it which gave you to feel in that state, to desire after the Lord, to turn from vanity, to long for communion with him, etc. Oh that you were there now, as you have been in times past! For there is no other thing we testify to you of (or desire to draw you to) than that which was the root and strength of your life in those days.

Therefore, come back to the life; know that which formerly gave you life. Has it moved on? Then stay not behind, but follow on! Oh, know the Lamb who is the leader! For this is the great duty of duties—to follow him whereso-ever he goes. He may (in his tender mercy) visit you in Egypt, in Sodom, in Babylon, but these are not the places of his rest, nor should they be so esteemed, simply because he once appeared, visited, touched, and refreshed the soul there. His dwelling place is Zion, his holy city is Jerusalem, where the Christians dwelt with him before the apostasy, and where those that are redeemed out of the apostasy are again to dwell.

Therefore, lose no more time in disputings, in thoughts, in reasonings, in consultings, with that mind which will never advise the soul for its good. Rather, wait on the Lord that you may come (through his leadings) to the true sense of his seed, to the feeling of the nature of his eternal light and life in the heart. This will put an end to disputes, yes, and scatter the disputing mind, and powerfully determine the controversy in the pure sense and demonstration of the Spirit. And he that knows anything of this, let him abide here, wait here, live here, dwell here, and breathe to the Father here, watching narrowly over that which would lead from here, and draw the mind into another way, wisdom, and spirit. And O poor soul, if the Lord touches your heart, and opens your eye, you will see your beloved, who is the "choicest among ten thousand," and there nothing like him for excellency of nature. Indeed, this is felt, it is experienced, and it is testified unto you in the love, and in the truth.

It is not the words of the letter, nor the observation of all that is in the letter, that can give life; but his voice gives life. The words that he speaks (at any time) are Spirit and life. So this is what we live upon—not the bread which we can make, not the things we can gather or comprehend from the letter, but the words which proceed from the mouth of God. Now, this seed is his mouth, in and through which he speaks to our souls, who fear before him, and wait upon him, in his own eternal and everlasting ordinance. And here we meet in substance, in life, in freshness, in purity, and in power. And this testimony is given forth to you in the love of God, from his tender heart, which knows your present state, your needs, your wanderings, your deep prejudices and settled hardness against his truth. Nevertheless, he remembers the days of your youth, and cannot give over seeking after you, and crying unto you. Oh, when will you turn? When will you hear? When will you wait to feel life in the Spirit?

A Word of Caution

The following is a word of caution to those who are at any time touched with the power of Truth, how they can afterwards hearken to and let in the enemy, and thereby have the good seed stolen away, the true sense lost, and the mind filled with prejudices and stumbling blocks.

The Truth of God, being received into the inward parts, is found to be of a living, powerful nature, working mightily there for the cleansing and redeeming of the heart. And this is certainly witnessed—that even as the mind joined to deceit is thereby defiled, so the mind joined to the truth of God is purified by its power and virtue. Now, having felt this, and being filled with the love and goodwill of God to the souls of others, how can we help but testify to others who stand in need of God's truth (and its cleansing property and virtue)?

Now, when the Lord gives forth his sound in power and life, it many times pierces deeply through the earthly veil, and reaches to his own within, which, being reached, answers the testimony, saying, "It is Truth!" Here is a beginning of the work of God in that heart, the soul being touched with his truth, feeling it inwardly, and yielding in some measure to the overcoming virtue and power of it.

But then comes the subtle one, whose design and labor is to undermine and overturn the work of God in the soul. He begets doubts and jealousies and questions, both concerning us, and concerning the doctrine taught by us, to suggest into the mind that it is not of God. In this way, the enemy brings the dispute into another part of man (besides where the truth got entrance), and there he easily sways the mind to judge against its own former feeling, and to turn from that work that was begun by God. In this way many poor hearts are entangled and carried back into captivity, who began to feel the stirrings of truth in their hearts (wherein is the power of redemption) which would have redeemed them as well as others, had they received it in the love of it, and become subject to it.

It is a precious thing to receive from God a spirit of discerning, which gives the ability to discern his Spirit from the spirit of deceit. Yes, it is impossible to be preserved in the right Spirit and way, except as this is felt. For how can the Lord be received in all the motions and operations of his Spirit? Or how can the contrary spirit be turned from in all its subtle devices, twistings, and reasonings in the mind, unless there be a discerning in the true light of the Lord, what is of the one, and what of the other?

And you that desire not to be deceived, sink deep

beneath the thoughts, reasonings, and consultations of the earthly mind, that you may meet with something of the kingdom and power (which carries its own evidence and demonstration with it), and may be gathered into it, and find a sense, knowledge, and judgment there, which never was deceived, nor can deceive. For the pure religion, the pure knowledge, the right judgment, the living faith, begin in the power and demonstration of the Spirit, and must remain within these limits. These things are separate from flesh, apart from man, out of his will, out of his wisdom, out of the compass of man's comprehension. And he that does not leave this ground never meets with the life, power, and virtue of truth. He may meet with a body of notions and formed knowledge, wherein he may talk of the fall of man, and restoration by Christ (even very exactly, according to a literal description). But the life, the true knowledge, the powerful virtue, is another thing altogether, and it is met with in another country, where man cannot travel, except as he is stripped of himself, newly formed, made and brought forth in Another.

Therefore, you who desire after the Lord (who desire to be his, and to feel him yours, and to know his truth in the life and power of it), wait for the demonstrations of his Spirit. Learn to distinguish inwardly between the teachings from his Spirit and the teachings of another spirit from the letter.

Question: But how may I, who am weak and full of doubts and fears, keep in the sense of truth, and come to a certainty that I am not deceived?

Answer: To you, who present this question in the uprightness and simplicity of your heart, I have something to say:

1. Mind how you were touched; mind how you were reached; observe what ear was opened in you, and breathe to the Lord to keep that ear open in you, and the other shut. For this I can assure you in the truth of God, that with the ear which the Lord opened to truth (which you felt his Spirit unlocking in you, and letting in truth), I say, with *that* ear you shall never be able to let in anything afterwards contrary to truth. But if the enemy can open the other ear, the ear that will hear his prejudices, jealousies, doubts, fears, and temptations, and let them in, it will thrust out that which entered at the other ear. Now, can you not distinguish, O poor soul, between that which brought some sense of truth into you, and that which rises in you against truth? Oh, fear before the Lord! Oh, watch and pray, that when the tempter comes, you enter not with him into temptation, and so lose your union and growth in that which is invaluable!

2. Keep your eye and heart upon the preciousness of what you felt. Oh remember how fresh, how warm, how living it was, how it reached, how it overcame, how it melted! The remembrance of this (cleaved to in the mind) will be a strength against the temptations and subtle devices of the enemy.

3. Meddle not with the things that the enemy casts into your mind. Consider not whether they be so or no. He that considers of a temptation (in many cases) has let it in, and is overcome already. When Eve did but hearken to what the serpent said, how soon was she lost and gone! The enemy many times brings temptations beyond the state, capacity, and ability of the soul to determine. These things, at present, are too high for you. You have not yet received a proportion of life from God to determine them by, and if you run beyond your measure, and seek to determine things in your mind (which are beyond your reach), you will surely run into the snare.

4. The present determining of these things would not be of so great advantage to you as you may believe. Why so? Because the enemy has many temptations and devices of the same kind (as well as of other kinds) which he would bring one after another. And when he brings a second, a third, etc., that which engaged you to consider the first, would engage you also to consider the rest. Therefore the way is to keep out of him, in the upright sense of what the Lord wrought in you. For in this measure the Lord is with you, and abiding there, you are out of the enemy's reach. But being drawn by the enemy to consider things that are out of your reach, you therein lay yourself open to his snares.

5. Mind what was forbidden you, or required of you, in that time when you felt the warmth from God. For there is then a heavenly voice, and a heavenly vision in the heart, though the enemy turns the mind, as much as he is able, from heeding it. There is then oftentimes something of the worldly nature and course discovered, or something of God's will made manifest. There is something that you do, or have done, which you then see to be not of the Father, but of the world. And perhaps there is something of the Father which you know you ought to become subject to, but you are afraid of the cross, or shame, or would rather have more clearness first. Oh call this to mind afterwards! And if ever you would receive life, and come into union with God's truth, and receive his Spirit and power, and be established therein, then become obedient to the heavenly vision! Consult not with flesh and blood, but enter into the obedience of that very thing which was forbidden or required, be it little or much. This is the right way that your mind should be exercised in. And if your mind be exercised faithfully here, the Lord will strengthen you against the tempter when he comes with his temptations and subtle objections. But if you falter here, and

become unfaithful in the little, you are not likely to meet with more, nor with the preservation of the Lord in the little. And indeed this is the cause of the miscarriage of many, because they have not received and loved that little thing which was made manifest, but rather had pleasure in unrighteousness, and so lingered in pleasing the spirit of the world (both in themselves and others) when they were called by the Lord to leave it, and travel out of it.

6. Wait for the renewings of life and true sense in you from God. Wait for another visit; wait for another touch and demonstration of his Spirit. Where did you meet with it? Go there again, wait there again, and look up to the Lord to stay your spirit till he appears again.

But oh, take heed, that before the light arises again, before the life stirs again, you are not already gone (by hearkening to temptations) into an incapacity of knowing or receiving it. For this is the way of the Lord, the experienced way—after he comes, after the touches of his truth, then comes the tempter with his reasonings, deceits, likenesses, etc. Now the Lord is trying you, to see how your heart will stick to him. If you come off from the temptation, if you stand clear of the enemy, the Lord will appear to you again, to strengthen you, comfort you, open more to you, and lead you further in the way of life, nearer to the power and purity thereof. But if you draw back from that wherein the Lord began to work, the Lord's soul has no pleasure to appear any further to you, or to work any further in you.

And one thing I will tell you: if you let not in the enemy's temptations, but abide (under the clouds, under the storms, under the tempests, under the confused reasonings, fears, doubts, and troubles), looking towards the Lord, waiting for him, and not making a league with the enemy against him in the meantime, then the Lord will certainly appear. And when he does appear, you will find one of these two effects: Either the power of the enemy's objections, or temptations, will be so broken that you shall not then heed them; or they will be so answered by the appearance and light of the Spirit of the Lord, that you shall be satisfied about them. Now, which of these is the better for you, the Lord God knows, and you are sure to receive it from him in that hour. He will not leave you, but secretly support you in the meantime, as your eye and mind are towards him.

The light and power of the Lord, when it arises, scatters and breaks into pieces (in the mind) that which was very powerful before. And then, the soul does not so much care to consider or know that which the enemy before made it believe was so necessary to know. For mark: that which causes me to grow is the feeling of life, the sense of the Lord's presence and power with me, the living knowledge, the knowledge which quickens and gives life. Now, when the life springs, when the light shines, when the Lord, in the power and precious visitations of his truth reaches to my heart, this is present with me. Then what matter to me those objections and prejudices which the enemy casts into my mind? No, I cannot heed them, being taken up with another thing of a deeper nature! For this have I often found by experience: all that troubled me, and all that I doubted, vanishes in a moment, when that which puts an end to all thoughts, reasonings, and disputes is present with me and prevailing in me.

Again, it pleases the Lord at other times (when he sees good) to open the mind, and let it into the light of those things (the mind waiting upon him, and letting them alone till his season) which of itself it could never have waded through. Thus also have I seen the objections and stumbling blocks concerning this precious people, concerning their seed, way, doctrine, practices, etc., opened unto me in the clear light of God, and in the holy demonstrations of his Spirit. Indeed, I have manifestly seen, and been fully satisfied, that what was objected in my own heart, and is objected to in the hearts of others, has been from the subtle accuser of the brethren, who bears false witness against them, and would draw as many as he can to partake in his false testimony, and become false witnesses against God, his truth, and his people.

Therefore beware, all you that desire after the Lord, to meet with the rest and satisfaction of your souls in him, how you be prejudiced against the way whereby God has appointed to work in you, and in all others. For he has sent his Son to give life, and he will not give life by another. And he has appointed that his Son shall be received as a seed, as a seed of life, though as a little grain of mustard seed; yet in this way he must be received. And in this, his low appearance, he has the presence of God with him, and his power and authority. And what he (this little seed) requires, teaches, forbids, etc., must be observed. But there is no one upon the earth that can acknowledge or submit to this, except he become a child also, yes, a very little child. Man's spirit, man's wisdom, man's knowledge, man's religion, man's zeal, etc., is too big to enter here. Men are too wise, too knowing, too rich from scriptures and experiences, to submit to this, even as the Scribes and Pharisees were with Christ's appearance, doctrines, and preachings, when he appeared among them in that body of flesh. Therefore, come into the true feeling, out of the dead knowledge into the living sense, where life, power, righteousness, yes, the peace and joy of the kingdom, is tasted of, and in some measure witnessed by those who bow down in spirit before the least and lowest appearance of Jesus—the lowest degree and measure of him whose life is King and Lord over death forever.

An Objection Against the Light

Objection: Many do believe, and in that belief do object against us, that what we call the light or seed is no more than man's natural conscience.[1]

Answer: I can grant that it is natural, in a sense, but not in the intended sense. It is a seed, indeed, of God's nature, of Christ's nature, but not of man's nature. It is that which stands as a witness in man against him when he falls and transgresses. It is a light indeed that shines within his conscience, but it existed before his conscience was, and is of a higher nature. Man is earthly (with his understanding, knowledge, reason, judgment, conscience); but the light that shines in him (even in his dark, hard, unregenerate, earthly heart) is heavenly, such as his darkness cannot comprehend, though it shines in his darkness.

Do you desire (in true understanding) to know what it is? Then feel it; come out of the darkness where it finds you, into that light where it dwells, and then you will know it indeed, and be able to judge it better. Now I will tell you how we know it to be the light of the new covenant: because we find it discovering to us the new covenant, and leading us into it. We also find it showing us the sins against the new covenant, and furnishing us with power from God against them, and preserving us out of them. And with this demonstration,

---

[1] This was a common criticism against the early Quaker's teachings regarding the indwelling seed or light of Christ. It was objected that the light to which they directed all men's hearts and minds was nothing more than the natural, innate moral conscience. But the Quakers saw and understood a clear distinction between the natural conscience (a faculty of the created soul) and the eternal light of Christ that shines, convicts, and teaches from *within* the conscience. For a thorough treatment of this objection, see Robert Barclay, *Apology for the True Christian Divinity*, The Fifth and Sixth Proposition, section 16. (Available through Quaker Heritage Press in print and online).

indeed, our hearts are satisfied; though we could also say much more concerning this thing, whose testimony fully settles the matter to the full satisfaction of the soul, wherever it is heard and felt.

Some Questions and Answers Concerning the New Covenant — to open the nature and way of it, as it is experientially felt in the heart, and witnessed to in the holy Scriptures.

Question: What is the New Covenant?

Answer: It is a new agreement between God and the soul, different from that former agreement, which was between God and the people of the Jews. It is a precious, glorious covenant, containing precious promises on God's part, and is as easily to be obtained on the creature's part as can possibly be. It is a covenant of the eternal love of God—of life, peace, and rest to the soul. It is the power of the Lord stretched out for the soul, to deliver it from Egypt, carry it through the wilderness, bring it into the Holy Land, and give it its proper possession and inheritance there, maintaining it therein against all its enemies. Yes, this covenant contains very precious things, which the soul finds great need of, and rejoices in the sense and presence of, such as: writing the laws of God in the heart, putting his fear in the inward parts, yes, putting his own Spirit within, to be a fountain of life and strength there, whereby he causes the soul to walk in his ways, and preserves it from departing from him. Likewise, in this covenant God becomes the teacher who creates in the soul a capacity to learn, and causes it to heed and profit. And in this covenant there is a forgiving of iniquity, and a remembering of sins no more, with the destroying and rooting out of that which caused sin, and a healing of the backslidings of the soul.

Question: How is this covenant made with the soul?

Answer: In Christ, the seed, who is all in this covenant. He is the light of it; he is the life of it; he is the power of it; he is the righteousness and sanctification of it. By coming into him, the soul comes into this covenant; by abiding in him, it abides in this covenant; by growing up in him, it grows up in this covenant.

Question: Is this an absolutely free covenant? Or are there any terms or conditions required of the soul in it?

Answer: It is absolutely free in its own nature. It comes from the free love of God; it contains in it the free love of God; it is freely offered to all to whom it is offered; it is freely given to all to whom it is given. There is no price; nothing of the creature is required for it. All that is required is the creature's receiving of it, and giving up to God in it. But in the receiving and giving up to it, much will be required of the creature, without which he can never come to truly receive the covenant, abide in it, or reap the blessings contained therein. Of this the Scriptures abundantly testify, together with the experiences of those who know and feel the nature and virtue of the covenant.

Question: What things are required in this covenant according to the Scriptures, and according to the experiences of those that enter into it, and reap the fruits and benefits of it?

Answer: 1. This is required: that when the Lord calls, when the Lord quickens, when the Lord touches the heart, opens the ear, and gives a faculty and ability of hearing, that then the Lord be hearkened unto diligently. The ear which God has opened must be kept open to him, and that power whereby he opens the one ear and shuts the other must be kept close to, and the Lord waited upon therein. In this way, the true ear will be more and more opened by him, and the other ear (which is apt to hearken to and let in the enemy) will be more and more shut.

Who is there among us that has not felt the Lord God requiring this of us? And as he has been answered, the work of God has gone on in us. And as he has not been answered, the work has gone backward and not forward. And the Scripture bears witness to the same, as in Isa. 55:1-3, where the free covenant is proclaimed, yet there is something even there required: "Hearken diligently; come and eat that which is good, and let your soul delight itself in fatness. Incline your ear, and come unto me; hear, and your souls shall live; and I will make an everlasting covenant with you, even the sure mercies of David."

2. Repentance is required—turning from the old, unclean nature and spirit, and touching it no more, but cleaving to that which has power against it, and preserves from it. This also is felt and witnessed to be required of by God now, and was also testified to of old, as in 2 Cor. 6:17-18. "Touch not the unclean thing, and I will receive you, and will be a father unto you, and you shall be my sons and daughters, says the Lord Almighty."

3. Faith, believing the testimony of truth, and receiving the Spirit's baptism, is required. He that will enter into this covenant must believe the testimony of the gospel (the record of God concerning his Son) with the faith that comes from

him. And he must be circumcised, baptized, renewed, and changed by him. Now he that does this shall be saved, as Christ promised. Mark 16. But he who has the power of life and salvation did not promise that any should be saved otherwise.

4. Obedience of the gospel, subjection to Christ in the rule of his Spirit, and keeping of his commandments, is required. For as the first covenant required the obedience proper to it, so the second covenant requires the obedience proper to it. And as there was no salvation or standing in the first covenant without the obedience thereof, so neither is there in the second, without the obedience thereof.

He that will enjoy the peace, the righteousness, the justification, the life, the power of this covenant, must live in the Spirit, walk in the Spirit, and fulfill the will of the Spirit. He must keep to the seed, keep to the anointing, so that the evil one cannot touch him, so that the interrupter, the slayer, the destroyer of life in the heart, has no power over him, as he does over any who are outside the limits of this covenant. For within the covenant is all the good, but outside of it are the evil things, the dangers, the temptations, the snares, the death and destruction of the soul. And whoever wanders outside of the covenant cannot help but meet with them. Therefore there must be a great care to abide in that which has gathered, in that which has quickened, in that which gives the true sense and understanding, and keeps out of the wrong. How tender, how free was the love of Christ to his disciples! Yet he bids them to abide in his love, and tells them how they should do it: "If you keep my commandments, you shall abide in my love, even as I have kept my Father's commandments, and abide in his love."

Question: But how shall the soul be able to perform all these things? Are they required of it in its own strength, or does God undertake to perform and work all in it?

Answer: Not at all in its own strength, will, or wisdom (for these are eternally shut out of this covenant), but in the strength, life, and power, which flows from God in the covenant.

Question: How then shall the soul receive this strength, life, and power?

Answer: By embracing it as it comes, cleaving to it, panting after it, patiently mourning and waiting for it. By not despising the little, and looking after more before the little be received, but thankfully entertaining the beginnings of life, the beginnings of the holy instructions, the first drawings away from the spirit and nature of this world, in whatever it be. He that disputes not concerning the thing, but receives it just as it appears, in simplicity and uprightness, watching thereto, he shall be blessed of the Lord, and meet with the desire of his soul in the Lord's season, when the Lord has fitted and prepared his heart for it.

Now, this is such a small and narrow door, such a poor and low beginning, that the wisdom of man can never enter it. And if there should be a little entrance through it (through the overcoming power of life), yet man's wisdom will often quickly drive the soul back again. 'Let me know the doctrine first,' says the wise man; 'I will understand the doctrine thoroughly before I will change my present way.' No, says Christ, "He that does his will shall know of the doctrine." John 7:17. You shall know a little, which will reach to your heart. There you must begin, and being faithful there, you shall know further of the doctrine. But if you are unfaithful there, you will stumble and be prejudiced against the doctrine, and never be able to know it. Oh, the mystery of life! Oh, the hidden path thereof, which none can learn but those whom the Father teaches! But many think to learn in that mind which was always, and will ever be, shut out. 'If Christ would lay his doctrine before them, and make it good to their understanding, then they would receive it.' No, no; they must bow to Christ, to his name, to his power, to his will, to his way of manifesting his truth; for he will not bow to theirs.

Question: What are the sins against this covenant, and what effects do they have?

Answer: The sins against this covenant are chiefly unbelief in the power, and disobedience to the power, which are of a deeper nature than the sins against the first covenant, and have more dangerous effects. The refusing of this covenant is more dangerous than the refusing the covenant of Moses. And the breaking of the covenant here, that is, turning back from God (through a heart of unbelief), is more dangerous than the breaking of the first covenant.

Question: But can this covenant be broken? Has not God undertaken all in it?

Answer: This covenant is an agreement between God and the soul, wherein things are required of the soul, through the life and strength which flows from the covenant. And the soul may hearken to the enemy and not to the Lord; it may walk after the flesh and not after the Spirit; it may lust after high knowledge and hidden things of the kingdom (as those of old who pried into the ark); it may draw back from the Lord in those respects wherein it had formerly given up to him, etc. Now, these and such like things are breaches of the covenant. These are sins against it, which draw down judgments upon the soul at present, and at last will result in an utter casting off, unless the soul be brought back by the judgments into the agreement again with the Lord in truth and uprightness.

Now, it is true that the Lord does all in the covenant according to his good pleasure, but he has appointed a way of working out the life and happiness of the soul, to which it is his good pleasure to keep. And his way is Christ, his seed. From this seed, all the love, mercy, care, and tenderness of God flow. And to this seed, the soul must come, and here the soul is to abide, that it may enjoy and possess these things. But if the enemy can (by any means) draw the soul out from here, he draws it from its own life and strength, and from the sweet blessings and influences of the holy and free covenant. Now, the Lord has not given power to the enemy to force the soul from here; rather he gives power to the soul to abide with him here, and in the hour of distress, if it cries to him, he helps the helpless, and lifts up a standard against the enemy.

Now, all that desire the sweetness of this covenant, the life, the virtue, the blessings of it, oh wait to feel and receive something from God, and in that gift learn to fear before him, and walk worthy of him, and do not grieve or provoke his Spirit. For he has the power of life and death in his hand, and with whomever he has sufficient cause, he may turn from and cut off. And to whomever he will, he may extend mercy as far and as long as he pleases; for it is his own, and he may do what he will with it. Only know this, God is love; God is tenderness, infinite tenderness. Yes, his compassion is beyond imagination or comprehension, and he hates putting away. The poor mourning souls that cry unto him, feeling their need of him, and gasping after him, he cannot cast off. But the wise, the confident, the conceited, from their own apprehensions of Scriptures, that think themselves safe by virtue of the covenant, and yet are enemies in their minds to the light of the covenant, these are out of the covenant at present (in their own imaginings and conceivings), and are in the most danger of any I know. May the Lord in mercy cause his light to shine, his life to arise, his power to be manifest, and thereby lead into, and preserve in, his everlasting covenant, according to his good pleasure. Amen.

Question: What is the house of Israel and Judah, with which this new covenant is to be made? Is it the Israel and Judah according to the flesh, that is, the Israel and Judah according to the old covenant, or according to the new?

Answer: When the old covenant passed away, the consideration of Israel and Judah after the flesh passed away also. The new covenant is fitted for and made with the new Israel and Judah. So now, as the apostle said, "He is not a Jew that is one outwardly, nor is circumcision that which is outward in the flesh; but he is a Jew who is one inwardly," etc. This gospel breaks down the outward consideration between Jew and Gentile, and brings up another consideration in both; so that the promises and blessings are not to either in their old state, but to both as they are gathered into, and spring up in, the new seed.

Question: Is this covenant faultless? Does it mend that which God found amiss in the first covenant? Does it keep more firmly to him than the other did? Is there no falling away from it?

Answer: Yes, it is faultless. It does help the defects of the other. It does keep more firmly to God. There is no falling away from it by those with whom it is fully made, and who are established in it. But in the passage and travel, there is danger to the soul which is not faithful and watchful, lest it be drawn from that which gives it a right to, and entrance into, the covenant. For even as the beginning is in the faith, and in the obedience, so is the continuance, growth, and progress. Thus the gospel was preached, "He that believes, and is baptized, shall be saved." This believing includes not only a beginning to believe, but a going on therein, and a continuing to the end. For so is the promise and word of Christ, "He that continues to the end shall be saved." But if any man draw back from the Lord, from his Spirit, and return into the way of death with the other spirit, the soul of the Lord will have no pleasure in him.

Objection: But then this also is like the first covenant, depending upon the creature, and is as defective as the other was.

Answer: No, this covenant does not depend upon the creature, but upon God's love, mercy, and power, which has no limits in this covenant. It depends upon the seed of his life, upon the power of his Spirit freely dispensed to the creature. Nevertheless, the creature that will reap and enjoy this, must come to it in the faith and power which is of the seed, and in the same must abide with it. For God forces none to come, but draws and makes willing. Neither does he force any to stay, but he persuades and makes willing to stay. This is the manner of his working in the day of his power. But now, if the soul hearkens to the other spirit and his drawings, and departs from the Lord, and will not hearken and be won again, the love and pleasure of the Lord will turn from it, even according to the law of this covenant. For there is a law of this covenant, according to the nature of it (according to which the Lord works), as well as there was in the other covenant.

Now, search the Scriptures concerning this thing. Is there any promise of salvation except by coming to the Son? Or is there a promise to them that come without abiding? Did not Christ tell his own disciples that as they were in the vine, in his love, so they must abide there? This was the law his Father gave him, and the same law he gave to them. It is natural to man to backslide, and if he backslide from that wherein is the life and virtue, how can he not but miss the life and virtue of it? Therefore, in this covenant, the Lord has provided that which will heal the backslidings, and which will powerfully preserve him, etc. But man must come to it (he must come to the Son, he must come to the waters), and he must also abide there. Yet even this is not required of him to do of himself, according to the law and course of the old covenant, but rather it is required of him in that new ability which is in the new seed of life, wherein he is daily to receive it. Yes, it is with him and near him, daily drawing him into, and preserving him in, the life, and within the limits of the covenant, even as the tempter is drawing him into sinning against the covenant, and so into death.

Question: What does God promise to do for the new house of Israel and Judah in this new covenant?

Answer: He promises to put his laws into their mind, and to write them in their hearts. (Oh, happy is he that knows these laws, this mind, this heart, and this manner of writing!) He promises to be their God, and that they shall be his people.

He promises to become their teacher, and such a teacher as all shall know him, from the least to the greatest. He promises to take away that which is able to hinder the good things of the covenant—for he will be merciful to their unrighteousness, and their sins and iniquities will he remember no more.

The Reason for Misunderstanding the Scriptures

Question: What is the ground of men's misunderstanding and twisting of Scriptures?

Answer: 1. A lack of acquaintance with God's Spirit, and the right way of waiting upon him to receive a true understanding of them. For though men may go as far as to know and confess that the Spirit of the Lord is the only revealer of the things of God, and the only right interpreter of his own words, yet the same man who confesses this may not certainly and distinctly know the Spirit of the Lord. He may not know when he is receiving the interpretation of a scripture from the Spirit, or from his own understanding, or from a spirit that is contrary to him. For there is another spirit near man, whose nature, work, and delight is to cause man to misunderstand and misuse the Scriptures. And this enemy can warmly and clearly bring Scriptures to him, with a purpose to deceive and mislead him. Now, he that hugs and receives everything that rises up within him easily runs into the snare of the enemy. Therefore, a man must watch and wait and fear and pray, that he may distinguish between the nature and voice of spirits in himself, that so he may know (in the light of the Lord) when the Lord speaks, and also when the mysterious spirit of deceit strives to speak like the Lord.

2. A lack of acquaintance with God's truth in the love, life, and power of it. For he that knows truth, and has received from God the thing of which the Scriptures speak, how easy is it to him to understand the words that speak of that thing! But he who has the knowledge of the thing from the words alone, how easy is it for him to misunderstand the words!

3. The opinions, apprehensions, ways, and practices of men, which they have taken up in the dark, and in which their minds are engaged, are a great obstacle to the right understanding of Scriptures. For there has been a cloudy and dark day, or a great night of darkness upon the earth, wherein the light, which leads to the soul's rest, has not shined clearly in men's spirits. And so, in this cloudy darkness, men have wandered from mountain to hill, seeking their resting place. And now, some have settled on one mountain, some on another; some on one hill, some on another, saying, 'Here is the resting-place.' And so, when the Spirit of the Lord comes and cries, 'Depart you, depart you; this is not your resting-place, for it is polluted,' they cannot hear. Why so? Because they have already believed otherwise, and think they have found their rest.

Some Questions Concerning Deceit and Deceivers

In the truth there is no deceit, and they that are in the truth are out of the deceit, and abiding there, are out of the reach of deceivers. But they that are out of the truth, are in the deceit already, and are liable daily more and more both to be further deceived, and to help to deceive others.

Question: What is deceit, and who are deceivers?

Answer: That which appears like truth, but is not—that is deceit. And they who are in a form of godliness, but are without the Spirit, life, and power of it—they are deceivers.

Question: Who are most susceptible to deceit?

Answer: The simple, the heedless, the careless, the gullible; those who do not wait upon the Lord in the light, power, and demonstration of his Spirit. These (through good words and fair speeches, and appearances of things) are easily led aside from the truth itself into some likeness or resemblance of it.

Question: What is the time of deceit?

Answer: The night; the cloudy, dark time, when the enemy has raised his fogs and mists in the minds of men—this is his time of deceiving their hearts.

Question: Is it now night or day?

Answer: It is night with some, and day with others. Where the light is arisen, there it is day. Where the darkness covers and possesses the minds of men, there it is night.

Question: How may a man know whether it be night or day with him?

Answer: By waiting to feel something of the life of God arising in him, and by turning and hearkening to his witness.

Question: How may a man come out of the darkness of the night, into the light and brightness of the day?

Answer: By joining to the first glimmerings and breakings forth thereof upon him. The least light of truth has the same nature, virtue and properties with the greatest. Though it is not the same in degree, yet it is the same in kind. And he that will come to the greatest, must begin with the least. Light makes manifest; the day discovers both the things of the night and of the day.

Have you made a discovery of either kind, either of that which is good, or of that which is evil? Either of that which is of the worldly nature and the evil one, or of that which is of the heavenly nature and the Holy One? Then join in immediately in the virtue, strength, and power of that which makes the discovery, and your spirit will find there an entrance into the light of the day. And going on faithfully in this, the light will daily more and more break in upon you, even until it has gathered your spirit out of the blackness, darkness, and deceit of the night, into the beauty, brightness, and truth of the day.

Question: How may a man be preserved from deceit and deceivers?

Answer: By abiding in that which uncovers them to him, and preserves him out of them. By dwelling in that light, in that life, in that power, in that truth, into which they cannot enter. For it is God, it is his seed, his nature, in which the wicked one finds nothing, and into which he cannot enter. And he that abides in him is safe in him. But he that goes forth out of the life, out of the light, out of the seed, out of the power which preserves, out of the holy anointing which keeps the eye open, he easily runs into, and is entangled in, the deception of unrighteousness.

A Question Concerning Miracles Answered

Question: If this be a new dispensation of the life and power of God, even of the preaching of the everlasting gospel again after the apostasy, why is it not accompanied with outward miracles now, as formerly it was? I say *outward* miracles, because it is indeed accompanied with inward miracles. For the lame, that could never set foot on the path of life, do now walk; the eyes that were blind are opened, and do now see; the ears that were deaf have been unstopped, and do now hear; the lepers inwardly, who were overspread with sin and corruption, have been washed, cleansed, and healed by the pure power; yes, the dead inwardly have been quickened, raised, turned to him that lives for evermore, and have received life from him, and do live in him and with him. Now, these are mighty things, wonderful miracles, even the substance of both the miracles which were done under the law, and those which Christ himself wrought outwardly. For it is not outward healing which is the true salvation, life, and power, but these outward miracles point to that which must work inwardly; so that man might take notice of it, know it, come to it, wait upon it, and be made partakers of the inward health and salvation. Yet seeing that Christ was then pleased to put forth his power outwardly, in order to point to and bear witness of the inward, why does he not do so now?

Answer: The nature of the present dispensation does not require it. For the present dispensation of life is to bring men to the seed of life which is within them (which is the sum and substance of all former dispensations). And to bring them to this, there need not be anything of a miraculous nature outwardly, but only the witness, demonstration and enlightening of the Spirit inwardly.

Now, when the outward law was to be received, then the Lord saw need of outward miracles to confirm it. So it was also in the prophets' days, while that dispensation held, up until the coming of Christ. And when Christ came in the body prepared by the Father, it pleased the Lord to confirm, by outward, visible demonstrations of his power in him, that this was he. Likewise afterwards, the apostles having the doctrine concerning that appearance to preach and testify to the world, the Lord was also pleased and saw good to confirm it by miracles. But now there is no new doctrine to be preached. The doctrine concerning Christ is the same now that it was then, the very same that the apostles preached. Neither is there any need of confirming it now, for it is generally believed among Christian professors of all sorts. For as to Christ's birth, preaching, holy life, dying (offering himself up as a sacrifice for sin), rising, ascending, sitting at the right hand of the Father, etc.,—who doubts these things? But under all this knowledge men still hide their sins, their lusts and corruptions, serving not the Lord (not truly fearing, believing in, and obeying him), but his enemies, and are become corrupt like the heathen. These are Christians in word, but as to holy walking and the power of the endless life, they are as far from it as the very heathen.

Therefore, the Lord has now visited the world in this state, and sent forth what he judged necessary for it in this state, that is, not a ministry to preach again the same doctrine (under which the Christian world has corrupted themselves), but to point to the seed of life, in which is the light and power to uncover, lead from, and wash away this corruption. And with this ministry there goes forth a power to reach the heart and raise the witness in all that fear the Lord. Thus the inward witness confirms it, and the mind is inwardly satisfied, and comes to know the truth and turn to it.

Now, this (and the effect of it) is beyond outward miracles, and beyond the satisfaction or assurance which they can offer. For such miracles leave a dispute in the mind (for notwithstanding all the miracles Christ showed, there was still a dispute and dissatisfaction in the minds of many concerning him). But he that feels the thing itself in the true seed, where the demonstration and certainty of the Spirit's assurance is received, this one is past dispute, and is gone (in measure) into the nature of things, beyond that satisfaction which miracles can afford. He is out of that state and mind which asks a sign, or seeks confirmation by a sign.

A Brief Account Concerning Silent Meetings

This is a great mystery, hidden from the eye of man, who has run from the inward life into outward observations. He cannot see that this is required by the Lord of his people, or acknowledge any edification therein, or benefit thereby. But to the mind that is drawn inward, the thing is plain, and a true building up in the life of God, and a fellowship one with another is therein sweetly felt. For there is precious refreshment from the presence of the Lord received by them who singly wait upon him according to the leadings and requirings of his Holy Spirit. Now, if the Lord please, I will open the thing a little more for the upright-hearted.

After the mind is in some measure turned to the Lord, and his quickenings are felt, and his seed begins to arise and spring up in the heart, then the flesh is to be silent before him, and the soul is to wait upon him (for his further appearings) in that measure of life which is already revealed. Now, this is a great thing to know the flesh silenced, to feel the reasoning thoughts and discourses of the fleshly mind stilled, and the wisdom, light, and guidance of God's Spirit waited for. For man is to come into a poverty of self, into true humility, into the nothingness, into the silence of his spirit before the Lord. He must come to put off all his knowledge, wisdom, understanding, abilities, all that he is, has done, or can do, that he may be clothed and filled with the nature, Spirit, and power of the Lord.

Now, in this measure of life which is of Christ, and in which Christ is and appears to the soul, there is the power of life and death. There is power to kill the flesh, and power to quicken to God. There is power to cause the soul to cease from its own workings, and power to work in and for the soul what God requires, and what is acceptable in his sight. And in this God is to be waited upon and worshipped continually, both in private and in public, according as his Spirit draws and teaches.

For the Lord requires of his people not only to worship him privately, but also to meet together to worship him, in the seasons, and according to the drawings, of his Spirit. And those who are taught of him dare not forsake the assembling of themselves together, as is the manner of some, but rather watch against such temptations and snares of the enemy.

And this is the manner of their worship—they are to wait upon the Lord, to meet in the silence of flesh, and to watch for the stirrings of his life and the breakings forth of his power among them. And in the breakings forth of that power they may pray, speak, exhort, rebuke, sing, mourn, etc., according as the Spirit teaches, requires, and gives utterance. But if the Spirit does not require to speak, and give to utter, then everyone is to sit still in his place (in his heavenly place I mean), feeling his own measure, feeding upon it, receiving from it, into his spirit, whatever the Lord gives.

Now, in this is edifying, pure edifying, precious edifying.

The soul who waits in this way is hereby particularly edified by the Spirit of the Lord at every meeting. And also there is the life of the whole felt in every vessel that is turned inward to its measure. For the warmth of life in each vessel does not only warm the particular, but they are like a heap of fresh and living coals, warming one another, and a great strength, freshness, and vigor of life flows into all. And if any be burdened, tempted, buffeted by Satan, bowed down, over-borne, languishing, afflicted, distressed, etc., the state of such is felt in Spirit, and secret cries ascend up to the Lord for them. And many times these find ease and relief in a few words spoken, or even without words.

Now, as for absolutely silent meetings, wherein there is a resolution not to speak, these are unknown to us; rather, we wait on the Lord, either to feel him in words, or in silence of spirit without words, as he pleases. And that which we aim at, and are instructed to by the Spirit of the Lord as to our meetings, is that the flesh in everyone be kept silent, and that there be no building up except in the Spirit and power of the Lord.

Now, there are several states of people. Some feel little of the Lord's presence, but rather feel temptations and thoughts, with many wanderings and rovings of mind. These are not yet acquainted with the power, or at least they do not know its dominion, but still feel dominion of the evil over the good in them. And this is a sore travailing and mournful state, and our meetings to such as these (many times) may seem more for the worse than for the better. Yet even these, while turning, as much as they may away from such things, and cleaving (or at least in truth of heart desiring to cleave), to that which witnesses against the flesh, have acceptance with the Lord herein. And continuing to wait in this trouble and distress (keeping close to meetings, in fear and subjection to the Lord who requires it, though with little apparent benefit), do reap a hidden benefit at present, and shall reap a more clear and manifest benefit afterwards, as the Lord wastes away and wears out in them that part wherein the darkness has its strength.

God is to be worshipped in spirit, in his own power and life, and this is at his own disposal. His church is a gathering in the Spirit. If any man speak there, he must speak as the oracle of God, 1 Pet. 4:11, as the vessel out of which God speaks, as the trumpet out of which he gives the sound. Therefore, there is to be a waiting in silence till the Spirit of the Lord moves to speak, and also gives words to speak. For a man is not to speak his own words, or in his own wisdom or time, but rather the Spirit's words, in the Spirit's wisdom and time, which is when he moves and gives to speak. And seeing that the Spirit inwardly nourishes even when he does not move to speak words, so this inward sense and nourishment is to be waited for and received when there are no words. Yes, the ministry of the Spirit and life is more close and immediate when it is without words than when it is with words, as has been often felt, and faithfully testified to by many witnesses. Eye has not seen, nor ear heard, neither has it entered into the heart of man, how and what things God reveals to his children by his Spirit when they wait upon him in his pure fear, and worship and converse with him in Spirit. For then the fountain of the great deep is unsealed, and the everlasting springs surely give up the pure and living water.

Chapter IX

Life and Immortality
Brought to Light by the Gospel

Two Questions Concerning God's Teaching

Question: What is the reason that others cannot learn, nor become subject to, the same spiritual truths which God makes manifest to us, and subjects our spirits to?

Answer: The reason is because they do not learn the same way that God teaches us. And so, though they may have many advantages above us in natural abilities, learning, etc., and study hard to know much, yet not coming into the right way in which God's Spirit teaches, they never come to learn the truth.

Question: But what is the way wherein God teaches you?

Answer: This is the way God teaches us—by giving us an understanding to know him that is true, and by opening an ear in us to hear his voice. And so, being kept within the limits of that understanding and that ear, we come to hear and know aright.

"Take heed," said Christ, "how you hear." Oh, the Lord has made us sensible of the weight of that scripture! And we have often experienced that it is easy to hear amiss, and read amiss, and pray amiss, and believe amiss, and hope amiss; but it is hard to do any of these aright. Therefore, we are taught to wait for the stirring of the waters, for the moving of God's Holy Spirit upon our spirits. Only then is healing virtue and ability felt and received from him to perform what he requires.

Thus, when we read the Scriptures, our eyes are towards him, and we watch against our own understandings, against what we could gather or comprehend of ourselves. And we wait to feel how he will open our spirits, and what he will make manifest to them when they have been opened. And if he drops down nothing, we gather nothing; but if he gives light, then in his light we see and receive light. So in praying, we wait to feel the birth of life (which is of the Father, and which the Father hears) breathe in us; and so far as the Spirit of the Father breathes upon the soul, and it breathes to the Father, that far we can pray. But when life stops, we stop, and dare not offer up to God any sacrifice of our own, but only what the Father prepares and gives us. So in eating and drinking, and whatever we do, our heart is retired to the Lord, and we wait to feel everything sanctified by his presence and blessing, and indeed, here everything is sweet unto us. And in whatever God enables us to do, we narrowly watch to that direction of Christ, "not to let the left hand know what the right hand does." For we are nothing of ourselves, nor can we do anything of ourselves. Therefore, whatever is done in us, is done as we feel the grace of God, the virtue and power of his life, working all in us.

And in this temper of spirit we find nothing too hard for us. For the strength of Christ is always at hand, even in the midst of our weakness; and the riches of the kingdom are always at hand in the midst of our poverty and nothingness. And his strength works, and our weakness does not hinder the glory of him that works through it. And so we are assured, by a constant sense and daily experience, that it is not by our willing or running according to our wisdom and strength, that we can attain anything, but by God showing mercy to us in Christ. We therefore daily wait at the posts of God's heavenly wisdom, to feel the gate of mercy and tender love opened to us, and mercy and love flow in upon us, whereby we obtain what our hearts desire and seek after. Blessed be the Lord forever!

And truly here in the springings of love and openings of mercy from our God, we have fellowship with the Father and Son, and one with another, in the Holy Spirit of life. And we testify of these things to others, that they also may come into the same fellowship, and be of the same faith which flows from, and abides in, the power and life eternal.

May the Lord guide all tender, breathing, panting spirits here, that they may be satisfied in the goodness and loving-kindness of the Lord, and may eat abundantly of the fatness of his house, and drink of the rivers of his pleasures, and no longer wander up and down in their own barren thoughts, apprehensions, and conceivings upon the Scriptures.

The Threefold Appearance of Christ—Namely: Under the Law, In the Body of Flesh, and in His Spirit and Power.

First—His appearance under the law. Various were the appearances of Christ under the law. Sometimes he was as an angel, or in the likeness of a man (as to Abraham, Jacob, Joshua, and Moses, etc.). Also, the appearances of God to the prophets in visions were often the appearances of Christ; as particularly, that glorious appearance of God sitting upon a throne, and his train filling the temple, and the Seraphim crying, "Holy! Holy! Holy is the Lord of hosts; the whole earth is full of his glory!" Isa. 6:3. This was an appearance of Christ to Isaiah, as is manifest by John 12:41, where the Evangelist (relating to that place) uses this expression: "These things said Isaiah, when he saw his glory, and spoke of him." Also, he was the angel of God's presence who went before the Jews in all their journeys and travels out of Egypt, through the sea, in the wilderness, and in the time of the Judges, and who wrought all their deliverances for them, as is signified in Isa. 63:9, "In all their afflictions he was afflicted, and the angel of his presence saved them," etc. So too with the three children, he appeared in the midst of the fiery furnace in a form like the Son of God. Dan. 3:25.

Now, indeed, the whole law was a shadow of him who was to come to be the substance of it, and to perform inwardly in the heart that which the law represented in outward figures. Thus Moses and all the prophets were forerunners of him who is the great prophet of the spiritual Israel of God. All the priests, especially the high priests, were types and forerunners of him, and were meant to end in him, who is the high priest over the household of God forever. The judges and saviors were types of him who is the great Savior and Redeemer, for they saved not by their own strength, but by his Spirit and power coming upon them, so that the yoke (which was made and brought upon them by their rebellion against the Lord, and disobedience to his law) was broken because of the anointing.

David, Solomon, and the good kings were types of him — David, in his conquest over his spiritual enemies; Solomon, in his ruling Israel in peace, after he had conquered their enemies.

Circumcision was a type of his circumcising the heart, that his children (his holy seed) might love the Lord their God with all their heart, and live.

The Passover, and blood of the lamb, was a type of his blood sprinkled upon the conscience, which preserves against the stroke and power of the destroyer; and so God passes over all such, when he visits for sin and transgression.

The outward Sabbath was a type of the pure rest which Christ gives to those that believe in his name. For indeed, they that truly believe in him do enter into rest, and cease from their own labors and workings of themselves, and witness God's working in them, "both to will and to do of his good pleasure."

The outward law in the letter, written in tables of stone, was a shadow of the inward, living, pure, powerful, spiritual law of love and life which God writes in the hearts of his chil-dren, which constrains them to obedience, and enables them to do all that God requires of them with ease and delight. For truly the yoke of his law is easy, and the burden of his commandments is light. They are not at all grievous to them that are under, and in subjection to, his Spirit. For when the mind is gathered, and brought from under the spirit and power of darkness into his Spirit and power, oh, how easy it is to believe, to love, to obey, etc.! Indeed there is nothing but love, and faith, and obedience, and life, and righteous-ness, and holiness, and pure power, and peace, and joy here. "For the old things are passed away, and all things are become new in Christ," to them that are in the new creation in him.

So too Canaan, the Holy Land, represented the land of life, or country of life, into which God gathers, and in which he feeds and preserves all the living, whom he gathers out of the territories of death and darkness. And the plenty and fullness of the land of Canaan, and the sweet rivers therein, signified the abundance of rich things, and the rivers of God's pleasure, where his redeemed ones drink as they come to live and dwell and walk and sup in and with him.

Jerusalem, the holy city, was a figure of the New Jerusalem, the spiritual Jerusalem, the heavenly Jerusalem, which is the mother of all who are born of the Spirit. The hill upon which Jerusalem was built signified God's holy mountain, whereupon his city is built. The inhabitants of the outward Jerusalem signified the inhabitants of the new and inward Jerusalem. The temple signified Christ's body, and the bodies of the saints, which are temples in which the Holy One dwells in the midst. The altar in the outward temple signified the altar in this inward temple, which all the true, inward, spiritual Jews have right to partake of, and none else. The fire in the outward temple, and the candlesticks, and the lights which were never to go out, signified the holy fire in the spiritual temple, which comes from heaven, and with which all the spiritual sacrifices are to be offered up. The candlestick is to hold the light (and the priests to keep the lamps burning) or God will remove it out of its place. So too the holy garments of the priests signified the robes of righteousness, innocence, and purity, with which the people of God under the gospel (who are a royal priesthood to him) are to be clothed.

The ark signified that which holds the law of the new covenant, and the pot of manna showed with what kind of food God fed and nourished the soul in the wilderness, before he brought it into the Holy Land. For indeed, Christ appeared to, and was with, that people in the wilderness, in a cloud by day, and in a pillar of fire by night, which signified the leadings of God's Spirit in the day of the gospel. Isa. 4:5. And he was the rock that followed them, and the manna of which they did eat, and the water of which they did drink. For they did eat and drink of the heavenly things in a figure, and as their spirits were at any time opened, they had a taste and sense of the true food, in and through the figure. Yes, doubt-less, at sometimes they had a sense, and did eat of the same spiritual food of which we now eat, "and did all drink of the same spiritual drink" of which we now drink, 1 Cor. 10:3-4. For they were not only all under the cloud, and did not only all pass through the sea, but they were also all baptized in the cloud and in the sea, having a sense of the pure power of the Lord, and of his outstretched arm made bare for them.

Likewise there was Aaron's rod that budded, laid up in the ark, which is the evidence of the true priesthood and ministry forever. This priesthood is not to be spurned against, but still to be acknowledged and honored, as of God. In this ark were also the tablets of the law, which represented the true ark, wherein are the tablets of the law of life, which God writes by the finger of his Spirit, and appoints to be kept in the spiritual ark forever.

Above the ark was the mercy-seat, with two cherubim of glory, one at each end of it, spreading their wings on high over the mercy seat. Between these God dwelt or sat, and he met and communed with Moses, and with the priests under the law, when they came to worship him and inquire of him. This was a figure of the true mercy seat under the gospel, where the true priests (the true circumcision, the spiritual Israel of God) have access with boldness to the throne of grace. And through the high priest of their profession, they may obtain mercy and grace to help in time of need.

So too under the law, all the sacrifices (the sin offering, the peace offering, the thank offering, the heave offering, the wave offering, the whole burnt offering, the meat offering, the drink offering, etc.) signified Christ, the one true offering who comprehends them all, which the spiritual people (the priests of the gospel) are daily to offer up to God. And the sweet spices, frankincense, and odors signified the sweet seasonings of the gospel sacrifices with grace, with salt, with the Spirit, with the fresh breathings of life, with innocency, meekness, tenderness, zeal, faith, love, etc., which yield a most pleasant scent in the nostrils of the Lord. Oh, how precious it is to read the figures of the heavenly things with true understanding! But to read *through* the figures (with the eye of life, with the eye of the Spirit) into the invisible substance,—this is sweet, precious, and heavenly indeed!

Second—Christ's appearance in a body of flesh. When the time of these shadows drew towards an end, and the fullness of time was come, he who thus appeared in several types and shadows now came down from the Father, debased himself, and clothed himself like a man, partaking of flesh and blood. In all things he was made like unto us (except for sin; for he was the Lamb without spot) humbling himself to come under the law, and under the curse, that he might redeem those that are under the law (and under the curse) by fulfilling the righteousness thereof, and bringing them through into the everlasting righteousness.

Now, in this body he finished the work which his Father gave him to do. He fulfilled all righteousness (the righteous-ness of the letter, the righteousness of the Spirit) that he might bring his people through the righteousness of the law or letter, into the righteousness of the Spirit and power, that is, the righteousness of the new life. His whole life was a doing of the will of the Father who sent him. And when the Spirit of the Lord was upon him, moving him to preach the gospel, he preached the gospel in the Spirit and power of the Father, and went about doing good, and healing all that were oppressed of the devil, as his Father's Spirit led and guided him. For he did nothing of himself, or in his own will, or for himself; but did all in the will and time of the Father.

Thus he did always please his Father, and seek the honor of him that sent him. He was obedient unto death, even the death of the cross, being willing to drink of the cup which his Father gave him to drink. And so, having finished his work, he returned from where he had come and sat down at the right hand of the majesty on high, being exalted above all principalities, and powers, and dominions, both in this world, and in that which is to come.

Thirdly—Now, the third appearance of Christ (which these two outward appearances made way for) was his appearance in Spirit, even his pure, inward, heavenly appearance in the hearts of his children. This he bids his disciples to wait for, telling them, "that he would not leave them comfortless, but would come again to them." They had known the appearance of the bridegroom in the flesh, and he was to go away. It could not be helped; it was necessary for them that he should go away; but (says he), "I will come again." The same power and presence that is now with you in a body of flesh, shall visit you in Spirit, and so abide with you forever. For he that is now with you shall be in you, and until that time you shall have sorrow, and be like a travailing woman. The world, in the meantime, shall rejoice; "but I will see you again, and your heart shall rejoice, and your joy no man will take from you." And was it not so? Did not Christ send the Spirit, the Comforter? Did he not come in the Spirit and power of the Most High to be with them always, even to the end of the world? Did he not bid them "stay and wait at Jerusalem" for that appearance of him in his Spirit, and not go about his work and message till he came in the power and authority of his Father to go along with them? And did not their hearts rejoice when he came with joy unspeakable, and full of glory? Did they not then have the joy and peace which passed all the understanding of man, which joy and peace none could take from them? Yes, truly, in the kingdom, Spirit, and power of our Lord Jesus Christ there is a seeing eye to eye.

Truly this administration of the Spirit and power of the gospel is exceedingly glorious, and they that come into it come into the glory and heavenly dominion and authority of the Lord Jesus Christ (and so are made kings by him, and wear crowns in his presence, though they still cast them at his feet), and are changed from glory to glory. These behold, as in a mirror, the glory of the Lord, which none can do but with the eye that is in some measure changed and glorified.

Now, this dispensation of the gospel, Spirit, and power, began in the apostles' days, and the church was exceedingly chaste, pure, and beautiful then, without spot or wrinkle. But there was a falling away after this, and a thick dark night, and a very great and universal apostasy from the Spirit and power of the apostles. Many departed out of the fear of the Lord into high-mindedness, and did not keep their standing in the faith, and love, and obedience of the truth; but held to a form of godliness outside of the power.

Concerning Mount Sinai and Mount Zion

Was not Sinai the mountain that could be touched, an earthly mountain, from which came the ministration of the outward law, or letter, which led to bondage, condemnation, and death? Does not the apostle Peter say, concerning the law as so administered, "that it was a yoke too heavy for them or their fathers to bear"? Acts 15:10.

Is not the gospel's Zion a spiritual mountain, a heavenly mountain, a mountain that cannot be touched by human senses, a mountain from which comes the ministration of the Spirit, the ministration of liberty, the ministration of life, the ministration of the glory that exceeds? Is this not the holy mountain, upon which the holy city (the New Jerusalem) is built, and where the King of Righteousness rules in right-eousness and peace over all his subjects, and where he makes them the feast of fat things, and sups together, eating and drinking the bread and wine of the kingdom, even the living bread, and the fruit of the living vine?

"You are not come (says the apostle) to the mount that might be touched, and that burned with fire, nor unto black-ness, and darkness, and tempest, and the sound of a trumpet, and the voice of words, etc., but you are come to Mount Zion, and unto the city of the living God, the heavenly Jerusalem," etc. Heb. 12.

Now, Mount Sinai was that mountain of earth which the voice and presence of the Lord shook at the ministration of the outward law. But there is an inward earth which is to be shaken also, even the nature which transgressed, the nature that was subject to sin and under the curse, the earth which brings forth briars and thorns. Into the earth the plow of the Lord must go, to break it up and overturn it, that there may be a new earth formed, fit to receive the heavenly seed, and bring forth fruit to God. Yes, not only the earth, but also the heavens, are to be shaken and removed. "But yet once more, says the Lord, I shake not earth only, but also heaven; which signifies the removing of those things that may be shaken, that those things which cannot be shaken may remain."

There is that which is changeable, and there is that which is unchangeable. The old earth and the old heavens are changeable; the new heavens and the new earth are unchangeable. There is a changeable mind, a changeable spirit, a changeable nature, a changeable will, a changeable wisdom, a changeable reason and understanding (which blows this way and that), and a changeable knowledge of God, which man learns not from the Spirit of the Lord, but after a traditional way, by hunting with his own mind, and drinking knowledge into that part which is old and earthly. There man kindles his own fire, with which he warms himself, gathering unto himself peace and joy, hope and confidence, etc. But when the Lord appears, and his voice is heard (when he arises to shake terribly the earth, yes, and the heavens also), all these will be shaken, and will fall like untimely figs at the rushing of a mighty wind and terrible tempest.

For the day of the Lord, the day of his pure appearance, the day of the brightness of his rising, will be upon all that is high and lofty, and upon all that is proud and lifted up above the pure seed. Every cedar of Lebanon and oak of Bashan that is high and lifted up, every high mountain and hill that is lifted up, every high tower, and fenced wall, etc., shall all feel the terror of his majesty, and only that which is of the pure seed, gathered into the seed, and changed into the nature of the seed, shall stand. Nothing else shall be able to dwell with the devouring fire and everlasting burning. And so it may be very well said, "Who may abide the day of his coming; and who shall stand when he appears? For he is like a refiner's fire, and like fuller's soap; and he comes with his fan in his hand, to fan away the chaff. And he shall sit as a refiner and purifier of silver, to purify the sons of Levi, and purge them as gold and silver, that they may offer unto the Lord an offering in righteousness... pleasant to the Lord," Mal. 3:2-4, which none can do but those that are purified by him.

Oh happy will they be, whose religion and worship in that day will stand the trial, and bear the fire! And oh, blessed forever be the Lord, who has come near for judgment, and is a swift witness against all deceit and unrighteousness; but is a justifier of those whose consciences he has sprinkled with the blood of Jesus.

But now, as the Lord takes away the old, so he brings in the new. As he removes the old earth and the old heavens, wherein dwelt unrighteousness, so he forms and brings forth the new heavens and the new earth, wherein righteousness dwells. And here the kingdom is known and received which can never be shaken. Here is the Mount Zion, which shall never be removed, and the Jerusalem whose stakes or cords shall never be plucked up or broken. Here is the city which has everlasting foundations, whose builder and maker is God. Blessed are they that come and dwell here, who are not come to the mountain that may be touched and shaken and removed, but to the holy mountain of God, upon which all the buildings of life are raised, and upon which they stand firm forever. For the Lord of Hosts, who has created the new heavens and new earth, has created Jerusalem a rejoicing, and her people a joy, and they shall be glad and rejoice in him, forever and ever. Amen

The Temple and Sacrifices Under the Gospel

God's temple under the gospel is the light of his Son, the Spirit of his Son, and those souls which are renewed, and built up as a habitation for him in the Spirit of his Son, and also those bodies in which renewed minds and spirits dwell. God is light, and he dwells in light. God is Spirit, and his building is holy and spiritual, for he dwells in nothing that is dark or corrupt or unclean.

Now, that which is sacrificed or offered up to God must be clean and pure. No unclean thought, no unclean desire, nothing that is earthly or fleshly or selfish must be offered up to God, but rather the pure breathings of his own Spirit. For whatsoever is of him, and comes from him, is accepted with him. But whatever man can invent or form or offer up of his own, or of himself, though it be ever so glorious or highly esteemed in man's eye, yet it is an abomination in the sight of the Lord.

Thus all the sacrifices of the Gentiles (or the heathenish nature) are rejected. And thus all the sacrifices of the outward Jews (or of the religious mind and nature, without the true life) are rejected also. "With what shall I come before the Lord," said the prophet of old, "and bow myself before the high God? Shall I come before him with burnt offerings, with calves of a year old? Will the Lord be pleased with thousands of rams, with ten thousands of rivers of oil? Shall I give my firstborn for my transgression, the fruit of my body for the sin of my soul?" Mic. 6:6-7. What was the answer of God? No, no, this is not the way to come to pardon of sin, or to acceptance with the Lord. Rather, come to that which teaches what is good, and shows what the "Lord requires of you, O man!" which is "to do justly, and to love mercy, and to walk humbly with the Lord." Come there in the teachings of God's Spirit, and worship there, and there you shall witness forgiveness of sins, and acceptance with the Lord. Mic. 6:7-8 and Isa. 1:16-18. For it was not offering sacrifices of old (appointed under the law) that would do the thing, nor is it men's pleading the sacrifice of Christ under the gospel, but rather a coming to that Spirit which teaches holiness, and being subject to that Spirit, and offering in that Spirit (to the Father) what proceeds from him. So that God's building in the Spirit is the only true temple, and the sacrifices or offerings in the Spirit are the only offerings of the new covenant.

Here every groan or sigh towards the Lord after that which is pure, every supplication in the Spirit, every acknowledgment of the goodness of the Lord in a true and pure sense, are of a sweet savor in the nostrils of the Lord. Indeed, hospitality, relieving the poor, or doing anything that is good out from the good and holy root, are sacrifices acceptable to the Lord. Read these following scriptures, and if the Lord opens your eyes, you may thereby come to see both what the temple and the sacrifices are. As for the temple, see 1 Cor. 3:16 and 2 Cor. 6:16. Isa. 5:7,15. Eph. 2:21-22. Heb. 3:6. Rev. 21:22. John 4:23. Psa. 90:1. Then for the sacrifices, Psa. 1:14-15 and 51:16-17 and 141:2. Mal. 1:11. Heb. 10:8-9. Rom. 12:1. 1 Cor. 6:19-20. 1 Pet. 2:5. Heb. 13:15. Phil. 4:18.

Concerning God's Election

Now, as concerning God's election, observe this: that it is in Christ, and not out of him. For it was the intent of God to honor his Son, even as his Son honored him. And this was the honor which God gave him—that he should be his salvation to the ends of the earth, that whosoever believed on him should not perish, but have everlasting life. That he should be the way for all mankind to come to the Father, through faith in him. For, as in Adam all died, so in Christ all might be made alive; and in Adam all men were shut up in death and condemnation, so the free gift might come upon all, and the way of life and redemption be opened to all, in him.

Mind the figure, the brazen serpent, which was not lifted up so that a certain number might be healed, and no more. Rather, it was lifted up that everyone that was wounded, everyone that was stung with serpents, might look up and be healed.

So too was Christ lifted up, that every sinner that was stung with sin and with the serpent might look up to the physician of souls and receive virtue and healing from him, according to that precious scripture, "Look unto me, and be you saved, all the ends of the earth." And, "Whoever is thirsty, let him come; and whoever will, let him come and drink of the water of life freely." Yes, God stands ready, by his Holy Spirit and quickening power (which is near men), to kindle the true thirst in them, and to make them truly willing.

But to open this thing yet further: there is a predestination, election, calling, justifying, and glorifying. There is a predestination unto holiness, an election in that which is holy, a calling out of darkness into light, a justifying and glorifying in the light, through the renewing and sanctification of the Spirit. All of these God orders and manages according to his good will, and according as he has purposed in himself; but he is not the decreer, nor the author of sin or rebellion against himself, which is the cause of the creature's condemnation.

Now, all things are as present with God before they were; for God did foreknow Adam's fall (though he was not therefore the author of it) before it came to pass. And he foreknew how his power and love and mercy should work towards men and for men, in and through Christ. He knew how far he would visit men with his love, and how far men would resist and strive against his holy and good Spirit. And he determined how long his Spirit should strive with nations and persons, for indeed, with some he would long wait to be gracious, and with others he would be quicker and more severe, according to their provocations.

Indeed, God's love, mercy, power, and his good Spirit are his own, and he may show forth the operations of them towards men according to his pleasure. And who can say unto him, 'What are you doing?' Can he not do with his own what he pleases? And because he may show mercy as long as he will, and harden as soon as he will (as he sees cause), may it not be truly said, "That he has mercy on whom he will have mercy; and whom he will he hardens?" But he does not harden without first giving them a day of mercy, visitations of mercy, following after and forbearing them in mercy, and seeking by the riches of his goodness and long-suffering to lead them to repentance, that they might escape his wrath. Indeed, to suggest that God hardens any from a mere will in himself, because he desires to destroy the far greater part of men, this the Scriptures do not declare, but rather abundantly testify against. For how long did God strive with the old world (in the days of Noah), even to have saved them, whom afterwards he did destroy? And how long did he strive with that people of the Jews (yes, and with other nations also)? "As I live, says the Lord," (and he speaks his heart), "I desire not the death of the wicked, but rather that they might return and live. I am not the destroyer, I am the Savior, and my delight is not to destroy, but to save." "O Israel, your destruction is of yourself, but in me is your help!" Truly, no man's blood will lie at God's door, but at his own.

Therefore, as God has prepared a Savior, so there is no lack of love, or mercy, or power on his part, to draw men to the Savior. But this is the condemnation: that men harden themselves against the drawings of his Spirit, and against the operation of his holy light and power when it appears and is willing to work in and upon their hearts. Scripture does not declare that man's condemnation is because the light does not shine in his heart, but rather because light does shine and men love darkness more than the light. For indeed a measure of light appears and shines to all men, witnessing against and drawing away from the darkness. And in the end it will be clearly manifest that God's Spirit did indeed strive with all, and that they who have refused him would not be turned from their darkness to the light of the Lord. Every mouth will be stopped before him, for all men that perish are justly condemned, having refused and neglected so great a salvation. For truly the light of the sun of God's everlasting day, and the sound of his Spirit visiting dark man, reaches throughout all the earth, and his voice extends to the ends of the world.

Question: How may a man make his calling and election sure?

Answer: By making Christ sure to him, in whom the calling and election is; for the Lord chooses only in him, and refuses or reprobates only outside of him.

Question: How may I make Christ sure to me?

Answer: By receiving him, giving up to him, parting with all for him, and waiting upon him in the way and path of life till you feel the power of that broken in you which would separate from him. For then what danger is there, when the soul is naturally become the Lord's, rooted in his love, circumcised in heart to love the Lord above all, even with the whole heart and soul? Certainly the love of the Lord cannot help but flow in great strength to that soul, and what can come between? But now, while there is still something not given up, something yet standing in which the enemy has a part, and by which he may enter, then the state of that soul is not fully sure. For there may be a going back from the saving life into that wherein is the destruction of the soul, and whoever goes there meets with perdition and destruction, so far as he travels that way.

In the path of death there is death; in the path of life

there is life. God is no respecter of persons, but he is a respecter of his seed, and of his eternal covenant of life, which stands firm in his seed forever. Here is life for every soul that feels the drawings of the Father, and comes to his Son for life, and abides in him. But there is death for every soul that does not come to this, but rather departs from the Lord through a heart of unbelief. So the way of God is eternal and immutable; he cannot deny himself. He that believes in the Son has life; he that believes not is in the death and condemnation which belong to the unbelief.

Now, do you desire to know your election? Then wait to know and distinguish between Jacob and Esau, Isaac and Ishmael, in yourself. For these were outward figures and allegories of something inward. Feel Esau, the profane one; Ishmael, the scoffer at the wisdom, way, and seed of God. You must feel these, who are cast off by God, cast out also of you. And then feel Isaac, the seed of the promise; feel Jacob, the plain birth of life, raised up in you, living in you, and you in it. And then you will feel the election, and will be in the election. And as his seed is sure to you, and your union with it, and standing and abiding in it is sure, so your election is sure.

Election is a deep mystery, and none can read the scrip-tures about it (which indeed are hard to understand, but easy to twist) except those who can read in the seed, life, power, and openings of the Spirit of the Lord. These read things as they are; but other men only read things as they apprehend and conceive them to be. For the knowledge that God has given his people is above all the knowledge that can be searched out, gathered, or comprehended by all the men upon the earth.

Chapter X
The Ministration of Spirit and Power

There are chambers of imagery in many people, and strongholds, reasonings, imaginations, and high thoughts, exalted above the pure seed and measure of life in their hearts. For every true Christian, every true believer, has received something of Christ's Spirit, some proportion of grace and truth from the fullness of Christ, which is as leaven and salt, to leaven the heart, and season the mind and spirit. But all do not distinctly know this, nor have all that do know it become subject to it in such a way that it does lead, command, and rule in them. Instead, there is something else which holds captive. The enemy of the soul has the rule and dominion in many men's spirits. And though they profess godliness, still they keep the seed under in them, so that their souls are kept back from the redemption and deliverance which they could partake of in and with the seed. So it is that many talk of the gospel (and speak great words of Christ, and redemption by him) who do not know "immortality brought to light," nor the dead raised by him, to live to God and praise his name.

Now, in these chambers of imagery, in these strongholds, there are many pleasant pictures, many images of heavenly things, which men form in their minds from their own imaginations and conceivings upon the Scriptures. For men reading the Scriptures outside of the life, Spirit, and power which gave them forth (but rather with that which is natural), do not come to the true, pure, heavenly, living knowledge. These obtain only a natural knowledge, according to which they believe and worship, and so they bow down before the apprehensions and imaginations of their own minds. And so one believes and worships one way, and another believes and worships another way. And truly, here men worship what they do not know; but they who are the true Jews, know what they worship. For indeed, salvation is of the true Jews, who worship neither at this mountain, nor at the other mountain, but only in Spirit and in truth, even in the life and power of our Lord Jesus Christ.

Thus it is with all men in their several professions of religion in the darkness, in the apostasy from the true life and power, which all sorts have erred and wandered from, but few have returned to. Oh, few have found the pearl of price which has been long lost! Instead, they have contented themselves with a literal relation and knowledge about the pearl, without knowing and possessing the pearl itself. Yes, this was the state of darkness the Lord found us all in when he came to visit us. For the strong man had his strongholds in us, whereby he held us captive in the bands of death, and free from that righteous life and power which we thirsted after. But when the stronger man came, he battered his strength, he assaulted and took his strongholds. He broke all his reasonings, knowledge, wisdom, and subtlety, wherein he trusted, and made spoil of his goods, and delivered the captive from under his hand.

For truly, when the mighty day of the Lord came upon us, and his pure, heavenly light shone in our hearts, God searched Jerusalem as with candles, discovering the most hidden things of Esau's nature inwardly. Then all the knowledge and wisdom, all the understanding and experiences, which were treasured up in us outside of the pure life, outside of the truth (which lives and abides), were found to be dead. And these were condemned to death in us, and so cast forth, even as the treasures of Egypt and Babylon, and were thrown to the bats and moles (who either creep up and down in the earthly nature, or soar aloft in the dark dreams and imaginations of the night of darkness and apostasy). For when the true light shines, it discovers what the day is, and what the night is, and also the things which are of the day, and the things which are of the night.

Now, when the Lord thus appeared unto us, and caused the light of his Son to shine in us, many of us quickly came out of Egypt, turning our backs upon the darkness. We went willingly into the wilderness, to travel along with the Lord, and to be exercised and fitted there for the good land, the land of the redeemed, the land of the living, the land which flows with milk and honey (which is pure, heavenly food). For those that come there find the excellent vine, which bears the heavenly grapes, of which is the wine of the kingdom, and the true olive, which yields sweet oil, and houses which they did not build, wherein are many dwelling places of rest and pure glory.

But there were others, who were unwilling to come out of Egypt, or to forsake the idols and ways of worship in Egypt and Babylon, whom the enemy long held captive in their thoughts and reasonings, and in the disputings of their minds. Now, these suffered much, and felt many of the strokes and dreadful judgments of the Lord poured out upon that spirit in them which held them captive, and upon them for their hearkening and joining to the subtle reasonings and suggestions of that spirit. For the enemy uses all his strength and subtlety to the utmost, to hold his captives in subjection to him, and under his power, as long as he can. He keeps every hold, he strengthens every reasoning and every thought and imagination of the mind against God's call, against the appearances of his Spirit in the heart. 'Do not go yet!' (says the enemy), 'Your way is not yet plain before you, your light is not yet clear enough!' 'Your objection or consideration is not yet fully answered. You are to try all things! And there is still this, or that, or the other consideration, which you have not yet tried, or considered fully and satisfactorily to your own heart.' Thus many pure drawings of the Father (in which there was light sufficient for the soul to follow) have been lost, and the soul thereby has missed the hand which was put forth (in the tender love of the Lord) to help and save it.

Question: But some may say, 'What have you learned of the Lord more than we, or more than you knew before, when you walked among us, and practiced the ordinances which we practice? Have we not good directions from the Scriptures?'

Answer: There are three things I shall mention (besides many others, which might be mentioned) which the Lord has taught us since his Spirit and power has appeared to us, and led us out of the darkness, which are these: He has taught us to believe; he has taught us to obey; and he has taught us to pray to him in the name of his Son.

Objection: Did you never learn these before?

Answer: No, not as the Lord has taught us now. There was indeed some true faith from the true seed in us, and some true obedience, and some pure breathings to the Father in the days of our former profession. But we knew not the root from which they came, so as to turn to it, and abide in it. Thus the holy desires, and the true sense in us, were often made a prey of, and we remained in need and in barrenness in a strange land, and could not enjoy, possess, or retain, what was freely given to us by our God and Father in Christ. For still there was a fleshly wisdom, a fleshly comprehension, a fleshly nature, mind, and knowledge (which in that day we thought was spiritual, as others do now), which rose up over it. But when the Lord turned us to the light of his Spirit, and by the light and power of his Spirit broke the bonds and chains of darkness in us, then we could believe in him who appeared, and (in the strength and virtue received from him) we could obey him, yielding our members instruments of righteousness to do his will. And in the Spirit of the Son (which we then received in the faith, even the heavenly Spirit, the most excellent Spirit) we could pray to the Father—first, sighing and groaning before him, and afterwards, pouring out our requests and supplications to him, with giving of thanks.

Question: How did the Lord teach you to believe? Or what did he teach you to believe now, more than before?

Answer: It is written in the prophets, "All your children shall be taught of the Lord." And in the new covenant it is promised, "They shall all know me, from the least to the greatest."

Now, as we were brought by the Lord into the light of this covenant, we were taught thus to know him and to believe in him and his Son, as he was made known. So that we knew the Father revealing the Son, and the Son revealing the Father. Our hearts were drawn to believe in both, as they were both revealed in us, and to us, and the revealing was in the Spirit of both, in the light of both, in the life of both, in the power of both, which Spirit, light, life, and power, are one. And he that indeed knows the Son, knows the Father also. And he that indeed knows the Father, knows the Son also.

So now to us there is but one God and Father, "Of whom are all things, and we in him;" and "one Lord Jesus Christ, by whom are all things, and we by him;" and but one Spirit and one power of life, which we have received of the Son and Father, through which we believe and lay hold on the pure, eternal power and strength of the Almighty, which redeems and saves the soul.

Question: How did the Lord teach you to obey?

Answer: Truly, the Lord has taught us obedience in such a way as we never learned before—putting his laws into our minds, writing them in our hearts, and giving us his good Spirit to dwell in us, to quicken and help us to obey and perform his holy laws. And those two commandments (upon which the whole law and prophets hang), namely, "To love God with all our hearts, and our neighbors as ourselves," this he has inwardly written in our hearts, and taught us to observe and obey. So that now we have no other God but him, who brought us out of spiritual Egypt by his outstretched arm and holy power revealed inwardly for us, as it was outwardly revealed to the Jews, whom God redeemed out of outward Egypt.

Question: How did God teach you to pray? Surely you never learned the Lord's prayer, for you do not practice that among you.

Answer: As God brought us into a truly sensible condition, so we came to feel our poverty, and the need of our souls, inwardly and spiritually.

Now, waiting on the Lord in this sense, when we meet together, and when we are alone also, the Lord breathes upon us, and kindles in us fervent desires and longings of soul after that which is pure, and to be delivered from that which is impure, and that we might be ingrafted more and more into Christ. We desire that judgment and condemnation might pass upon all that is not of God in us, and that our hearts might be so united to the Lord that we fear his name fully. For we feel and observe that all our life and strength flow from the union of our souls with the Lord. Therefore, above all things, we cry out for that, and for separation from that spirit which captivates into the things of the earth, and in the earthly mind and nature.

So, we watch unto prayer, and watch for help from God in our calling upon him. We are deeply sensible that we have need both of watching and praying continually, for the enemy is so near, and the soul's snares and dangers are so many.

And truly, Christ, our Lord and Master, who taught his disciples to pray formerly, has taught us also to pray that very prayer, though not to say the words outwardly in the will of men, or in our own will. Indeed, he has taught our hearts to breathe after the same things, even that the name of our heavenly Father might be hallowed or sanctified more and more among all that call upon his name in truth, and especially in our own hearts. And we desire that his kingdom come more and more, that he might reign more in men's spirits, and the kingdom of sin and Satan be thrown down, so that his will might be done, even in our earth, as it is done in the heavenly places, where all the hosts of God obey him. And we look to him for that proportion of the heavenly bread whereby our souls may live to him, and necessary food and outward provision also, according as he sees good, who cares for us.

Now, as we are kept in the light, and watch to the light which discovers all things, we can see what we are kept out of. And if at any time we are entangled and so trespass against the Lord, then we are taught to beg pardon, and to wait where pardon is to be received, through our advocate, even as God has taught us to forgive. Yet this does not embolden any of the little ones to sin, but they pray that they may not fall into temptation, and instead witness deliverance from evil, which the enemy watches to ensnare them with.

Now, we witness this to be true religion, and undefiled before God, and we are sensible that the Lord has taught us this. Surely he is with us in our faith (which he has given to us), in our obedience, in our praying to him in the name of his Son, in our watching, in our waiting, in the silence of our spirits before his mighty and glorious majesty.

Oh that you all knew our God and his Christ in the same covenant and power of life wherein it has pleased him to make himself manifest to us! Oh, awake, awake out of your dreams; come out of the night of sin and darkness into the light of the day! And be not offended that I call them dreams of the night, for they are no better than dreams before the light of the day. Oh, be not contented with dreams concerning God, with dreams concerning fellowship, remission, justification, peace, sanctification, concerning the help of God's Spirit in prayer, etc.

Ah friends, dear friends, let go of the dead for the living! Away with dead knowledge, dead faith, dead hope, dead prayers, dead understanding of the Scriptures, dead strivings after holiness, which shall never obtain the promise! Come to feel that seed raised in you, in the true retired waiting upon the Lord, which shall certainly obtain the promise in you, as your minds are united to it, and come into the true sense and subjection under it.

Concerning the Gospel State

The Gospel is a ministration of the new covenant, or a spiritual ministration of the substance of all that was shadowed out under the law. There were many things under the law, but in the gospel God has gathered all into one. In Christ there is but one seed, one Spirit, one life, one power, which redeems, one circumcision, one baptism, one faith, etc. The law was given by Moses, and its ministration continued through the prophets, until the seed should come, who was to put an end to the law and the righteousness thereof (as in the letter), and bring in the righteousness in the spirit, which should last forever.

The gospel is by Christ, by whom God spoke in the last days, who is the beloved Son, the prophet and high priest of God, who is to be heard forever. Christ taught his disciples, while he was with them on earth, in that body of flesh which his Father prepared for him. And afterwards, by his Spirit (or holy Anointing), he continues teaching his children, and bringing them up in the virtue, life, and power of the new covenant, giving them a new heart and spirit, and causing the old nature of the earthly Adam to die in them, and pass away from them.

The law was given to the outward Jew, and is contrary to the nature in man, who seems willing to obey, but will not. The law was also given to check that part (or nature in man) which is above the seed, to which were given all the outward shadows and types.

But in the gospel, which is the power of God to the redemption of the soul, that part is done away, and the seed is raised, and comes to live in the soul, and the soul lives in the power that quickens it, in and through the seed. So here the life, virtue, and nature of the seed overshadows all, and changes all in the gospel ministration. So that here is a new heaven and a new earth wherein God reigns, and where right- eousness dwells. The old things, wherein unrighteousness dwelt, and wherein the devil reigned, are done away, and so his kingdom is destroyed and laid waste in man, and the kingdom of Christ is set up, exalted, and established.

Then the mountain of the Lord's house comes to be known on top and above all the mountains and hills; and then is the flowing of the enlightened soul there, to learn of the Lord in his holy sanctuary, that it may know his ways and walk in his paths. Then is the voice of the true Shepherd heard, and the law known (the law of the Spirit of life in Christ Jesus) which comes out of Zion. Then is the day of the Lord known—the mighty, terrible, shaking day of the Lord, which is then upon all flesh, silencing it in the dread and awe of him who is holy and pure. And the seed is then raised to life and power, and the Lord alone is exalted in that soul.

Then, after this shaking, after the work of this terrible day of the Lord in the heart, when God has purged away the filth and blood of the defiled soul and spirit by his Spirit of judgment and burning, then that which is left shall be called holy, and dedicated to the Lord, even in everyone that is written and reckoned by God among the living in his Jerusalem. And all God's tabernacles and dwelling places on his holy mountain, and in his holy city, he will cover with the glory of his presence. And in all their assemblies (by his cloudy pillar, and by his shining flame), God will be a defense around them, before which brightness Satan, with his devices and fiery darts, shall fall like flashes of lightning. Indeed, his storms and winds shall not be able to prevail against the dwelling places which God builds on this his holy mountain of peace and salvation.

Then the rod of the stem of Jesse is known, and the branch which grows out of his root, and the Spirit of the Lord resting upon him. "For grace and truth came by Jesus Christ," and where this grace and truth are received, and his everlasting covenant is entered into, there the same Spirit is poured forth and rests. And true judgment is set up in the heart, and the soul is established in the righteousness and peace of his kingdom.

So, if any lack wisdom, let him ask in faith, for it is presently given from the Spirit of wisdom which is poured out upon the seed. This is a Spirit of understanding and knowledge, and of pure, heavenly fear, which makes the fear of the Lord come alive in the understanding, and (being understood and observed) keeps the heart clean, teaching it to avoid and keep out of all that defiles. Here there is not so much as a touching of unclean things by any of the sons and daughters who are led by God's Spirit, and live and walk in the Spirit, but a following of the law of the Spirit of life in Christ Jesus fully and perfectly.

Yes, in this day the feast of fat things is made on God's holy mountain! And in this mountain the veil of the covering (spread over the heart) is done away. Isa. 25:7. For in the seed there is no veiled covering, but rather an opening of the unveiled eye to see the unveiled life and power, even the revealed arm of the Redeemer.

"Who has believed our report; and to whom is the arm of the Lord revealed?" This was said in the old covenant, in the law dispensation, but it is not said so in the new covenant, in the gospel dispensation. For the veil is done away in Christ, and the children there with open face behold (as in a mirror) the glory of the Lord. And here the seed is revealed, and the soul comes into the seed, and becomes one with the seed, which is felt to break the serpent's head. And then says the soul, "Lo, this is my God who I so needed, and so long waited for! Oh, he is come, he is come to judge my heart in right-eousness, and to bring down all that has kept the seed under in me! I feel him, my soul's salvation, and my heart is glad in him! And now I know the land of Judah" (for that land outwardly was but a figure of the inward), "and the strong city that is there!"

Chapter XI

Christ's Baptism

*"He that believes, and is baptized, shall be saved;
but he that believes not, shall be condemned."
Mark 16:16.*

This is a very weighty scripture, and it is necessary for every Christian to rightly understand it, that he may so believe, and be so baptized, as to witness salvation by the gospel of our Lord Jesus Christ.

Now, what believing is this which is here required as necessary to salvation? Is it anything less than a believing in the Lord Jesus Christ from a true sense of his power to save, which the Father has given him? Is it not an inward believing, a believing with the heart? And what baptism or washing is it which saves? Is it not an inward washing, a washing of the soul, a washing of the heart, a washing of the conscience from dead works to serve the living God? Does outward washing save the soul? Inward washing does; baptizing into the name does. Bodily exercise profits little; but godliness (the inward renewing and washing of the heart and mind) profits greatly.

There is one faith and one baptism. Eph 4:5. Is not the one faith inward and spiritual? Is not the one baptism so also? I am certain that he that believes and is baptized in this way shall be saved. But he that believes not, remains in the filthy, unwashed state, in which there neither is, nor can be, salvation, but rather judgment and condemnation, death and destruction, forever. Now consider:

> *...the Divine longsuffering waited in the days of Noah, while the ark was being prepared, in which a few, that is, eight souls, were saved through water. There is also an antitype which now saves us, baptism—not the removal of the filth of the flesh, but the answer of a good conscience toward God—through the resurrection of Jesus Christ. 1 Pet. 3:20-21*

The apostle Peter shows what the baptism is which saves, even that which is the "antitype," or which inwardly or spiritually answers to Noah's ark. The Greek word is *antitypous*, which signifies antitype, or that which fulfills the type; it is the substance, which comes instead of the figure or shadow. And so it is more properly and naturally rendered (as the old translation has it)—"The baptism that now is, fulfilling that figure, saves." For just as Noah's ark saved the bodies of those that were in it when God came to judge and destroy the old world, so now the inward washing saves those that are washed thereby from the wrath and destruction which will come upon all that are unwashed.

Now, lest any should misunderstand and misapply his words, as if he spoke concerning an outward baptism or washing, Peter explains himself in the following words: "Not," says he, "the removal of the filth of the flesh," not the outward washing of the body, that is not what saves; but rather that baptism which brings about the answer of a good conscience towards God, by the resurrection of Jesus Christ. For this is the effect of the inward baptism—sin is washed away by the water of life, by the blood of the Lamb, and that which is new, that which is renewed, rises up out of the water that washes away sin. Then the pure and good conscience answers to God, and the soul knows and partakes of both the death and resurrection of our Lord Jesus Christ. And so, being baptized by the one baptism, even the baptism of Christ, into the one body, the soul comes into the state and fellowship of the living. Another apostle also speaks of the inward washing, even "the washing of regeneration and renewing of the Holy Spirit," by which, says he, "God according to his mercy saved us." Tit. 3:5.

Elsewhere, the apostle Paul speaks of a "circumcision made without hands," and tells wherein it consists, namely, in putting off the body of the sins of the flesh. Moreover, he shows how this is effected, that is, not by Moses' circumcision, but by the circumcision of Christ. Col. 2:11. And truly, those who are circumcised in this way are the true circumcision, the spiritual circumcision, who worship God in the Spirit, and have no confidence in the flesh, but rejoice in Christ Jesus who circumcises them. Now, in the very next verse Paul speaks of baptism, of being "buried with Christ in baptism, and of rising with him through the faith of the operation of God, who raised him from the dead." What is this baptism? Is it inferior to the circumcision spoken of just before? Is it not also without hands? What is it that buries into the death of Christ, and raises into the life of Christ through the faith of the operation of God? Is not this the one spiritual and heavenly baptism, with which the one body is baptized by the one Spirit? What does outward circumcision avail? Does it avail anything? What does outward washing avail? Does it avail any more than outward circumcision?

But the inward circumcision of the inward Jew, and the inward washing of the soul from sin, does avail very much.

Now, as for Matt. 28:19, where Christ expressly commands baptizing, it is a very weighty question, and worthy to be considered, what baptism he there commands. For if it be outward baptism, they greatly err who believe it to be the inward and spiritual baptism. But if it be the inward and spiritual baptism which Christ intended in those words, then they greatly err who think it to be the outward. Now consider the words in the fear and weight of God's Spirit.

It is said, "Go teach, baptizing," but it does not say, baptizing with water, but rather "baptizing in the name," or rather (as the Greek has it) "baptizing *into* the name of the Father, and of the Son, and of the Holy Spirit."

Now, to baptize with water is one thing, and to baptize into the name is another, as all who experience the spiritual baptism know it to be. For the word of faith turns men from Satan to the power of life, and then as they receive the power, and are made partakers of the power, they are baptized into the power and virtue of life. And so they are buried by the power of his Spirit with this heavenly baptism, into death unto sin, and by the same power are made alive unto righteousness. Thus the name of the Lord (the name of the Father, Son, and Spirit) comes over them, and they rise up in it unto life and righteousness, and so are dead unto sin, and alive unto God.

Now, any outward circumcising or washing can be only a figure of this, but the inward circumcising and washing is the thing itself. For Christ did not send his able ministers of the new covenant to minister the letter, or to minister the figures of things, but rather to minister the Spirit, (else how were they able ministers of the Spirit?), that is, to minister the substance. They were not to minister a circumcision or baptism which might be shaken and pass away, as outward and elementary, but rather to minister the circumcision and baptism which cannot be shaken. This is the circumcision and baptism of the gospel, the circumcision and baptism of the Spirit, the circumcision and baptism of the kingdom, which is never to be shaken and pass away as elementary, but to stand and abide forever. Read Heb. 12:26-28, and consider how all elementary and outward things that could be shaken were to be shaken and pass away, so that those things which were of a higher nature (even of the nature of the kingdom) might remain and be established in their stead.

And indeed, even as the inward circumcision could not be thoroughly and singularly established while the figure thereof remained, the same may be truly said concerning the inward baptism. By this it may appear that the baptism of water cannot be the baptism which Christ intended in this place, because the baptism here spoken of was to continue to the end of the world. But the baptism of water is clearly of an outward, elementary nature as can be shaken (as well as circumcision), and so was to be shaken in due time, that that which could not be shaken might remain.

Objection: Against this it is objected that the baptism of the Spirit cannot be the baptism spoken of in this place, because the baptism spoken of in this place is commanded; but the baptism of the Spirit was never commanded.

Answer: Surely this is a great mistake. Was the inward washing of the heart never commanded? The gospel is a ministration of inward things, and the inward things are strictly commanded there. Can any man be saved without inward baptizing? And is he not commanded to receive inward baptizing? Does he not sin if he will not wait to receive it, and give up his heart and soul to be baptized by God's Holy Spirit?

Oh, if the eye were opened in people to look into the gospel ministration, and into the inward nature of things, this might easily be demonstrated to the least babe there. For indeed, to the Lord, the gospel existed before the law, and could not be annulled by the law. So this ministration of the Spirit's baptism (in nature and kind) was long before John's baptism, and could not be annulled by any outward ministration of baptism, but rather abides the same forever. And this baptism is to have its place in the gospel state, where all figures and shadows of things pass away, and that which is true, lasting, and substantial, fills up its place.

Now, the baptism of the Spirit, or the spiritual washing and circumcising the heart (which is all one in substance), was called for and required of the Jews under the law, and it was their sin not to answer God's call and requiring therein. Consider these following scriptures, with many more of the like nature: "Break up your fallow ground, and sow not among thorns." Jer. 4:3. Again: "Circumcise the foreskin of your hearts, and be no more stiff-necked." Deut. 10:16. "Make you a new heart and a new spirit; for why will you die, O house of Israel!" Ezek. 18:31. (Is this not all one in substance with that scripture, "He that believes and is baptized, shall be saved"?) "O Jerusalem, wash your heart from wickedness, that you may be saved! How long shall your vain thoughts lodge within you!" Jer. 4:14. "Rend your hearts, and not your garments." Joel 2:13. "Wash you, make you clean, put away the evil of your doings from before my eyes.... Come now, and let us reason together, says the Lord: though your sins be as scarlet, they shall be as white as snow; though they be red like crimson, they shall be as wool. If you be willing and obedient, you shall eat the good of the land;

but if you refuse and rebel, you shall be devoured with the sword, for the mouth of the Lord has spoken it." Isa. 1:16-20.

Is this not the true baptism, and the remission of sins, which comes thereupon? Is this not the blessing on the baptized state, and the curse on the unbaptized state, which extends both to Jew and Gentile (for with God there is no respect of persons)? Oh that men could read the Scriptures of truth, with the true Spirit and with the true understanding! For these things, which were written to the people of the Jews, were written for our learning. Indeed, precious things may be learned from the Scriptures by those whose eyes are opened by the Lord, and who keep close in their reading to that which anoints and opens the eye. But otherwise, man cannot help but misunderstand and twist them to their own great danger, or to the ruin and destruction of their souls.

Objection: The baptism of the Spirit cannot be intended in Matt. 28:19 because this baptism is to be administered by men; but the baptism of the Spirit was never administered by men, but rather by Jesus Christ.

Answer: The apostle says that "God had made them able ministers of the new covenant, not of the letter, but of the Spirit. For the letter kills, but the Spirit gives life." 2 Cor. 3:6. Now mark—they were made able ministers by God of that which gives life, and that they did minister the Spirit by the laying on of hands is manifest, Acts 19:6, and in many other scriptures.

Indeed the apostles were not able of themselves, or by any virtue or strength of their own, to beget men unto God, or to baptize men into his name and power; but their suffi-ciency was of God.

Consider: Paul was sent to the Gentiles to open their

eyes. Acts 26:18. Now, opening the eyes of the blind is just as peculiar to Christ as baptizing with the Spirit can be. And when Christ gave his apostles commission to teach, baptizing, he told them, "All power in heaven and earth was given me" and he bid, "Do not depart from Jerusalem, but wait for the promise of the Father. For John truly baptized with water, but you shall be baptized with the Holy Spirit not many days from now," (Acts 1:5) and then they should receive power. Power to do what? To baptize with water? Or to baptize into the name with the same baptism wherewith they themselves were baptized? See Matt. 28 together with Acts 1.

Now, if the commission given to the apostle in Matt. 28:16, etc., was to baptize with water, then Paul was inferior to the other apostles. For he, though he had seen the Lord, and was sent from him to open the eyes of the Gentiles, yet he was not sent to baptize with water, as he expressly says, "I was not sent to baptize" (that is, outwardly with water), "but to preach the gospel." But if the baptism intended by Christ was inward and spiritual, even into the name, virtue, life, and power of the Spirit, then Paul had the apostolic commission as fully as any of the rest, and the grace and power of God did work as mightily in him to this end, as in any of them.

But men are as much mistaken about the teaching required by this commission as they are about this baptism. For this teaching is not a literal teaching of things, or a discipline into an outward knowledge and way, but rather a teaching in the Spirit and power. And he who God enables to teach in Spirit and power, he also enables to baptize into the same Spirit and power. Yes, indeed, when the life and power ministers (the word spoken being mixed with faith in them that hear), it brings the earthly part under, and brings the life and power of the Lord Jesus Christ over the heart and spirit. This is true baptism, and is the substance of the figure or shadow which was before the figure of both baptism and circumcision, and remains when they are gone.

Objection: The baptism in the commission was to all nations, but the baptism of the Spirit fell only upon a few at the beginning.

Answer: The promise of receiving the Spirit is upon believing, and it extends to everyone that believes. "He that believes in me, as the Scripture has said, out of his belly shall flow rivers of living water; but this he spoke of the Spirit, which they that believe in him should receive. John 7:38-39.

Likewise, Peter said to that great assembly to which he preached, to which there were added about three thousand souls, "Repent and be baptized, every one of you, in the name of Jesus Christ, for the remission of sins, and you shall receive the gift of the Holy Spirit. For the promise is unto you, and to your children, and to all that are afar off, even as many as the Lord our God shall call." Acts 2:38-39.

And this is the one washing which all the flock are washed with, and so baptized into the one pure, living body. This is the substance of the figure, which substance belongs to the gospel state, even though God also made use of some figures in the breaking forth of that gospel day, and even inclined their hearts then to make use of them.

Objection: The baptism in the Matt. 28 commission cannot be the baptism of the Spirit, because it is to be administered in the name of the Spirit.

Answer: The Greek word is not 'en,' which signifies in, but rather 'eis,' which signifies into. So that the baptism commanded here is to baptize *into* the name, into the

Father's name, into the Son's name, into the Spirit's name, by turning them from darkness to light, from the power of Satan to God. Then the power and life of God's Holy Spirit comes over their hearts and minds, and breaks the power of Satan, and washes the conscience from that which is dead, and plunges or dips them into that which is living.

But that there was also a baptizing with outward water, that I do not deny. And that it was used as a type or shadow to the weak and ceremonial state the Jews were in (when Christ sent forth his apostles to gather them out of the law state into the gospel state), I am also satisfied. But it has been since corrupted, and set up above its place by those who have fallen from the power and life. And everyone should consider and wait on the Lord to know what God requires, and what he will accept of him. For the kingdom of God stands not in food and drink, or any outward washing; nor does it come in the way of man's observation, but in a heavenly seed, and in the Holy Spirit and power of life. Happy are they who are made partakers of, baptized with, and led by, the Spirit of God. Indeed, God will try every man's religion, work, and practices, by the true measuring line. Blessed is he whose religion will bear that trial!

It is a great matter to know the gospel state and ministration, the gospel Spirit and power, the gospel church and ordinances, the words of the holy prophets concerning the day of the gospel, the words of Christ concerning the kingdom and power of God, the words of the apostles concerning the mystery of faith, and the Word which was from the beginning.

Indeed, these are weighty things, and of great importance, about which men may easily miss and twist the Scriptures, unless they are enlightened by the Lord in the renewing of their minds, and their eye kept to the holy anointing, so that they do not run ahead, and so imagine and conceive of themselves according to their own ability of understanding.

The Pharisees had a great deal of knowledge and under-standing of the law of God, and prophecies of things to come from the words of Moses and the prophets. But not having the true key of knowledge, "they erred, not knowing the Scriptures" (despite all their diligent reading and studying them), nor the power of God."

Oh, consider! The Pharisees little thought they would have killed the prophets, had they lived in their days. No, they greatly condemned their fathers for doing so, and yet they themselves crucified Christ. And many now little think they would have crucified Christ had they lived in the days of his flesh; and yet they disdain, reproach, and persecute the appearance of the same Spirit, life, and power, as it now appears in his saints.

Question: What is it that must be washed in the gospel state? Is it the outward or inward man? And what is the inward man to be washed with?

Answer: Consider this scripture seriously, and may the Lord give you the true understanding—"In that day a fountain shall be opened for the house of David and for the inhabi-tants of Jerusalem, for sin and for uncleanness." Zech. 13:1. Does not this scripture speak of the gospel state? What foun-tain is it that is opened in the gospel state? Is it an outward fountain of outward water which washes away sin and uncleanness? The Lord knows of what nature sin is, and with what water it must be washed away, and he therefore opens that fountain in the gospel state with which it is proper to wash it away.

Now, that there was a figurative washing away of sins by John's baptism, I do not deny. For John's was a baptism unto repentance, and by it they professed repentance, and were to "bring forth fruits worthy of repentance." Matt. 3:8. But the "antitype", (1 Pet. 3:21) or fulfillment, is not the washing away the filth of the flesh or body, but rather an inward baptism, which so washes inwardly that the answer of a good conscience is presently felt in the sight and presence of God. And then the soul truly knows with what kind of water it was washed.

Oh that people knew and experienced the baptism which is the substance! Then they would not idolize that baptism (or outward washing), which in its nature can be no more than a sign, signification, or representation of that which is the substance!

Now consider: Did the Jews know the inward circumcision? And do you know the inward baptism any more than the Jews knew the inward circumcision? Read that scripture, Rom. 2:28-29, and the Lord apply it home to your souls—"He is not a Jew who is one outwardly, neither is that circumcision which is outward in the flesh; but he is a Jew who is one inwardly, and circumcision is that of the heart in the Spirit, and not in the letter, whose praise is not of men, but of God." Now, may not the Spirit of God say in these our days (yes, of a truth the Spirit of our God does say so, and many have heard his voice so speaking), 'He is not a Christian who is one outwardly, neither is gospel baptism that which is outward in the flesh; but he is a Christian who is one inwardly, and the gospel baptism is that of the heart in the Spirit, not in the letter, whose praise is not of men, but of God.' The Jews praised the outwardly circumcised, and you praise the outwardly baptized; but God praises the inwardly circumcised and washed.

Objection: But the baptism of the Spirit is a promise, and not a duty.

Answer: That the baptism of the Spirit is a promise is granted; but it is also a duty to receive the promise, and to give up to be baptized by him. For John said, "I indeed baptize you with water unto repentance, but He who is coming after me is mightier than I, whose sandals I am not worthy to carry. He will baptize you with the Holy Spirit and fire." The baptism of the Spirit is the inward purging away of sin and filth by the Spirit and its fire, or by the "Spirit of judgment and burning." Isa. 4:4. Those who were baptized by John were afterwards to expect and wait for this baptism, that with the Lord's fan their floor might be purged, their chaff burnt up, and the wheat gathered into the barn. Matt. 3:12.

Now, we indeed grant that Moses' circumcision was God's ordinance, and that John's baptism was God's ordinance. But to assert that either of these is a gospel ordinance —that Moses' circumcision is the circumcision of Christ, or John's water baptism is the baptism of Christ—this we conscientiously and groundedly deny. Indeed, God's Spirit (in the Scriptures) declares a difference between them, as particularly, between John's baptism and Christ's. Matt. 3:11. Moreover, to set up the shadow of a thing instead of the thing itself is not the way to glorify Christ, or the gospel dispensation. For Christ is the Son, who did not come forth with Moses' circumcision, or with John's baptism (who were both servants), but with the Spirit and power of his Father, with which he circumcises and baptizes inwardly and spiritually.

The Testimony of God's Spirit

O Lord, open my lips, and my mouth shall show forth Your praise. For You do not desire sacrifice, or else I would give it, nor do You delight in burnt offering. The sacrifices of God are a broken spirit; a broken and a contrite heart— these, O God, You will not despise. Psa. 51:16-17

Inquiry 1: What rule did David have from the law of Moses to say that God did not desire sacrifices, nor delight in burnt offering? Did not God desire and require that his people perform these things under the law? And did he not accept them, and delight in them, when they performed them aright, in faith and obedience to him? Was not the Lord pleased with Abel's sacrifice? And did not God smell a sweet savor in Noah's sacrifice? How could David say in truth, and from a true Spirit, that God did neither desire them nor delight in them?

Inquiry 2: Should not David try this Spirit which spoke these things in him, whether it was of God or no? Should he receive a testimony from any spirit so directly contrary in appearance to the foregoing testimonies of God in the holy Scriptures, without a full and certain evidence and demonstration that it was the Spirit of God?

Inquiry 3: How was David to try this Spirit, whether it was of God or no? Was he to try it as to whether it spoke according to the testimony and law of Moses, which certainly was of God, and was given by God for a law or rule to the Jews? If he had tried it in this way, would he not have judged it to be a different spirit from the Spirit of Moses, speaking contrary to the law and testimonies which God gave forth by him?   For indeed, sacrifice and burnt offering was strictly required there, and God often testified his acceptance of it and delight in it. So that God did accept and did delight in these in one respect, and did not accept nor delight at all in them in another respect, for his aim was at another thing, and at other sacrifices, which David clearly saw. And so David's eye, mind, heart, and spirit being gathered inward, even to where God's eye and heart was, there he had a clear sight, and gave a certain testimony concerning what was, and was not, acceptable in the eye of the Lord. So he says, "God did not desire sacrifice, nor delight in burnt offering," Psa. 51:16, though the language of the law of Moses speaks far otherwise, where circumcision, sacrifices, and such outward things are expressed as of great value with the Lord.

Inquiry 4: Now, may not the same Spirit, or the children of God in the same Spirit, say to the Lord in this day (concerning things of the same outward nature)—'You desire not such outward things, else would we perform them. You delight not in outward shadows of the things of the kingdom. You desire not outward washing the body with water, or eating and drinking of outward bread and wine, which avail no more than circumcision and the Passover. If your delight was in things of this nature, and you did require them of us, oh how willingly would we be found in the practice of them before you! But your delight is in that water which washes the soul from its filth, and in the souls that are washed with it. And you desire to see your children feeding on the living bread, the bread which comes down from heaven, and drinking the wine which refreshes, and makes glad the heart of both God and man.'

The Lord has likewise shown us clearly that outward water, bread, and wine, are not the substantial, the spiritual, the heavenly water, the heavenly bread and wine. Rather, these are of the nature of the things that were to be shaken, that those things which cannot be shaken may remain in the gospel state and kingdom.

Oh therefore, let men take heed how they build, or how they judge concerning the appearances of God, by their own apprehensions upon the letter of the Scriptures. But let everyone be careful to build upon the rock which is Christ, upon his Spirit, his life, his power inwardly revealed, which the birth, being kept to, reveals in and to us. For no man, by his own conceivings and apprehensions upon the letter, ever knew, or can know, the Spirit and voice of the Lord. For man is dead, dark, and corrupt, except as he is quickened, enlightened, and his heart sanctified by God's Holy Spirit. What can a dead man see? What can a dead man hear? Can he hear the living sound before he is quickened by it? Do not the Scriptures speak of spiritual things? And can the natural man understand them? Can man's unholy mind understand the words of God's pure, holy Spirit, which were given forth through vessels that were sanctified (some from the womb), and when the Spirit of the Lord was upon them?

Oh that men saw their need of the Lord to open their hearts, and that flesh might be silent in them! Oh that they might come to witness the birth of God's Spirit, and the precious understanding of heavenly things which is given therein! And then that understanding which is not precious, nor living, nor of God, but of themselves, would not be of so great value with them. For indeed, through this great mistake, many (some of whom are zealous and knowledgeable according to the esteem of men) reject that which is of God, and set up that which is of themselves, even of their own apprehending and conceiving, all of which will be bitter-ness and sorrow in the latter end, when that eye shall be opened in them which is at present closed.

Blessed is he who can truly say, 'The Lord has opened an eye in me, even the true eye, the pure eye, the living eye, and with that eye I now see! But the eye with which I saw before, I now see not. And now I know the difference between seeing the same things with my own eye, and with the eye which God has given me. So that now, my earnest desire and prayer to the Lord is to keep open in me forever that eye which he has opened, and also to keep that eye shut which he, in his tender mercy to me, has been pleased to close up in me.

And truly, this is the ground of the great difference between us and others with regard to the things of God. For though we acknowledge the same things, and speak of the same things, yet we do not acknowledge them alike, nor speak of them alike. Why so? Because we see them with different eyes, and so have a different sense of them. Others call things true and so acknowledge them as they apprehend them from the letter. We call things true as they are demonstrated to us by God's Spirit, and as we feel the virtue, life, and power of them from God in our hearts.

Chapter XII

A Further Testimony
Concerning the Work of God
Upon Our Hearts

We are a people (many of us) who have been greatly distressed for lack of that life and power which was revealed in the apostles' days. We are a race of travelers, who have been traveling out of the nature, wisdom, spirit, and course of this world (which is vain and passes away), towards our resting place. We have wandered from mountain to hill, from one way of religion to another, seeking after him whom our souls dearly loved. Indeed the watchmen have often laughed at us and mocked us, wishing us to return to them; but that would not still the cry of our souls, which were sick with earnest desire, not after formal ways of religion, but after life and immortality, that it might be again brought to light (as it had been in the apostles' days), and that our souls might be made partakers of it.

Now, after many a weary step and deep sickness of heart, when we had come near to despair of ever finding and enjoying what our souls so sorely longed after, it pleased the Lord at length in his tender mercy to appear among us. And by the directions of his Holy Spirit, he taught us to turn our minds inwards, showing us that what we sought without was to be found within. Indeed he told us that there (within) was the kingdom of God, which was not to be found by observations without, but by meeting with, and being subject to, the light and power of life. And when we were concerned how to discern it from the darkness and deceit within, this answer was given us from the Lord: 'Its nature will discover itself, for it will find out and reprove whatever is reprovable, and furnish the soul with strength against it.'

Oh, what a blessed sound from the Lord God of life, who thus drew our hearts to wait upon him, and showed us how to wait, and what to wait for, and where we might meet with what our hearts so exceedingly desired and panted after! And truly, as our minds were thus turned inwards, the holy light did shine upon us from the Sun of righteousness, and the pure life and nature from the Son of God did spring up in us. We felt the power of God revealed in our hearts, and the old image of sin and unrighteousness daily defacing, and our souls being created anew (in Christ Jesus), into the holy and heavenly image. Here we felt the mercy of God, the same which saved his people in all ages, reaching to us also, and we found his Spirit regenerating, renewing, and washing us, with the water and blood which cleanses. And as we were regenerated and renewed more and more, so we were also washed more and more, and came more into fellowship with Christ in his death, and were also raised up by him more and more into his life, and taught to set our affections more on things above, and less on things below. For the things below are of an ensnaring and entangling nature, in which the minds of the sons of men are held captive, until they meet with that royal, excellent, noble Spirit and power, which breaks the chains and fetters of darkness, and redeems out of them. And now we can testify (in a true sense, and in the evidence and demonstration of God's Spirit), that not by working, willing, or running of ourselves—not by any works of righteousness which we had done or could do—but by the tender mercy of God visiting, and by the operation of his Holy Spirit upon us (in and through regenerating, renewing, and washing us from that which defiled and stained our souls), we were saved from the wrath to come, and from the ways of transgression wherein we walked, before our God thus visited us.

Now, it is the sincere desire of our souls that this tender mercy of God might take effect on others also, and that they might likewise be taken by him to the place where wisdom teaches her children, and where the true redemption of the soul is witnessed, and the true knowledge of the Father and of Christ (which is life eternal) is given and received. It is our earnest desire that people not be hardened unto destruction, and deceived in their souls by a foolish and vain religion, wherein is not the substance, but only some show and appearance thereof, which cannot really satisfy that which is indeed begotten and born of God's Spirit.

Some Inquiries to be Seriously Considered

Inquiry 1: Who do truly and rightly know and own the Lord Jesus Christ? Is it they who only know and own him as he is outwardly described and spoken of in the Scriptures, but do not know him inwardly revealed in their hearts as the Word and power of eternal life? Or, is it rather they who not only know him according to a literal description in the Scriptures, but also as inwardly revealed by the Father, witnessing him formed within them, and their hearts changed into his holy and heavenly image, by the virtue of his inward appearance, and the operation of his Spirit and power in them?

Inquiry 2: Who do truly and rightly know the death and resurrection of Christ? Is it they who know only the relation of these things in the Scriptures, but are not made conformable to his death, nor raised up by him in the power of his life? Or, is it rather they who are buried with him (by the holy baptism of his Spirit) into death, and who, through the Spirit, have mortified the deeds of the body? Indeed, these witness the holy seed of life raised and living in them, and find themselves raised and made alive to God in and through the power of the Father revealed in them.

Inquiry 3: Who do truly and rightly confess Christ to be the Lord and King, Priest and Prophet, of his people? Is it they who confess it only from the reading of it in the Scriptures? Or, is it rather they who witness him exercising these things within them? Indeed, do they not truly know Christ who experience him overcoming and reigning over sin and death in them, and ministering as in his temple, offering spiritual gifts and sacrifices to his Father, and also prophesying there, opening and revealing the mysteries of his kingdom?

Inquiry 4: Do they, or can they, truly know Christ's voice who never experience the Word of life speaking in their hearts? Where does the false prophet speak? Does he not speak within? And where does the true Shepherd speak? Does he not speak also in the heart? And do not the sheep hear, know, and distinguish his voice there?

Inquiry 5: Who are ingrafted into Christ? Can anyone be ingrafted into him, except as Christ is inwardly revealed and made known, insomuch as he sensibly feels the pure, holy root of life bear him, and its sap springing up in him, causing him to bring forth fruit to God in due season?

Inquiry 6: Who prays in the name of Christ? Is it he who says these (or such like) words in his own will—"Hear me, O Lord, for Christ's sake," or, "I beg of you in Christ's name who is worthy," etc.? Is it not rather he who prays in the child's nature, with the Father's breathing upon him, in the Spirit of the Father which is given him, and in the time and will of the Father? He that does but sigh or groan in and from the Spirit, does not that sigh or groan ascend up to the Father in Christ's name? Alas, how outward is men's religion! But the inward streams and currents of the true, pure, and heavenly religion they do not know.

Inquiry 7: Who do truly and rightly believe in Christ? Do any do so, or can any do so, but those who first feel the life from which the true faith springs? Oh that all the faith in men were dashed, except for what comes out from life, unites to life, and abides in life!

Inquiry 8: Whom does Christ gather from the barren mountains? Is it not his sheep—his poor, distressed, scattered, wounded, fainting, and almost famished sheep? What are the mountains he gathers them from? Are they not the several dead ways, worships, and professions of religion without life? And out of whose mouths does he rescue them? Is it not out of the mouths of the shepherds that have made a prey of them, who have not fed them with life, but rather with words, with dreams, with apprehensions of their own mind concerning the things of God?

Inquiry 9: Who are Christ's kindred according to the Spirit? Who is his mother, sister, and brother? Are any so except they that do the will of the Father? And is this obedience a working according to the law, or the righteousness of the law? No, it is the nature and righteousness of the gospel, which flows out from him who is righteous.

Inquiry 10: Are there two Christs, one manifested without, and another revealed within? Or is it the same Lord Jesus Christ, who, in the days of his flesh, appeared outwardly, and was afterwards manifested within as the mystery of life and the hope of glory? And is he not also, in this our day, revealed and made known within unto us, by the same eternal Spirit?

There are a great many who profess the gospel state, and that they are in Christ, and under grace, and freely justified by grace, so that they look upon their sins as covered by the Lord, and not imputed to them, etc. Many profess these things, and yet do not at all know what they mean truly and rightly, as in God's sight. For it is a great matter to be in Christ, even to know him that is true, and to be in him that is true. It is a great thing to come out of darkness into his light, out of death into his life, out of Satan's kingdom, and out of subjection to sin, into Christ's kingdom, and into subjection to his Spirit. "If any man be in Christ, he is a new creature; old things are passed away, and all things become new." Is this true? Does he that is in Christ witness this? And he that does not witness this, is he in Christ?

Oh, how many are deceived about their being in him, and of their hope in him! For how few of those who talk of being in Christ know what the new creation in him means, or what it is to have Christ formed in them! How few know his Spirit by receiving it, and by their union with it! And "if anyone does not have the Spirit of Christ, he is not His." Rom. 8:9.

Oh, how few truly know what it is to be under grace. For

grace is that which has dominion over sin, and which gives dominion to those that are under it. "Sin shall not have dominion over you," said the apostle, "for you are not under the law, but under grace." Therefore, do not yield your members as servants or instruments to sin. You did so when you were free from righteousness, but now do not let sin reign in your mortal bodies, seeing that grace gives you power over it, and makes you free from it unto righteousness.

So, the justification by grace is only to those who are taught by grace. The grace of God brings salvation, redemption, and justification to these, and to no others; for sins are blotted out, covered, and not imputed in those who receive grace, hear the voice of it, and obey it. "Hear, and your souls shall live." In hearing this grace (by which God teaches), souls come to light in his sight, and the living are justified by him, and in the living way and path of life sins are blotted out, and a garment is given which covers the nakedness. This garment is to be girded about the soul, and kept close on, or the nakedness and shame will appear and be seen again.

So, to believe in the name of Christ, and to run to his name, and trust in his name, and pray to the Father in his name, and obey in his name and power—these are great matters, and very few of those that make profession of them truly know them. For his name is living, and his presence, heavenly virtue, and power is in it. They that know his name, know that which is above every name. They know that which has an authority from God to bring all things under (both in the heart and also in life and conduct), that God alone may be exalted.

The gospel state is a great state, a high state, a state not of shadowy things, but of the everlasting kingdom, where the substance of the things under the law is possessed by those that are there, as they grow up in the gospel power and covenant.

Concerning Some Particulars

Concerning the "form of sound words"—2 Tim. 1:13

Not only the "form of sound words," but also the good knowledge of the heavenly things themselves have been miserably lost and buried in the ruins of the great apostasy. Now, though men have had the Scriptures, yet lacking the Spirit of God, and not knowing how to turn their minds to him and distinguish his voice from the voice of their own spirits and reasonings (yes, and of the enemy also, who lies in wait to steal into men's minds false apprehensions from the Scriptures), they have not come into a clear understanding either of the things or words of Scripture. Instead, with the knowledge and apprehensions of things which they have gathered, they have many times been ready to fight against Christ rather than antichrist. So it is that their confessions of faith, and their expositions of Scriptures have been mixed things, more suiting to their own beliefs and apprehensions than the true nature of the things themselves. Yes, by this gathered knowledge they have been in great danger of opposing the pure administration of God's truth, which is from and in the light and power of his own Spirit. Likewise, the churches that such men have gathered and built up, have been built by way of imitation of something that was done formerly by the power and authority of the Spirit, but not in the same power, life, and authority. The same might be said of their ordinances and duties, wherein they have erred very much.

It is true, some of you have rejected some wood, hay, and stubble, and we acknowledge the Lord's goodness to you in that you have gone so far. But there is yet more to be rejected! All imitations, and knowledges, and interpretations of Scripture outside of the pure life are to be laid aside, and the Spirit of the Lord is to be waited upon in the light which is of him. Here the mind is to be turned and truly learn to abide.

Oh professors, you would know much more of him if you were acquainted with him in his own way, and worshipped him in the everlasting ordinance, which is the pure light of his Son! For this light was before the letter, and brings the soul nearer to the Lord than the letter can, and gives a fuller communion with the Lord in Spirit than can be had or enjoyed through words or conceptions of things. And the purpose of the letter's testimony is to bring the soul into the Spirit and power which is the administration of the gospel.

Concerning Doctrines

Men lay the great stress upon owning doctrines according to their apprehensions of them, but they must yet come much further out of Babylon, out of man's spirit and wisdom. Truly they must come more into the pure fear and waiting upon God, more into the sense and power of truth, and into the light and knowledge which is there, before their doctrines will be owned by the Lord. And this springs in my heart in true love and tenderness, and in melting compassion concerning you: Oh that you held onto the head! I question not whether you hold notions about the head, according to your understanding of things; but to hold the head is a far deeper thing indeed.

Again, a man may apprehend his doctrines to be right, as to the main substantial things, when indeed they are not so. For the doctrines of the gospel are mysteries.[1] Faith is a

---

[1] Penington uses the word mystery to refer to something that is forever hidden from the natural mind, but revealed by the Spirit of God.

mystery; the love of God in the Spirit is a mystery; obedience to the truth is a mystery; the right confession of Christ in and through the Spirit is a mystery; the worship of God in Spirit is a mystery; justification, sanctification, and the peace and joy of the Spirit, all are mysteries of the kingdom, and it is easy missing and misunderstanding these things, but hard to come to the true knowledge of them. And indeed, if any of the true, inward, spiritual knowledge of these things is received at any time, it is hard retaining it, no, impossible to do so rightly, except in that light and power which gave it.

Truly, this is the great mystery of religion, namely: to begin in the Spirit, and so to travel on in the pure light, life, and knowledge thereof, and not to entertain or mix with anything of the flesh. But now, if a man does not have the Spirit of Christ, or if he is not able to distinguish the Spirit of Christ in its voice, motions, and workings from the other spirit, and from his own wisdom and understanding, then when he reads a scripture, he may easily err and mistake about its doctrines. He may let in something of his own, or of the other spirit's forming, instead of that which is the pure truth of God. And then, this thing which he has so let in will cause him to misjudge concerning the truth, and often make him a great enemy to it.

This was the case of the Scribes and Pharisees and great priests in the time of Christ. They studied the law, gave interpretations of it, being appointed by God to preserve the people's knowledge. By their understanding of the law and prophets, Christ could not be the Messiah, for, plainly, his appearance disagreed with the law and the prophets according to their understanding of them.

So that, whereas many say, "Our religion consists, first, in right apprehensions of Scripture, etc." we, on the other hand, cannot help but testify (as we have been convinced by the Lord), that a man must first receive the Spirit before he can have right apprehensions about the mysteries of God, Christ, etc. For the Spirit searches the deep things of God, and no one knows the things of God except by the Spirit. Therefore, there is a necessity for people first to be turned to the Spirit of God. This is the first step in the way to true, saving knowledge.

Concerning the Work of Light

Christ, who had all power given him by the Father, and authority to send forth messengers to preach the gospel of his salvation, sent forth his apostles and servants to testify of and declare it. Now, that which they were to preach and testify of was the one "who was from the beginning," even the "eternal life, which was with the Father, and was manifested unto them." And this is the message which they heard from him, and were to declare to others, "That God is light, and in him is no darkness at all." And this Word of faith, this Word which was from the beginning, this Word which reconciles the soul to God, they were to preach as being "near in the heart and in the mouth." And the intent of their preaching and testifying of this was to turn men to it, from the darkness within to the light within, from the power of Satan within to the power of God within. See Acts 26:18.

Now here, being turned to this light, it discovers the darkness, the lost state, the captivity, the bonds, the misery of the soul, and enables the soul to long after the Savior. And not only this, but the light also shows the Savior whom it causes the soul to long after, and in the waiting upon the Savior in the light which is of him, it gives also to partake of his salvation.

And now, God having demonstrated this thing to us,

showing us what it is, and giving us to partake of the precious virtues of it, how can we call it anything less than a measure of Christ, a measure of his Spirit, the seed of the kingdom, the heavenly leaven, etc.? For we know and experience it assuredly to be that very thing which Christ described in his parables. Now, that thing in man which is offended at us for this, we know to be not the true birth, but rather the birth of another wisdom, which is to be cast out with its mother. And indeed, it will be a happy day for you if ever you come to witness the casting of it out. But this you will never witness until you come to know, and own, and become subject to Christ within, to the pure commandment and Word of life in the heart, to the law which comes out of Zion, and to the testimony and word of the Lord from Jerusalem. And any that do not come to know the wrong birth cast out of them by the power, they will thereby be cast out with it.

Now, as for the idea that there are some glimmerings of light remaining in fallen man, directing him concerning many morally good things, such as to honor parents, to deal justly, to do as we would be done unto, etc., if it is meant a light distinct from the Spirit and divine nature of God, I desire you to manifest such an idea from Scripture. For Adam was to die the death that very day that he sinned. And death and the curse came upon his posterity, who are dead in trespasses and sins; but the light that discovers and leads out of evil is from Christ alone. That which makes sin manifest is his light. Now, I read in Scripture that the grace which brings salvation has appeared to all men, and that it teaches men to deny ungodliness and worldly lusts, and gives them strength so to do. I read that it is the work of the Spirit to convince of sin, and that the Spirit of the Lord strived with the old world to reduce them from their evil ways, and that he gave the Jews his good Spirit to instruct them, (though they rebelled against him). But that there are some glimmerings of light distinct from the Spirit of Christ, teaching fallen men to do good, and some corresponding strength in man to walk accordingly, I do not read in Scripture.

It is the promise of the new covenant that God will write his laws in the heart, and whatever measure of his law is written in any man's heart, it is so done by him alone. For man is dead unto God's law naturally, and his eye is blinded by the god of the world. So then, that which opens man's eye to see what the law says, this is the light of the Spirit. For that which makes manifest is light, Eph. 5:13, and that which may be known of God in the Gentiles is made manifest to them by the light of God in them. Rom. 1:19. This light shines in their darkness, and their darkness cannot comprehend it, but the light fathoms and comprehends the darkness, and is able to gather the mind out of it. For when the mind is made subject to the light (in the will which the light creates and begets through the eternal power which comes by it, and is present with it), it can be delivered from the darkness. And since this light comes from Christ ("for he is the true light, that enlightens every man that cometh into the world"), so it uncovers and makes Christ manifest in his nature and Spirit, and also leads and guides towards him. And he that is led to Christ in Spirit, and born of him in Spirit, cannot miss the benefit and virtue of what he did in that body of flesh, for such a one is gathered into and found in that which is of him.

Now, it is in and by this only that the soul receives that nature wherein the law is fulfilled. And the work of answering the law is through the renewing of the mind, and the bringing forth of a new nature, every degree of which is begotten and maintained by Christ, the power of God. But by the old corrupt nature or mind, no man can do the things contained in the law, for this nature is enmity against God, and is not subject to his holy law, neither indeed can it be. But the law is spiritual, holy, just, and good, converting the soul, and making wise the simple. This work it effects wherever it is written in the heart by the finger of God's Spirit.

And now, as for being complete in Christ in a relative way, while the heart is unmortified, and unsubdued to God, it is dangerous to mistake about these things. I do confess that sins are pardoned upon a true belief, and the soul enters into the covenant of life, and is accepted with the Lord as it finds entrance thereinto, and walks therein. And there is no condemnation to them that are in Christ, "who walk not after the flesh, but after the Spirit." But if there be a hearkening to the flesh, and walking after its lusts and desires, is there no condemnation then? Is not the justification in the covenant, and according to the laws of the covenant? Alas, how do men imagine concerning these things! And so, in their imaginations, they justify themselves in that wherein the Lord condemns them, and they do not know the way of the covenant, or the justification thereof. For there is a new covenant as well as an old (and the new is not like the old). And there is a walking with God in the new covenant, where every step in it his life justifies, and every step out of it his life condemns. For the Mediator of the new covenant justifies according to the new covenant, and never otherwise. Indeed, the way of God is perfect (the way of life, the way of reconciliation, the way of redemption), and the soul is only accepted and justified of the Lord therein.

Concerning the True and Pure Way of Life

This has been the cry of my soul from my childhood, even after holiness, after the presence of the Lord, after union with him, after the nature and image of his Son, after a separation from what was contrary to him, and a being brought forth in the power of his life. Now, blessed be the Lord who has revealed that which answers my cry. And in as much as my soul comes to partake of it, it is refreshed and satisfied with the supply of that which it thirsted and cried after.

And now my earnest desire is that all who have felt the true cry might also be taught of God, and learn aright how to wait upon him, and to walk humbly and in fear before him, that nothing come between them and the cry of their souls. Oh that they might be led by him into the enjoyment and possession of that which the true birth (which is born of the Spirit and is Spirit) naturally longs after!

Now, truly there is no other way to life and satisfaction than by believing in that power, and following that power, which raised Christ from the dead, for this power is to work the work in all that are saved. To feel this power revealed within, to have the mind turned to this power, to follow this power in the regenerating work and path, is the way to partake of its virtue, and to experience the redemption which is in it and from it. He that is born of the Spirit, and has his eye opened and daily exercised by the Spirit, such a one knows the Spirit, and is acquainted with his stirrings and movings, and is taught of God to distinguish them from the stirrings and movings of the evil spirit. In this way the soul does not quench the Spirit of God, nor grieve it when it moves, nor give way to the other spirit when it moves and allures.

Now, the spirit of deceit allures and guides men not so much by outward rules, as by an inward evil nature, and by the law of sin and death. So too, the Spirit of truth leads into truth by the newness and power of its own life revealed in the heart, by the pure instinct of life within, and by the law of God written in the nature of the new creature, which is nearer than outward words. For in the heart that belongs to him, God blots out what Satan had written there, and he writes by the finger of his Spirit what he would have the new birth read there. And indeed there is a kingdom of life, of righteousness, of true peace and joy (yes, of the holy power and wisdom of the Most High), for his children (who are born of his Spirit, and spring up of the immortal seed) to read.

Oh, why should men's eyes be closed, and their hearts hardened against the truth? Why should they cry out for Christ in words, and cry out against his life and power where it is revealed! Is this to kiss the Son? Can those who are guilty of this help but perish in the way of their soul's travels? Oh how many must perish by their resisting the power of truth, and the precious testimony of God's Holy Spirit who seeks to rescue out from that which captivates and destroys!

Christ came to destroy sin, he having received power from his Father to do so. He knows this power to be of a destroying nature, and that it will also destroy the soul, if sin is not (by the power of life) consumed and destroyed in the soul. Oh, how precious to us is that visitation of truth, light, life, and power, which searches out and discovers sin to the very root, and also destroys it! Oh, how glorious is that axe of the Lord Jesus Christ which is laid to the root of the corrupt tree, and is daily hewing and cutting it down that it might encumber the ground no more! For the heart is meant to become good earth, sanctified earth, circumcised by the Lord to bring forth good fruit, good grapes, and good increase of the good seed of life to the good gardener, who is worthy to reap the grace and mercy, love and goodness, wisdom and power, which he plentifully and daily sows in the spirits of his own. Glory to his name over all forever, who has exalted, exalts, and will exalt that which the several sorts of high professors, in their own wisdom, trample upon and despise.

Concerning the Perfecting of God's Work in the Heart

Is it not the will of God that his people and children should be sanctified throughout, in body, soul, and spirit? 1 Thes. 5:23. Is it not the will of Christ that his disciples should be perfect, even as their heavenly Father is perfect? Did he not bid them pray, "Thy kingdom come, your will be done in earth, as it is in heaven"? And would he never have them believe and expect that it should really be done in earth, as it is in heaven? Does not he who has the true, pure, living hope (which anchors within the veil), purify himself, even as He is pure?

Is not this the way to enjoy the promises of God's holy presence (who tabernacles in a people that are cleansed and sanctified), "to cleanse ourselves from all filthiness of flesh and spirit, perfecting holiness in the fear of God"? 2 Cor. 7:1. Will God dwell in an unholy temple? Will he dwell where sin dwells? He may indeed do so, when at any time they are tender and truly melted before him. He may be to them as a wayfaring man that tarries for a night; but he will not take up his abode there, walk there, sup there, and give them to sup with him.

Has not Christ received all power both in heaven and earth from his Father? Is not this the end of receiving this power, to bring down the soul's enemies, and to purify and sanctify his church, that it may be without spot or wrinkle or any such thing? Is he not the Captain of our salvation, anointed to fight the battles of the Lord? Where is the fight? Where is the strong man to be found, cast out, his goods spoiled, and the house emptied of him, and all that belongs to him? Is not Christ the author of faith and the finisher of faith? Does he not carry on the work of faith with power? And what is the work of faith? Is it not to fight with and overcome sin? Is it not to be too strong for the enemy and all his weapons? Is there not a whole armor of light, life, and salvation prepared? What is it prepared for? Is it not that the children of light should be wholly armed with it? Were there never any that were wholly armed with it? Are those that are armed with it afraid of the enemy, his power, his snares, his wiles? Or are they rather bold in the faith, following him who rides before them, conquering, and to conquer?

Oh that men's eyes were opened by the Lord! Then they would see the glory of truth in the pure light which shines from God's holy mountain. Then the dark doctrines of the night (which tend to the dishonor of Christ, his power and love, and to the upholding of the enemy's kingdom) would pass away, and prevail no more in the hearts of any that truly fear the Lord. Then they would quietly wait and hope for his salvation, that by the law of the Spirit of life in Christ Jesus, they might be made free from the law of sin and death, and not always be subject to it. For all whom the Son makes free, they are free indeed. And being made free by him, they may serve God in freedom of spirit, without fear, in holiness and righteousness before him, all the days of their lives. And then they truly know the power and virtue of the new covenant, and the defense which is in it, where the wing of the Almighty overshadows, and his salvation (revealed therein) is experienced for a sufficient wall and bulwark against the enemy.

Concerning the True Knowing of Christ

While people were in expectation and mused in their hearts concerning John the Baptist, whether he was the Christ or not, John answered the case, and told them how they might discern and know the true Christ. It is not he, said John, that baptizes with water, but he "that baptizes with the Holy Spirit and with fire." It is he "whose fan is in his hand," with which he comes "to thoroughly purge his floor, gathering the wheat into his barn, and burning the chaff with unquenchable fire." Now, he that knows the one that does this work, and experiences him doing this work in him, does he not know Christ? Oh, is it not precious to be baptized by him whom God has appointed to baptize? Oh the fan, the precious fan, wherewith Christ, who is the power and wisdom of God, separates the precious from the vile, severs the wheat and the chaff, gathers the wheat into the precious treasury, and lets out the unquenchable fire upon the chaff!

"Our God is a consuming fire," says the apostle. To what is he a consuming fire? Is it not to the chaffy, earthy, drossy nature in men and women? If you bring chaff to the fire, will it not burn it up? And as that is burnt up and consumed, then that which is pure, that which is born of God, can dwell with, and delight in, the devouring fire, and everlasting burn-ings. For God is not terrible to the child who is born of him, to him who is brought forth in the image and Spirit of his Son. But to the transgressing nature, to the seed of the evil-doer, who are naturally inclined to do evil, and are every day doing evil, he is terrible forevermore.

Concerning the Light which Enlightens Every Man

> *"In him was life, and the life was the light of men. And the light shines in darkness, and the darkness comprehended it not."—John 1:4-5.*

What is the darkness which does not comprehend the light? Is it not man in the unregenerate state? "You were darkness," says the apostle, speaking concerning them as they had been in that state.

Now, it pleases the Lord that in this darkness his pure light should shine, to gather man out of the darkness. For unless light should shine on man in his dark state, he could never be gathered out of it. And he that is turned to the light, and follows it, cannot abide in the darkness, but comes into that which gathers and preserves the mind out of it.

But of what nature is this light which shines in man in his dark state? It is of a living nature; it is light which flows from life; it is the light which has life in it; it is the life of our Lord Jesus Christ, of the Word eternal, which is the light of men. And he who comes to the true understanding may thereby distinguish it from all other lights whatsoever.

Now, there is a vast difference between this light and the reason and understanding of a man. For the natural man, with his understanding, is dead; but this light is living and powerfully operating in man, as it finds entrance, and as his mind is joined to it. He that is dead, indeed, knows it not; but he that is alive unto God, feels the virtue of it. This light is above all gathered knowledge whatsoever, and above all descriptions of things whatsoever. For the light is the thing itself, the substance itself, even of the nature of him from whom it flows. A man may get a notion from this into his mind, which he may retain the dead knowledge of. Yes, such a notion may quickly become dead in man. But he that dwells in the thing itself, knows and dwells in that which never dies.

Inquiries Concerning the Time and Work of Reformation

Inquiry 1: What did the time of reformation and substance (spoken of in Heb. 9:10) signify? Was it not the bringing in of the gospel, the day of Christ's Spirit and power, the day of his inward renewing and reforming, the day of taking his fan into his hand to purge his floor, the day of his laying the axe to the root of the corrupt tree that he may destroy the works of the devil in men's hearts, casting down and plucking up what his heavenly Father has not planted there? When Christ comes as a refiner's fire, and as fuller's soap, to purify the sons of Levi as gold and silver is purged that they may offer unto the Lord an offering in righteousness—is this not the time of reformation?

Inquiry 2: Who is the reformer? Is it not the Lord Jesus Christ? Does he not create anew? Does he not blot out the old image and form into a new lump? For if any man be in Christ, there is a renewing there, a new building there, yes, old things are passed away there, and there is nothing in him but what is new. He is faithful (in all his house) inwardly to judge, condemn, crucify, subdue, destroy whatsoever is contrary to the nature and Spirit of his Father, and to form and build up the spirits of his in that which is new and pure.

Inquiry 3: How, or by what, does Christ reform? Is it not by his Spirit and power, by his light and life and virtue? For nothing can change and reform the heart except that which is more powerful than the one who corrupted it.

Inquiry 4: Where does Christ reform and newly create? Is it not in the new covenant, in the faith and obedience of this covenant? Does he not, by the laws of the new covenant, break and annul the laws of the old covenant, and make void the covenant of hell and death? Does he not make an everlasting covenant of life and peace, even a holy, pure, living agreement between God his Father and the souls that belong to him? Thus, by his light he overcomes darkness; by his life he overcomes death; by his pure nature and Spirit he over-comes (chains down, subdues, and destroys) that which is impure, breaking the bond of sin and iniquity, and letting the oppressed go free from under it. Thus he manifests himself to be the Savior by his holy anointing, breaking the yoke of the oppressor. Isa. 10:27.

Inquiry 5: Whom does Christ reform? Is it not those who take his yoke upon them and learn of him? Is it not those who are turned to the light of his Spirit inwardly made mani-fest, those who are turned from the darkness, walking no more in it, but rather in his pure light? They that own his inward appearance in their hearts, and turn (from the enmity there) unto him, receiving his light, his law, his life, his Spirit, these are daily exercised and reformed in their hearts by him. But if any man does not receive his light, his life, his Spirit within, such a one is none of his; and he may reform himself as much as he can, but he knows not yet the day of the true reformation.

Inquiry 6: How are they to walk whom Christ has begun to reform? Is it not in that light, in that Spirit, in that covenant, in that grace, wherein and whereby he has in some measure reformed them? Is it not in the newness of the Spirit, and in the law of the Spirit of life? Here Christ walked before the Father, and here are we also to walk. 1 John 2:6. For indeed there is no pleasing the Father, or Christ our Lord and Master, outside of the virtue, life, and newness of his own Spirit.

Inquiry 7: Does not Christ give of his grace in the gospel? And does not his grace make a glorious change? Does not Christ appear gloriously in the hearts of his people, and in his assemblies who meet together in his name, and wait upon him in that which is pure and living?

Inquiry 8: Was not this glory brought forth in the days of the apostles? Was not great grace then upon them all? (I mean upon such as received and held the truth in the love of it.) Did they not witness the peace which passes man's understanding? Had they not received the holy and spiritual understanding from him that is true; and were they not in him that is true? Did they not know victory and dominion over sin and death?

Inquiry 9: Was not this glory eclipsed, and did not a great darkness come over it, hiding it from the sons of men, so that (for ages and generations) they knew not the true Spirit, the true light, the true life, the everlasting covenant, the holy gospel, the true church, the man-child, etc.? Have not these, with many other heavenly mysteries, been hid from man's eyes? And what has risen up since these things have been hid? Have not the shadows of the night taken place and overspread the Christian state, instead of the light of the day? Has not antichrist got up, and a false church appeared? And has not that which is tender and begotten of God been disregarded, pressed down, restrained, and persecuted, while false devotion and worship is set up instead of the true?

Now, who is wise to understand the appearance of the Lord, and the beginning of these things, which is in a way contrary to man's wisdom? He that will discern them must come out from following man's own spirit, nature, and wisdom in himself, into the sense and leadings of him who gives the true eyesight. The appearance of the Lord is inward and spiritual, and he who discerns it must have an inward and spiritual eye. It was said of old, by mockers and scoffers, "Where is the promise of his coming? For all things continue as they were from the beginning." The same spirit will say so still; and yet, to that eye which the Lord has opened, he is already come inwardly, spiritually, in his own pure eternal life and power. Surely the precious effects of his coming are made manifest in many hearts, blessed be his name. Yet he is further to appear in glory and pure brightness, and so we wait further for his appearance, both in our own hearts, and in the hearts of the children of men. We have met with our beloved, for our God, whom we have waited for, has appeared. The Sun of righteousness has arisen with healing under his wings, and we who have felt virtue and healing from him cannot but rejoice and testify of his salvation.

Oh that all that love the Lord Jesus Christ in any measure of sincerity did know the way of the gospel, which is in the Spirit, light, life, and power, which is eternal, even in the grace and truth which is in him! And his kingdom, which is spiritual, and not of this world, cannot be shaken by this world (nor his Mount Zion removed), but is indeed able to shake all nations and kingdoms which kiss not the Son, but oppose him. Psa 2:12. Blessed are they who are turned to the light of his Spirit, and who therein kiss and obey him.

Some Serious Inquiries Concerning the Spirit of Christ

Inquiry 1: Do you know the Holy Spirit of the Father? You may have read something concerning it, and have apprehensions in your mind about it, but do you truly know what it is by its inward appearances and operations in your own heart?

Inquiry 2: Have you received God's Holy Spirit into your heart? Have you let in Christ's Spirit when he has knocked at the door of your heart, and received him? For he that is a true child, most naturally breathes and cries for the Father's Spirit, and the Father also most naturally gives his Spirit to them that truly and rightly ask it of him. Luke 11:13.

Inquiry 3: Does the Spirit of Christ dwell in you? Has the stronger man cast the strong man out of you and taken possession of your heart, and does he dwell there? Then you may truly say that you are built up by God as a habitation for him in the Spirit.

Inquiry 4: Does God's Spirit lead you into all truth that you need know and walk in? Are you a true child, depending upon, and guided by, the Spirit of the Father? Can you not see your way except as he makes it known to you? Are you a follower of the spotless Lamb, in the same Spirit wherein he walked?

Inquiry 5: Do you live in the Spirit? Do you feel the Spirit of God to be a fountain of life from which life springs up into you daily? Do you witness that scripture fulfilled in you, "He that believes on me, out of his belly shall flow rivers of living water"? Have you received the living water from Christ? And has that living water become a well of life in you?

Inquiry 6: Do you walk in the Spirit, in his newness of life springing up in your heart? Do you know the difference between walking in the oldness of the letter, and in the newness of the Spirit?

Inquiry 7: Did you ever learn of the Father to know Christ? And did you ever learn of Christ to know the Father? And has the Father indeed revealed the Son to you, and the Son indeed revealed the Father to you? Or are you yet only in the dead and dry notions, or barren comprehensions about these things?

Inquiry 8: Do you know how the letter kills, and how the Spirit quickens and makes alive? And are you made alive by the Spirit, and born of the heavenly water and Spirit, and so become spiritual as the Scripture testifies, "That which is born of the Spirit, is spirit"?

Inquiry 9: Have you come under the ministration of the Spirit? Do you know what the ministration of the Spirit is? Or do you only know what the letter says concerning the ministration of the Spirit, but remain altogether ignorant of the ministration itself?

Inquiry 10: Do you know what the law of the Spirit of life in Christ Jesus means? Have you ever received this law, the law of the new covenant, the holy law of life written in your heart by the finger of God's Spirit? For the same Spirit that wrote the law of the letter in tablets of stone, writes the law of the Spirit in the fleshly tablets of the heart.

Inquiry 11: Do you still grieve the Holy Spirit, or quench it, or despise his prophesying in your own heart? For Christ is a king, a priest, and a prophet, and he ministers in his sanctuary, in his temple (which the holy renewed heart is), in and by his Spirit.

Inquiry 12: Do you know what the anointing is? Are you anointed with it? And does your whole ability lie in it, inso-much that you are daily sensible you cannot do anything of yourself, but must find God working in you, both to will and

to do that which is right in his eyes, for his own good pleasure?

Inquiry 13: Did your religion begin in the Spirit, in the living
ministration of the new covenant? Did your knowledge begin
in feeling God opening your heart by his Spirit, and giving
you the understanding whereby you might know him? Did
your faith begin in his power, and does it stand in the same
power to this day?

Inquiry 14: Does your worship stand in the Spirit, and in the
inward life of truth in your heart? Are you such a worshipper
as the Father has sought out and made so? Or are you a
worshipper of your own or other men's making? And do you
keep within the limits of the living and spiritual worship, and
not transgress the law thereof?

Oh, who would be mistaken and deceived about such
weighty things as these, of so great necessity and concern!
Who would miss God's Spirit, and the law and covenant of
life in Christ Jesus, and be only in a dream concerning these
things, without the true, demonstrative knowledge, possession, and enjoyment of them!

Concerning the Way of Holiness, or the Way of Life

Christ is the way, the only way to the Father; there is not
another. Now, everyone that will truly know Christ, and
come to Christ, must learn of the Father. It is written in the
prophets, "All your children shall be taught of the Lord;"
"everyone therefore that has heard and learned of the Father,
cometh unto me," said Christ. Here are two things necessary
for everyone that would come to Christ: one is hearing of the

Father; the other is learning what he teaches. For though a man does hear the living voice of the Father, yet if he does not learn and keep the instruction of life received from him, he may be drawn aside before he comes to the Son. But he whose ears are opened to hear the voice, and who feels the instruction of the Father to go to him in whom he has placed life, here the Spirit of the Father secretly draws in the inwards of a man's mind and spirit, away from that which is really dead, to that which is truly living.

Now, when a man is come to the Son, in whom the Father has placed the fullness of life, then he shall witness him to be the way to the Father, and he will teach him daily of the Father. And here is the state of true subjection to the Son experienced, whom the soul must hear (and of whom he is to learn) in all things. For here the Son discovers the inward darkness in man's mind, and breaks down that in him which is contrary to God, having a daily cross ready for that which is to be crucified in him, whereby he shall die daily to himself. And as he dies to himself, Christ will reveal himself more and more in him, and he shall feel the pure seed of life springing more and more up in him, and living in him, and he in it. And in and through this, he shall come more and more into union and fellowship with the Father of spirits, and the whole living body of his church and people.

Now, to learn of the Father to come to the Son, and to learn of the Son to know the Father, and to walk in newness of Spirit before him, and not in an old, dead knowledge and fleshly understanding, these are great mysteries. No one can learn such things by a literal conception and comprehension of things, but only as they are quickened, and as their minds and understandings are opened and kept open by the Lord. Therefore, this is the great skill and true wisdom—to know the Shepherd and his voice, and his manner of appearing.

And his way and manner of appearing is by visiting and reaching to the true birth, and by his power opening it, and thereby giving it to see, hear, and understand. And herein he also shuts up from the contrary nature, wisdom, and spirit in all men.

Concerning Separation from the Spirit and Ways of the World

There is a necessity of separation from the spirit, ways, and worships of the world, by those that will be the Lord's people. The outward Jews were to be a separated people from all other people (from their gods, from their worships), if they were to enjoy the favor of the Lord, and the blessings of the good land. God had separated them from all other nations, and they were not to mingle with them, neither in their worship, nor marriages, etc. So too the inward Jews, who are God's gathering of spiritual worshippers out of every nation, kindred, tongue, and people, are to be a separated and holy people to the Lord.

For when God cast off the Jews, he sought out worshippers in their stead, even a spiritual nation and holy people of inward Jews, instead of that outward people, outward place of worship, and outward land, which he cast off. Now, those whom God seeks to be the new, inward, spiritual worshippers, instead of the literal and outward, must come out of all other ways and gatherings upon the many mountains, to the mountain of the Lord's house, and to the place of his gathering. The command is express, "Come out from among them, and be separate; touch no unclean thing, and I will receive you," etc. 2 Cor. 6.

The primitive Christians were to separate from both heathen and Jews (even from their temple, priests, and ordinances, which were once of God), if they were to be true worshippers under the gospel, worshippers of God's seeking. And now, after the anti-christian corruption and darkness, Christians must come out of Babylon, that is, out of all forms of religion and buildings without the life and power, if they will be found worshippers in the day of restoration. For Babylon is the city of confusion, which is built, stands, and practices without the order and unity of the Spirit. And the command is as express to come out of Babylon (that is, to separate from all anti-christian ways and worships) as ever it was to separate from the heathen and Jews. For there is no true worship in God's sight except in the true way of separation from all false worshippers, who worship in forms and appearances of godliness, without the life and power.

Oh, blessed is he who is separated by the Lord from all that is not of him! But when one who does not know the Spirit seeks to separate himself, he differs from others only in the outward form and appearance of godliness, but remains one in nature and ground with those from whom he separates. Thus the Catholics, and all professing Christians who do not feel the true Spirit, power, and life, are but one in their nature and ground, regardless of however great their outward differences seem. And those that separate further and further (even to the utmost extent outwardly), being not separated by the Lord from that nature and spirit wherein the enmity lodges, they are still inhabitants of one and the same city (for the city of Babylon is very large). They remain daughters of one and the same mother, even the wisdom which is from beneath, which wisdom, in its highest exaltation, is far beneath the nature and true excellency of the pure and heavenly wisdom.

Oh, blessed is the religion, the worship, the separation, the fear of the Most High God, the faith, the knowledge, which begins in the Spirit and power (even in the evidence and demonstration of God's own Spirit), and which stands and abides therein! For here are the children of light distinguished and kept distinct (by God Almighty, who has made the difference) from all the children of darkness.

Chapter XIII

God's Teaching and Christ's Law

Preface

Christ, who came from the Father, and knew the way of truth and life everlasting, and was to guide men to the Father (being the only way unto him), preached the kingdom, and bid men to seek the kingdom. He taught and instructed them in many parables concerning it, and directed them where and how to find it.

The apostles (who succeeded Christ in the same Spirit and power wherein he ministered) likewise preached the same kingdom, declaring and describing what it was, and in what it consisted—namely, not in word, but in power, even in the power which shakes all that is to be shaken, but cannot be shaken itself. 1 Cor. 4:20, Heb. 12:28. Nor was the kingdom of God food and drink (or any outward thing), but righteousness, peace, and joy in the Holy Spirit. Rom. 14:17.

Indeed, the apostles did not preach in vain, for the life was inwardly revealed in many, the power inwardly revealed, the kingdom inwardly revealed, and the righteousness, peace, and joy of was felt. For such as truly believed and obeyed the gospel, received the kingdom which could never be shaken, and had an entrance ministered to them thereinto, according to their diligence and carefulness in the truth.

Now, afterwards a great darkness came over the world, and this glorious kingdom was again veiled, and the kingdom of darkness and deceit overspread the profession of Christianity. In this time, notions and outward knowledge took with men instead of the life and truth itself, wherein the kingdom and power stands.

But blessed be the Lord, the light of life again shines out of and over the darkness, and the kingdom is again received, and the entrance into it is again known. And now, from what has been seen and heard (and in measure enjoyed and possessed), a faithful testimony has been given forth. And blessed are they who hear the joyful sound; for it is no less than the sound of life itself, the power itself, the gospel itself, the Spirit himself, manifesting himself in, and speaking through, vessels according to his pleasure.

Now, they that receive this light, which is testified of, receive Christ; but they that despise and reject it, reject him, as will be made manifest in the day of the Lord. For this dispensation is indeed most precious, glorious, and living, being a dispensation of the seed and power of life itself. And by this seed God translates out of darkness, and the regions thereof, into the kingdom of his dear Son, and into his glorious image. This, reader, is the goal of my giving forth the following things, not that you may have only notions concerning them, but that you may, in truth, come to partake of the thing itself.

Concerning God's Teachings

"It is written in the prophets" (said Christ) "they shall all be taught of God. Everyone therefore that has heard, and has learned of the Father, comes unto me." John 6:45. For the prophets indeed had said, "All your children shall be taught of the Lord," and "they shall all know me, from the least of them to the greatest of them."

Now, whose children are they which shall all be taught of the Lord? And who are they that shall all know the Lord by the teachings of his Spirit, from the least to the greatest? Are they not the children of the free woman, the children of the Jerusalem which is from above, which is the mother of all that are truly living? Gal. 4:26. Now, all her children are begotten by the Father of life, and he takes care to teach them the true, pure, heavenly, living knowledge. These indeed know the Lord, being taught by the anointing to do so, and they indeed know the Son, the Father revealing him to them. For "no one knows who the Son is except the Father, and who the Father is except the Son, and the one to whom the Son wills to reveal Him." "Flesh and blood has not revealed it to you, but my Father who is in heaven," said Christ to Peter. Matt. 16:17. And it pleased God to reveal his Son in me, said Paul. Gal. 1:15-16. And how did Paul preach Christ among the Gentiles? Did he not preach him as a mystery hidden from ages and generations, which none but the Father could reveal and make manifest? And when he is known and made manifest, is he not known within, revealed within, made manifest within? Col. 1:26-27 and 1 John 1:2. Notice John's words: "The life was manifested." In this way they came to know Christ, and if they desired to bring others to the knowledge of Christ, they must bring them to the manifestation of the same life, and show unto them that eternal life which was with the Father, and was manifested unto them. ver. 2.

Now, in order that they might do thus, they were to preach the light to them (even this message, "that God is light, and in him is no darkness at all." ver. 5), and to turn them to the light, Acts 26:18, in which alone men can see and receive the life which is eternal. Men may know or comprehend many things concerning the Messiah from the letter, but they can only know the Messiah himself in the light which shines into their hearts. This is the light to which he sent his apostles to direct and turn their minds. For they directed them to the Word within, the light within, the life within, the Spirit within, to feel after the manifestation of God within. And so Paul directed the Gentiles to seek after and find God near, and not afar off. Acts 17:27. Oh, this is precious to find and feel God near, Christ near, in his light to see light, in his life to feel and enjoy life! For here (in the place of darkness, in the place of sin and death, in the place where dragons lay, Isa. 35:7) is the redeeming power to be felt, and the deliverance of the soul experienced by those that truly believe.

The Scribes and Pharisees had a knowledge that the Messiah was to come, but how did they come to this knowledge? Why, they had read so in the letter of the Scriptures. The professors of this age have a knowledge that Christ is come, but how did they come to that knowledge? Why, they have read so in the writings of the evangelists and apostles. But who has believed the report of life now, and to whom is the arm of the Lord (which is now stretched forth) revealed? Who has heard and learned of the Father to know the Son, and so to come to him, even from the inward revelation of his Spirit, and from the inward living knowledge which is thereby? Everyone, Christ says, that is taught of God (because of what they have heard and learned of the Father), comes to the Son. Now, everyone that is drawn in this way, and thus comes, is received by Christ, and given eternal life. And these know him who gives them eternal life, and who preserves and maintains life in them. But others have only a notional knowledge of him, and do not indeed know him that is true, nor are they in him that is true, even in his Son Jesus Christ, who is the very God and life eternal. 1 John 5:20.

And so, these that are taught of God learn of him to repent from dead works, and they do indeed repent. Others, however, through hardness of heart, do not so much as discern which are dead works, and which are not, in matters of worship. Others do not know the true difference between that which is dead, and that which is living, but death (unknown to them) lives and reigns in their very knowledge and apprehensions of things. Death reigns even in their faith, even in their duties, yes, in all they believe and perform to God. For as Paul once thought himself alive without the law, even when he walked according to the letter of the law blameless, so too many are now dead, in the midst of all their knowledges and practices from the letter, till they come to the ministration of the Spirit. "For the letter kills; but the Spirit gives life." 2 Cor. 3:6 and see ver. 3.

This therefore is the work of a true minister: to beget into the Spirit, and into the life. But oh, how little do men know what dead works are, and what it is to truly witness repentance from them! Men who are out of God's Spirit, light, and power, are so far from repenting for them, that they do not so much as rightly distinguish and discern them! Rather, they take that for living which is dead, kindling a fire for themselves, and compassing themselves about with sparks, thinking the warmth thereof to be the true warmth. Now, if men have not come to the true repentance from dead works, much less have they come to the true faith towards God. So they are yet in their sins, yet outside of Christ, having never learned of the Father to come to him. They are still in Egypt's spirit, in Egypt's wisdom, and in that they hold their religion. And whenever God appears in his Spirit and power, he will not be to them what they expect, but rather a dreadful stroke from him will come upon all their ways and worships, which are as abominable to God as they are pleasing to them.

But alas, what good are words to that ear, to that spirit, which is like the deaf adder, which will not hearken to the voice of the charmer, though he charm ever so wisely! Could the learned Scribes and Pharisees hear the voice of Christ in the days of his flesh? No, they could not; not in that disputing spirit. Can the learned professors, who are in the same spirit, hear the voice of Christ's Spirit now? No, they cannot. And if they that cannot hear the voice of the second Adam, the voice of the quickening Spirit, the voice of him who gives life to the soul, how can they live? And if they do not first receive life from Christ, how can they perform any living action to God? How can they worship in the Spirit and in the living truth if they are not first gathered into the Spirit and into the living truth? Oh, that men could consider aright these things, and wait on the Lord for the true understanding of them! For without the true knowledge of God and Christ (without that knowledge which is life eternal) men must necessarily perish. It cannot be otherwise; for only the true knowledge saves, and therefore they which do not have it must perish.

Concerning the Law of Christ

> *"And the coastlands shall wait expectantly for his law."*—Isa. 42:4.

What is that law which the coastlands were and are to wait for? Is it not the grace and truth which comes by Jesus Christ, even the grace in the inward parts, even the truth in the inward parts? The outward law was given by Moses to the outward Jews, but grace and truth comes by Jesus Christ. This is the law of the inward Jew, which the coastlands of the Gentiles were to wait for.

The apostle holds forth Christ to be the soul's master (he is the Shepherd, Lord, King, and Bishop of the soul), to whom everyone must give an account. Now, for what must men give an account to him? Is it not for the grace and truth which comes by him? If any man has received that, obeyed that, believing the sound, report, and voice of that, and so loved and followed it, will it not be said unto him, "Well done, good and faithful servant"? But if anyone has neglected and despised the grace (not improving the talent, but improving his own natural abilities, while God's talent lay wrapped up in a napkin, and hidden in the earth), will not that person be judged a slothful servant as to improving the talent, regardless of what he has done to improve his own natural gifts and abilities?

Now mind this: If Christ is an inward and spiritual master, what is his law but the inward teachings of his Spirit? Moses wrote, "A prophet shall the Lord your God raise up unto you like unto me; him you shall hear in all things;" and he that will not hear him (however secure and confident he may seem to himself in his state at present), shall be cut off and destroyed from among God's people. Deut. 18:15-19. The words, the voice, the motions, the leadings, the drawings, the commands of his Spirit, are these not the law to all that are spiritual? Here is the glory of the great Lord and King, and of the great High Priest over the household of God, in that he gives forth precepts according to his holy will and pleasure. Indeed, all his sheep know his voice and follow him, and all his children and servants observe and obey him.

"If we live in the Spirit, let us also walk in the Spirit," said the holy apostle. Here are the limits of the children of the new covenant. Here is the law of life (the law of the Spirit of life in Christ Jesus), the law of the new covenant, written in the heart, which none can read but with the new eye. The children of the flesh may read the letter, and comprehend concerning the letter, and gather rules and observations out of the letter, but the children of the new covenant alone can read the law of life in the heart. And this law is the path of life, the path of all that are renewed by God's Spirit, which the inward Jew is to read diligently, and in which he is to have his delight, and to meditate day and night. And this law is light, true light, pure light, spiritual light, yes, the light which is eternal and never varies. The commandment which comes from this light is a lamp, and they who receive it know it to be no less than life everlasting; for indeed, the commandments of Christ's Spirit are felt to be so. Now, this commandment, this law, this light, shines in the darkness at first, but afterwards, it shines out of the darkness more and more (as it is believed, received, obeyed, and walked in) unto the perfect day. See Prov. 4:18-19.

Question: But how may I wait for, come to know, and receive this law? I am not of the stock of the natural Jews, but of the coastlands of the Gentiles. How may I meet with and receive the law of life from Christ, or the grace and truth which comes by him?

Answer: The way of receiving it is to carefully mind that which enlightens and renews the mind, drawing it out of the nature and spirit of this world, and out of the ways, worships, knowledge, and customs thereof. Now, here the grace is met with; here the truth is met with; here the Spirit of life is met with; here the inward change is felt, and the new law is written in the heart and spirit. And here the mind comes to prove and know what is the good, acceptable, and perfect will of God. For God is the teacher in the new covenant, and his teachings are here, even in that which he renews. He gathers into his Spirit, and he teaches those that abide in his Spirit, and gives unto them eternal life, eternal virtue, eternal nourishment, in and from his Spirit. But they that may be great searchers into the written letter, and comprehenders from the letter, and practicers according to their apprehensions of the letter (not being gathered into nor reading in the Spirit), these miss eternal life, and the redeeming arm and power, and are not saved from sin by the blood of Christ. These are yet in transgression, darkness, and death, even until now. Now, the Lord, who knows all things, makes manifest their states and conditions unto them, so that they do not perish forever, but rather learn of the Father to know the Son, and of the Son to know the Father, and come to witness true life manifested in their own hearts, that they may have fellowship with the Father and Son therein. For he that is not turned from darkness unto light (from the darkness within in his own heart, unto the light which God causes to shine there) does not yet know Christ livingly and savingly, but remains only in notions and comprehensions which cannot save. For it is the life and power of the Lord Jesus Christ inwardly revealed against the power of sin and death, which alone is able to save the soul.

Now, consider with yourselves (all who would not be deceived in this matter), have you known this law? Have you received it in measure, and do you wait to know and receive it daily more and more? Then you are Christians indeed, and are of the house of Jacob, who walk in the light of the Lord, and in the light of the holy city, whose light is the Lamb. But without this law, without this light, without the inward writing of God's Spirit in your hearts, you cannot be inward Jews, nor children of the new covenant.

Of the Grace of the Gospel

The prophets of old "prophesied of the sufferings of Christ, and the glory that should follow." 1 Pet. 1:10-11. Now, what was the glory which should follow? Was it not the setting up of Christ's inward and invisible kingdom in the hearts of men? Was it not God's abundant pouring out of his Spirit, and filling vessels, so that the Spirit of grace and of glory should rest upon believers, even as it had done upon Christ? Was it not God's tabernacling in men, and becoming their God, and making them his people? Was it not the fulfilling of precious promises concerning the gospel state, whereby men should be made partakers of the divine nature (of the heavenly image), and be changed from glory to glory by the renewing Spirit and power? Was it not to have fellowship with Christ, not only in his sufferings and death, but also in his resurrection and kingdom, where the bread and wine of the kingdom is eaten and drunk, and the feast of fat things enjoyed? Is it not a glorious state to be translated out of the kingdom of darkness into the kingdom of the dear Son, and to dwell with Christ in the kingdom? Is it not to have fellowship (pure fellowship, living fellowship) with the Father and the Son, that the blessedness and joy of the soul in the gospel state may be full?

The law was a ministration of shadows, for under it were the various and many shadows of the good things to come, which were to be possessed and enjoyed in the days of the gospel. In the law there was an outward people (the outward Jews), an outward covenant, an outward land of blessings, plenty, and rest. There was an outward Zion, outward Jerusalem, outward temple, outward ark, outward table, outward laver, outward candlesticks, outward lamps, outward oil, outward anointing, outward circumcision and sacrifices, outward new moons and Sabbaths, outward kings, outward priests, and outward victories over outward enemies, etc.

But now, in the gospel, there is the substance of these things inwardly revealed, and inwardly possessed and enjoyed. There is an inward Jew (the new man of the heart), an inward covenant of life and peace, an inward land of blessedness, of rest, an inward Sabbath or day of gospel rest (which the true believer keeps in the faith, not bearing any burden, kindling any fire, nor doing any work of the flesh therein). There is an inward Zion, an inward Jerusalem or holy city, an inward temple (in which is the Holy of Holies), an inward ark, in which the law of life is treasured up, an inward table, inward laver, inward candlestick, inward lamp, inward oil, inward anointing, inward circumcision and sacrifices, and solemn seasons. Indeed, there is now an inward King of glory, an inward Prophet and Priest known, even Christ within, who gives victories and dominion over the inward enemies, and gives his to partake of his kingdom and priesthood. Rev. 1:6. Yes, and by his Spirit poured out upon them, he makes his children seers and prophets also, as it is written, "I will pour out my Spirit upon all flesh, and your sons and your daughters shall prophesy."

Now, was not this fulfilled after the sufferings of Christ in the flesh? And is it not daily more and more fulfilled as the sufferings of Christ, which are yet behind, are filled up in his body the church? Did not the glory then follow? Was not the gospel spirit and power then revealed and bestowed? And did it not bring into the gospel state? Were not the precious promises fulfilled therein? 2 Pet. 1:3-4. Are they not all yes and amen in Christ? Is not the veil or covering taken away in him? Is not the glory revealed in him? Is not the Lord one, and his name one in him? Is there not glory then in the highest, on earth peace, and goodwill among men, as well as goodwill in God towards men? Where is the enmity and wars, the lusts and fightings? Are not these things drowned in the love and in the peace, in the life and in the power which is revealed in the gospel state, and springs up in the gospel Spirit? They know not what spirit they are of, who would have fire come down from heaven upon the disobedient and gainsayers. To be sure, they are not of the gospel Spirit, not of Christ's Spirit, who came not to destroy men's lives, but to seek and save that which was lost, and to overcome by the overflowings of his love and tender visits of his life. And how do his true children make war in this day? Is it not with innocency, with meekness, with patience, with hearts of love, with long-suffering, with truth, with righteousness, like the followers of the Lamb, like the children of him who abounds within? Indeed there is a sword given, there is a threshing instrument, there are darts and arrows to be shot into the hearts of the King's enemies. Psa. 45:3-5. But these are not to destroy the creature, but rather to smite and wound that spirit which captivates it, so that the creature may witness deliverance and freedom from it. Nevertheless it is true, that they who join with that spirit, must partake of its judgments and plagues, even to destruction, if they so continue.

Now, this glory is wrapped up in the grace which is ministered by the gospel. Where grace is sown, the glory is sown (there is a true seed of the glory); and where grace abounds, the glory abounds. It was said concerning the first gathering of Christians by the apostles that "great grace was upon them all," Acts 4:33, and indeed, it was a precious and glorious state which they were gathered into and brought forth in. Now, the grace is revealed again, the grace is poured forth again, the grace has appeared, teaching and bringing salvation again. Does it not behoove everyone to know it and partake of it?—not to be content with words concerning the grace, but to know the grace itself, receiving it from the hand of him that gives it, and hearing the voice, reproofs, and instructions of it? "Hear, and your souls shall live." Whom should they hear? Are they not to hear Christ, the great prophet? How shall they hear Christ? Is there any other way besides hearing his grace teaching them, and hearkening to the measure of the gift of grace, which is by Jesus Christ? "The law was given by Moses" (all his people, all his children, all his family were to come under the law, to be governed by the law). "Grace and truth comes by Jesus Christ," (all his children, all his people, all his family are to come under the grace, to be governed by the grace) who is faithful in all his house, dispensing of his grace and truth to all his, even as Moses did of the law (committed to him) to all under him.

So then, all that desire to be truly Christians, let them wait to know what this grace and truth which Christ gives is, and to partake of it and come under it—under its teachings, under its influences, under its protection, under its government (by being subject to it; and in everything guided by it). In this they will come to know what that scripture means in the true and weighty experience: "Sin shall not have dominion over you, for you are not under the law, but under grace." Rom. 6:14.

A Question Answered Concerning Real Holiness

Question: Are not persons to be really holy[1] (really sanctified in Christ Jesus) who desire to be received by the Lord, and

---

[1]   The distinction here is between a true inward transformation of the soul and a mere positional or unexperienced, imputed holiness.

enjoy fellowship with him as sons and daughters in the gospel of his Son?

Answer: Under the law, the Jews were to be separated from the heathen, to be outwardly circumcised and cleansed by the water and blood of purifying (which sanctified to the puri- fying of the flesh), and not to touch any dead or unclean thing. Any such thing polluted them, and those that were unclean had to be kept outside the camp as unfit for the holy communion with God and his people, until cleansed.

Now, what did this signify? Did it not signify that pure and clean inward state which God requires under the gospel? Did it not signify the inward circumcision of the heart and spirit before the Lord, and the cleansing of the soul, mind, and body, before its appearing to worship in the inward and spiritual temple? Heb. 10:22. Is there not a Jerusalem under the gospel into which no uncircumcised or unclean thing is to enter, or appear before God there? Mark what the apostle says in Heb. 12. "You are not come to the mount that might be touched," to outward Mount Sinai, or Zion, to the appear- ance of God there; but you are come to the inward Zion, and to the city of the living God, the heavenly Jerusalem, and to fellowship with God and Christ there. ver. 18-22.

Now, what is the way to this holy fellowship and heav- enly communion? Does not God himself prescribe it? 2 Cor. 6:16-17. "Wherefore come out from among them, and be separate," says the Lord, "and touch no unclean thing, and I will receive you. I will be a Father unto you, and you shall be my sons and daughters, says the Lord Almighty." For God desired to have a people representatively holy in the time of the law (yet not destitute of inward holiness), and he will have a people truly holy in the time of the gospel. "He that defiles the temple of God, him will God destroy," but keep the temple clean, pure, holy, and then the Holy God will dwell and appear there, according to his promise, "I will dwell in them, and walk in them." And this is eternally true, and witnessed by clear and certain experience among those who know the Lord—that if anything that is unclean be touched, there is a defilement thereby, and there must be a cleansing felt before there is an experience of the presence of the Holy God, and enjoying fellowship with him again.

Now, this ought to be the great care of every renewed mind, even to keep out that which is unclean. The enemy will be assaulting, tempting, casting into the mind that which is unclean. But the pure, chaste mind must not entertain or touch it, but rather withdraw and retire from it into the place of safety, into the strong tower of defense, from all the assaults and annoyances of the enemy.

Now, blessed be the Lord, who has revealed and bestowed on his sons and daughters in these latter days, that light of his Holy Spirit, who searches the most inward parts. This Spirit discovers everything that is of a contrary nature to itself, turning and separating the mind from it, and bringing the mind, heart, soul, and spirit under that which is a cross and yoke to it, and has power from God to crucify and subdue it. In this way life and immortality are brought to light and come to reign in the heart, and death and uncleanness are swallowed up in victory. For this is the intent of the gospel, and of Christ's appearance, even to destroy sin, and bring up the holy seed, and establish the law of the new covenant, the law of love, the law of life, righteousness, and holiness, in which the renewed should walk before the Lord all their days.

Oh God forbid that the gospel of our Lord Jesus Christ (which is the power of God unto salvation) should not attain its end, or that the will of God not be fulfilled. For his desire is the sanctification of his people in soul, body, and spirit, 1

Thes. 5:23, that they may be wholly leavened with the leaven of his kingdom, and become a new lump to him.

May the Lord bring this to pass in the hearts of the children of men, bringing down all religions which do not have the true virtue in them. And may he propagate and establish that religion more and more which stands in the evidence, demonstration, virtue, and power of his own Spirit, so that men may be redeemed out of deceit in matters of religion, wherein the eternal condition of their souls is so deeply concerned! Amen.

Concerning the Law of Sin in the Fleshly Mind, and the Law of Life and Holiness in the Renewed Mind

What is the law of sin? Who writes it in the mind? And what is it when it is written? "When lust has conceived, it brings forth sin; and sin when it is finished, it brings forth death" Jam. 1:15. So that the first beginning of sin is evil lust, and the whole corruption that is in the world is through lust. 2 Pet. 1:4. Now, from where does this lust come? Is it not begotten in the mind and spirit by the tempter? And what is the law, both of the lusting, and of the sins committed through the lust? Is it not the lustful nature, the lustful will, the lustful wisdom, the lustful desires and passions, which the god of this world begets in the worldly part?

Likewise (on the other hand), there is a holy law in the holy and renewed mind. From where does this law come? Does it not come from God? Does it not come from the Holy One? Is it not he that blots out Satan's law, and then writes his own law in the hearts of his own? Now, what is his law? Is it not of a contrary nature to Satan's law? Is not God's law what he writes in the hearts of his children, teaching them holiness, requiring holiness, enlightening the mind unto holiness, manifesting the good, perfect, and acceptable will?

Under the old covenant the law was at a distance, written in tablets of stone, but under the new covenant the law is near, written in the heart by the Spirit and power of the Lord Jesus Christ. For he is King, the inward King, the spiritual King of his people, who comes to reform, and amend by his covenant. Now, because he found (under the old covenant) that laws outwardly written would never bring men into, and keep men in, subjection to his Father, therefore he writes inwardly by his Spirit and power, and visits with the inward eternal day, even the day of his power. In this way he makes his people willing to receive the law of his Spirit of life, which makes "free from the law of sin and death." For this law being inward and spiritual, and more powerful than the other, overcomes the other law, even the "law of sin and death" (though it be inward and spiritual, and inwardly written also), and sets the soul free from it. Rom. 6:18. and 8:2.

Now, these laws each have their strength from him that writes them. The law of sin and death has its strength from the god of this world, the prince of darkness, who rules in all that are disobedient to the Spirit and power of Christ. The law of holiness, the law of life, the law of faith in the power, the law of obedience to God's Holy Spirit, has its strength from the Holy One, from the Prince of life and peace. For Satan is near his subjects, and dwells in them, to act in them, and to make his laws of sin and disobedience forcible in them. Every motion and temptation to sin he kindles, and adds vigor to, that he may set on flame the wicked spirits of men after sin, vanity, pride, lust, uncleanness, cruelty, and all manner of wickedness. But the Lord also is near to the soul. The King of holiness, the King of righteousness and peace is near, to give strength to every holy desire in the heart, and to every motion of his Spirit towards that which is good and holy. Hence it is, that he that trusts God's Spirit, watching to and following the movings and drawings thereof, finds life flow in, virtue and strength flow in, to carry on effectually in whatever the Spirit of the Lord moves to. So that, if one come truly to know a motion, or to understand the drawings and leadings of God's Spirit, then strength is never lacking to him who gives up in the faith to follow the Lord.

Now this is the great skill of Christianity—to come inwardly to know the Lord, to know the inward appearances of the Shepherd, to know his leadings out into the pastures where eternal life is fed upon, and back into the fold of rest, which is no less than the bosom of love and life eternal. Now, the growth of the new man, the growth of the Christian state, is in the exercise under the law of life, under the law of the Spirit. For the Spirit exercises the mind by his law, and the mind is to give up to the exercise thereof, and to wait upon the Lord in it day and night, finding itself never without, but always under the law to Christ in everything. Indeed, how can a man do anything aright without the sense and knowledge of the inward law? How can a man fight aright with his spiri-tual enemies without understanding the law of fighting? For there is a lawful fighting and an unlawful fighting against the soul's enemies. The unlawful fighting is in the self-will, wisdom, and strength, according to one's own apprehensions and conceivings, which gains no real ground, and therefore they that so fight cannot overcome. The lawful fighting is in the faith, in the wisdom and guidance of the Lord, in his Spirit and power, and this is ever successful. So there is a lawful running and an unlawful running the race, which the apostle plainly implies when he says, "So run that you may obtain." 1 Cor. 9:24. So likewise there is a law of prayer, a law of faith, a law of love, a law of new obedience, a law of liberty (for the liberty under the gospel is not boundless, but bound by the Spirit), a royal law, which the King of glory writes, and keeps living in the heart. By this law his will is understood, and the way of life is known, which never can be understood by any but those in whom this law is written, even the law of the new covenant, the law of the Spirit of life in Christ Jesus.

Read and consider this seriously, for indeed it contains the very mystery of Christianity and redemption. For redemption is not by a notional knowledge of Christ, but by receiving and being subject to the law of his Spirit. Wait to know and understand whether this is not the law which David speaks of when he says, Psa. 19, "The law of the Lord is perfect, converting the soul. The testimony of the Lord is sure, making wise the simple. The statutes of the Lord are right, rejoicing the heart; the commandment of the Lord pure, enlightening the eyes; the fear of the Lord clean, enduring forever; the judgments of the Lord truth, altogether righteous." Certainly the law of the Spirit of life in Christ Jesus is all this, containing in it the commandment which is life everlasting, and the sure testimony, and all the holy statutes, judgments, and fear, which the soul needs to learn. It is indeed perfect, and able to convert, and instruct perfectly the converted soul. And here the scripture is fulfilled under this holy law of the Spirit and power of life, "They shall not teach every man his neighbor, and every man his brother, saying, 'Know the Lord'" (they shall not do so in this covenant, under this ministration, which is a ministration of Spirit and not of the letter); "for they shall all know me, from the least of them to the greatest of them." Indeed, they shall know by the teachings of my own Spirit, by my writing my law in their hearts, by my holy unction, which shall teach my children, my anointed ones, all that they need to know. 1 John 2:27, Jer. 31, and Heb. 8.

Chapter XIV

The Seed of the Kingdom

Question: What is the seed?

Answer: The seed of God is the word of God; the seed of the kingdom is the word of the kingdom. It is a measure of the light and life, of the grace and truth, which is of Jesus Christ, who is the fullness. It is a heavenly talent, or manifestation of his Spirit in the heart, which is given to man to bear an increase for God, in the virtue and strength of Christ. This gift, which God has placed in man to witness for himself, and to guide man from evil unto good (in the pure breathings, quickenings, and shinings of it), this is the seed, which is freely bestowed on man, to spring up and remain in him, and to gather him out of himself, into itself.

Question: Who is the sower of this seed?

Answer: God, in and through Christ. He is the good gardener. He, by the word which created all in the beginning, creates anew in Christ Jesus, renews his workmanship in man, and puts a measure of this word or Spirit of life in man's heart, whereby he renews him. Now, these that are

309

thus renewed by him are his workmanship, created in Christ Jesus unto good works.

Question: Where is this seed to be found?

Answer: It is found where God sows it, which is in the inward earth. It is an inward seed, and it is sowed in inward land or earth, that is, in the hearts of men. There the light of the word shines, there the life of the word is felt, stirring secretly in and quickening those that were dead in trespasses and sins. There the voice and call of the word is heard, calling from unrighteousness and sin, to righteousness and holiness.

Question: In what sorts of earth is this heavenly seed sown?

Answer: In all sorts—in thorny ground, stony ground, highway ground, and good ground. God's inward lightnings enlighten the inward world throughout, so that God has not left any man without a witness in his conscience against sin. And though man's conscience is corrupt, and his light has become darkness, yet God's witness in his conscience can never be corrupted, but whenever it shines in the heart, it gives true light there. Whenever it witnesses there, it witnesses the truth for God, and against man, and the corruption and searedness of his heart and conscience.

Question: In what sort of earth does it bring forth good fruit unto perfection.

Answer: Only in the good ground. It brings forth some fruit in other grounds, and the fruit it brings forth is good. The convictions are good, the desires begotten there by it, and which arise from it, are good. The leaving off of some bad things, and doing some good things, is good. But the thorns, the cares, the worldliness, and the fear of persecution—these spring up from another root, and are of another nature, and stifle and choke the seed in the thorny ground. But the good ground yields its whole nourishment to the good seed (and will not yield nourishment to any bad seed) so that the good seed not only springs up, but brings forth fruit to perfection.

Question: How may the ground that is bad be made good? Was not the ground which is now good, once bad? And may not the ground which is now bad, be made good?

Answer: God has shut up all men in unbelief, that he might have mercy upon all. Indeed, the heart that is now soft was once hard. The heart that is now believing was once in unbelief. The heart that now loves God, was once in the enmity. The plow of God, put into the thorny ground, tearing it up, and rooting out the thorns, will change its nature, and make it become better. "Break up your fallow ground; sow not among thorns;" said God to his Israel of old. Does not man, by care, art, and industry, change the nature of outward land or ground? Surely then, the Lord by the word of his power can change the nature of inward ground.

Now, for the clearer and plainer signifying of what yet remains on my heart concerning this precious seed of the kingdom of God, I shall consider it under these three headings: I. What is hid or wrapped up in this seed, II. The nature of the seed, III. The effects of the seed.

I. *What is wrapped up or hidden in this precious, heavenly seed?*

Indeed, there is so much wrapped up in it, as the heart of man cannot conceive, much less the tongue utter. Nevertheless, I have felt something, and it is upon my heart to answer this thing under the following headings.

First, the glory of the kingdom of heaven, the glory of the everlasting kingdom, is hid and wrapped up here as in a seed. In whatever way Christ appears, reigns, and shines, he does so here in this seed. Oh, the shooting forth and spreading abroad of this seed is indeed glorious and excellent! How can a man speak concerning it? The thing itself (being inwardly felt, known, and enjoyed) is so far beyond all words! What does the kingdom of God stand in? It stands not in word, but in power. The power is hid and wrapped up in this seed. The pure power of life is in this seed. The sword that pierces Leviathan, that wounds the serpent's head, that cuts Rahab and the dragon, is in this seed. Does the kingdom of God consist in righteousness, peace, and joy in God's Spirit? This is all in this seed, and is partaken of and enjoyed as this seed springs up and gains authority and dominion in the heart. Yes, the horn of God's anointed, the righteous and peaceable scepter of the Savior is known and exalted in this seed, as it springs up and spreads abroad in the life and virtue of the Father.

Secondly, the divine nature of God Almighty is hid and wrapped up in it. It is the seed of God, and it is the very nature of God. Therefore, the one in whom it springs, and who is gathered into it, born of it, and made one with it, partakes of the divine nature. Peter speaks of the great and precious promises by which the saints are made partakers of the divine nature. 2 Pet. 1:4. All the promises are to the seed of promise, Gal 3:19, to Christ the Son of God, to the seed of God, to the heirs of life and salvation in Christ. And these promises are all fulfilled to them, and enjoyed by them, who are ingrafted into, and made one with Christ, the seed. Now this cannot be, except by the grace, by the truth, by the light, life, Spirit, and power, which he sows in the heart, which are not many things, but are all contained and comprehended in the one seed.

Thirdly, the new covenant, even the holy agreement of the soul with God in Christ Jesus, is in this seed. Here is the covenant which God makes with the new Israel, by which he makes the heart new, and writes his law in it, and takes away the stony heart, and heals all their backslidings, and loves them freely, and puts his Spirit within them, causing them to walk in his ways and to keep his statutes and judgments, and do them. God gave Christ for a covenant, and the seed of grace and truth comes by Jesus Christ. All that receive this grace and truth from him (in the holy seed of the kingdom) receive the covenant; and they that walk in it, walk in the covenant.

Here, and here alone, the new creation in Christ Jesus is known. Here, and here alone, the coming to God by Christ is truly understood and witnessed. Here, and here alone, the law of the Spirit of life in Christ Jesus is written in the heart. Keep here, and you will never go outside of the holy agreement with God, for in this grace and truth, in this seed of life, there is nothing that disagrees with him. Here you live in the Spirit, walk in the Spirit, and do not (indeed cannot) fulfill the lusts of the flesh. There is nothing in this seed that will either displease God, or lead your soul aside from him. Rather, here the Lord guides the feet of his saints, and teaches all of them, putting his law of life and new obedience, and his Holy Spirit, into their hearts, so that none of their steps may slip. Here the way of holiness, by which God preserves from erring, Isa. 35:8, is known and walked in. Yes, here Christ is known and felt to be the way, the truth, and the life. The sheep that are gathered here, and come here, have returned to the Bishop and Shepherd of their souls, who watches over them, and powerfully preserves them, that they run astray no more.

Fourthly, all the graces and virtues of God's Holy Spirit are hid and wrapped up in this one seed. There is nothing God can require of the soul, nor anything the soul can desire of God, but what is hid and wrapped up in this seed. All that is needful, or all that can be desired, is the growing and spreading of this seed in the soul, and the soul's gathering into it, and its living, dwelling, abiding, and acting in it. And oh, the great difference between the soul's selfish striving, willing, and running to join to God, and God's joining the soul to himself in this seed, and his living, willing, and acting in the springing life of this seed! Now, to make this a little more plain and evident to the hearts of those that desire the true understanding of these graces and virtues, I shall give some particulars under this fourth heading.

First, the pure, living, heavenly knowledge of the Father, and of his Son, Christ Jesus, is wrapped up in this seed. God is light, and this seed, which comes from him, is not darkness, but light; and in the light that springs from this seed, God and Christ are revealed. Their divine nature springs up in the seed, and if one knows their nature, then they are truly known. Indeed, here we know the righteous Spirit of Christ, the righteous nature of Christ, the righteous life of Christ, and we feel him to be one with the Father, who begets of the same Spirit, nature, and life in us. And he that is born of the Spirit is spirit; and he that is united to the Lord is one spirit; and he that is united to the seed, to the measure of grace and truth from Christ (wherein and whereby the soul is united), is united to God, and ingrafted into Christ. And as the seed is formed in him, Christ is formed in him. And as he is formed and newly-created in the seed, he is the workmanship of God, formed and newly-created in Christ.

Secondly, faith, the true faith, the lively, effectual, saving, conquering faith, which gives victory over the world, and over the devil and his temptations, is contained or wrapped up in this seed. Faith is the precious gift of God, which is not found in man's nature, but springs and grows from the precious seed of the kingdom, which God sows in man's heart. Indeed, faith is a gift to be waited for and obtained from God. Therefore the apostle Peter, writing to the saints in his time, directs his epistle in this way—"To those who have received like precious faith with us, through the righteousness of God, and our Savior Jesus Christ." 2 Pet. 1:1. Faith is a precious thing, a righteous thing, a holy thing, of which God is the giver, and Christ is the author and finisher. This faith springs from the holy root, from the holy seed of life and righteousness which God sows in the heart. This faith (I speak not of man's ability of believing, or the faith which is found in man's nature) is the faith of God's elect. Tit. 1:1. The faith which God gives to them that are born of him, John 1:12-13, who are born of the incorruptible seed, by the Word of God, which lives and abides forever. 1 Pet. 1:23. And this Word, being near in the mouth and heart, and begetting, preserving, and increasing faith there (as is daily experienced), is therefore called the word of faith. Rom. 10:8.

Thirdly, the pure fear, the holy fear, the heavenly fear, which is of a clean and heavenly nature, and endures forever, is also in this seed. This childlike fear is a promise of the new covenant, and is given to the children of the new covenant— God putting it into their hearts from the seed of life springing up in them, which preserves them from departing from the Lord. Jer. 32:40.

Fourthly, the pure divine love is in it. As this seed springs, so love springs to God. As God is love, so the seed that is of him partakes of his love. There is no enmity in it, and no enmity or contrary will springs from it. This makes it so natural to the children of God to love, for they are born of that seed which came from the God of love, whose nature is love. Oh, how daily is it found, by sweet and certain experience, that this seed (springing up) teaches and enables to love! And they that have this seed springing up in them need not to be outwardly taught to love with brotherly love, for in the seed, and by it, and through it, they are taught of God to love one another. So that the soul needs nothing but the circumcising of the heart, the purifying of the heart, through the obedience of the truth, the cutting off of that fleshly mind, nature, will, and wisdom, which cannot love aright. Then the pure love will spring up fully towards the Lord, and towards the brethren. Deut. 30:6. 1 Pet. 1:22. Yes, it will be natural to love all, and that command of Christ will not be grievous—namely, to love enemies, even the greatest revilers, cursers, and persecutors. Mat. 5:44.

Fifthly, the pure hope, the hope of the upright, the hope which makes not ashamed, the hope which goes within the veil, and is a sure and steadfast anchor there, staying the mind upon the Lord, who keeps such in perfect peace—this hope is contained in, and springs from, the seed. For nothing but that which comes from God (from the holy seed of truth and righteousness) can stay the mind upon God. So that he that feels the seed, feels the hope, and keeping to the seed (to the holy root), the hope remains. So the mind being turned to the light, being turned from Satan's power to God, being turned to Christ, being turned to the appearance and voice of

the word of life within, being turned from the seed of wickedness and darkness, to the holy and righteous seed of the
kingdom, it is turned to that which begets a true and right
hope in the heart. This is not a hope in the flesh, but in the
holy and heavenly seed, and the work of righteousness and of
the kingdom, which is God's battle-axe and weapon of war,
whereby he brings down the flesh. This hope stays the mind
in every temptation, in every distress, in every trial, in all the
winds, storms, and waves of persecution that it can be
assaulted with.

Sixthly, the true patience, and its perfect work, Jam. 1:4,
is contained in, and given with, this seed. As God is patient
and longsuffering, so is this seed also. It is man that is of the
brittle, fretful, and impatient nature, but he that receives the
word of faith, the seed of faith, in it he receives faith and
patience also. To this one it is not only given to believe, but
to suffer also for the sake of Christ. And he that abides in the
seed, and feels the seed remaining in him, and its nature
prevailing, can never be impatient, whatsoever the Lord
allows to befall him.

Seventhly, here the true poverty of spirit is witnessed. He
is poor indeed who has sold all, and has nothing left him
except this seed, and the appearance and help of God in this
seed; which also is not in his own hands, but in the will and
disposal of God.

Eighthly, here true mercy towards others is experienced;
for he that is brought to the seed lives only by mercy; and he
that lives by mercy, and is daily what he is by mercy, cannot
help but be merciful unto others.

Ninthly, the true hungering and thirsting after righteousness arises from this seed. It is the seed of God, the birth of
God, which has a sense of the excellency of his righteousness,
and which hungers and thirsts after his righteousness.

Tenthly, to name no more, the cross which mortifies and crucifies to the world and to sin, can only be taken up in the seed, or by virtue of the seed. Indeed the seed is a cross, yes, it is enmity to the serpent's nature, spirit, and course. He that takes it up (with its will, its nature, its law of life), takes up the cross to the other nature, will, and the law of sin and death. So that if you miss the holy seed, you can have only a shadow or image of the cross. But in the true sense of, and subjection to, the seed, the cross of our Lord Jesus Christ is felt working powerfully against sin, effectually crucifying and subduing the whole course of the evil and sinful nature.

II. *What is the nature of the seed of God, or the seed of the kingdom?*

Answer: Though the nature of it has been largely signified already under the previous heading, yet I shall speak a little more expressly of it in several particulars, according to the Scriptures.

First, it is of an immortal, incorruptible nature. 1 Pet. 1:23. It is a seed that can never die in itself, though it may seem dead in man, or unto man, when not putting forth any of its hidden life or virtue in the man who has slain it as to himself. For the one who has rejected and slain the seed by which God gives life, is still dead in trespasses and sins, and cannot live till God breathe upon and quicken this seed in him, and so bring him to life by the seed.

Secondly, it is of a gathering nature. It has the nature of a net. Mat. 13:47. It gathers out of that which is contrary to God, unto God. It gathers out of the world, out of the sea of wickedness, out of the kingdom of darkness, out of a man's own nature and spirit, into God's nature and Spirit, and his light and kingdom, wherein the soul should dwell, and walk, and be subject to God.

Thirdly, it is of a purging or cleansing nature. It is of the nature of fire, of the nature of water, inwardly and spiritually. This seed is Spirit and life in a measure, and by it (or by God's Spirit which dwells and is revealed in it) he washes and purges away the filth of the daughter of Zion. There is strength in this seed, and virtue in this seed, against all the strength of deceit and wickedness in the other seed. And as the seed of the kingdom springs up, and is received and joined to in the holy fear of the Lord, it prevails over the contrary seed, and casts away its darkness, and purges away and burns up its filth, chaff, and corruption.

Fourthly, it is of a seasoning, leavening, sanctifying nature. It is like salt; it is like leaven. It seasons and leavens with life. It seasons and leavens with righteousness. It seasons and leavens with the image of God. Just as soon as it springs in the heart, it begins to leaven it. And if it be not neglected, or grieved, or hurt, or quenched (for it is of a most sensitive, tender nature), it will go on leavening more and more with the nature of truth, into the likeness of the God of truth. See Mark 9:50, Luke 13:21, and Col. 4:6.

Fifthly, it is of an enriching nature. It is a hidden treasure or pearl of great price. It makes the wise merchant very rich, who sells all for it, and buys the field with it. He that buys the truth, and will by no means sell or part with it, but gives up to it and makes it his treasure, oh how does it enrich his heart with that which is holy and heavenly! How rich does it make him towards God! Mat. 13:44-46.

Sixthly, it is of an increasing, growing nature. The one talent may be increased into more. The little seed, like a grain of mustard seed, will grow in the good ground beyond all herbs, and become a tree, a tree of righteousness of the Lord's planting, that he may be glorified. Mat. 13:31-32, chap. 25:16, chap. 13:23.

III. *What are the effects of this seed?*

Answer: The effects of the pure seed in the heart are very many, very great, very sweet, precious, and blessed, which everyone comes to experience, who experiences the growth and spreading of it. I shall mention only a few.

First, is a true union and communion with God the Father of our Lord Jesus Christ, the Father of this seed, and with all that are united to it. Union and communion with God is in this seed, and never out of it. For in the seed of the serpent, a man is separated from God, alienated from his life, and can never come near him or have fellowship with him. So in the holy seed, in the seed of life, in the seed of right-eousness, in the seed of faith, the soul is united to God, has access to him, the living fountain, and has fellowship with him in that which is living and holy of him. Men may imagine a union and communion with God outside of this, but none can truly unite to God, or have fellowship with him, except in the gift, in the grace, in the light, in the Spirit which is of God.

Secondly, this seed is felt springing up in the heart, and when joined to, it brings down and keeps down all that is contrary to God. This honor and power God has given to the seed of the woman (even to the least measure of it)—that it should bruise the serpent's head, and free the soul from captivity and slavery to the wicked one. Thus the soul, in the living sense, authority, and virtue of this seed, may refuse yielding its members, its faculties, its will, its mind, its under-standing, its affections, to sin and unrighteousness. Yes, the devil, the great red dragon, the god of the world, the mighty spirit and power of darkness, being resisted in this, is truly overcome. When any resist the devil in their own strength (in the strength of their own desires, abilities, and resolutions), they are still overcome by him. But they that resist the devil in the faith that springs from this seed will overcome him. So it is that sin is brought down, and temptation kept out, by the virtue and power of the life and authority of the Savior that springs up in this seed of God.

Thirdly, as it springs, and as its operations are felt and received, it brings into the image and nature of God. It blots out the devil's image in the mind, and renews like unto God and Christ. Yes, here we have the very mind of Christ, and are made one with the mind of Christ. As in the serpent's seed, the serpent's image and nature is put on; so in this seed, the image of God and Christ is put on. Yes, the serpent, the dark spirit, the wicked spirit, the deceitful spirit, is here put off, and Christ is put on. And whoever desires to know the real putting off of the old man, and the putting on of the new man (which is created in the righteousness and holiness of truth), must know it in this seed.

Fourthly, the seed brings the mind, the heart, the soul, the spirit, into the new obedience (into its own obedient nature), even to do the will of God with great delight and pleasure. "I delight to do your will," said Christ. This seed is of his nature. It is a measure, a proportion, a heavenly talent of his grace and truth, a gift of light and life from him who is the fullness. It is given to make willing (like him) to do the Father's will, and it really does so, insomuch that the soul which is thoroughly leavened and one with it, can also say, "I likewise delight to do thy will, O God! It has become my food and drink, for I am nourished and refreshed, and delight in the virtue that I feel spring in me, in doing your will." Indeed, it is not so at first, while there is a nature, a will, a wisdom contrary to the nature, will, and wisdom of God. Then obedience is hard, and the cross is still a sore yoke upon the neck. But that nature being subdued, and the nature of the seed coming up and prevailing, what can be more delightful to this new nature than to do the will of its heavenly Father, and to find the heart of the Father pleased with the child?

Fifthly, it brings into the understanding, sense, and enjoyment of all the precious promises, and all the spiritual blessings in Christ Jesus our Lord. All the promises are to the seed and are yes and amen in Christ, and the least measure of his life has a share therein. The seed, the everlasting seed, is the heir, and we who are joined to the seed, born of the seed, and growing up in the seed, are joint-heirs with Christ. So that every promise comes to be understood here, tasted here, enjoyed here. How full are the Scriptures of sweet and precious promises! Alas, what good is it for men to apply them to themselves, when they have no right to them, nor indeed rightly understand them, nor were they intended by the Lord to man's present state and condition! But to come to the true understanding of the promises, to be led by the Lord into that condition, and preserved by him in that condition to which the promises belong—oh, how sweet, comforting, and joyous is this! Indeed, in this seed all the curses of the book pass away, and all the blessings flow in and multiply on the soul day by day. So that this may well be called the blessed seed, for in it the soul is truly blessed, and filled with blessings by him who is able to multiply them upon the soul, and to guide the soul in the safe and right use and enjoyment of them.

But need I mention any more? Here is light, here is life, here is righteousness, here is peace, here is heavenly joy, here is the holy power, springing and bringing forth its fruits and precious operations and effects in the heart. Here is assurance of the love of God in Christ forever, and the knowledge that God will never leave nor forsake that soul which is joined to him, and abides with him in this seed. Such a soul will be kept by the power of God, through the faith that springs from this seed, unto perfect redemption and salvation. Amen.

A Brief Clarification Concerning the Imputation of Christ's Righteousness

God visits men by the light and power of his Holy Spirit in their dead and dark state, even while they are ungodly. Now, they that feel life, and in the quickenings of life, by the faith which comes from life, turn to the light and power which visits them, these are in measure transplanted out of the unholy root, into the holy root. Here they partake of the nature and virtue of the true olive tree, and the mercy of the Lord in and through his Son Jesus Christ is spread over them, and their iniquities are pardoned, and their transgression is done away for his name's sake. These are reckoned by God, not as in the old root and unholy nature, but rather in that root which they have laid hold of by faith, and are in union with it. Here they are reckoned in the eye of the Lord, and they are accepted and beloved in him in whom they are found, by him who transplanted and ingrafted them there. So that Christ is really theirs, and they are his. And what he did for them in his body of flesh has become theirs, and they have the benefit, and reap the sweet fruits of it. And if they sin afterwards, they have an advocate who pleads their cause with the Father, and who breathes livingly upon them again, and quickens faith in them, and gives them to turn away from that which ran after them, overtook them, and defiled them. So that in this state of true faith in, and union with, the Son, a fountain is felt to be open for sin and for uncleanness, which daily washes away the pollutions and stains of the mind, which it is susceptible to in the traveling state.

But now, to every claim of faith these things do not belong, but only to the faith which flows from the power of the endless life, and which stands in the power. The faith which is from the power is precious, having a precious nature and virtue in it, and very precious effects flow from it. For it is the substance of things hoped for; it is of a pure nature, which has dominion, and gives dominion over the wicked one. But the belief in Christ, or the applying of his righteousness, which is not of this faith, nor in the true light of life (but rather according to the creature's apprehensions concerning things), this is not of the same nature, nor does it have the same virtue, or produce the same effects. For, despite this kind of believing and hoping, men are still in their sins, and they are not washed away from them by the blood of Christ, nor remitted or covered by the Spirit of the Lord. And oh, that men were wary, and did take heed in this matter, that they might not miss the true pardon from the Lord!

For there is indeed a state wherein Christ's righteousness is imputed to persons reached by the power of the Lord, who are coming up out of the ungodly state into the true righteousness. And in the true growth, the soul daily grows more and more out of its own unrighteousness, out of the dark, corrupt image, into the righteousness of Christ, and into his pure image. Thus, Christ is formed in the hearts of them that truly believe, daily more and more. They receive him as a heavenly leaven, and giving up to be leavened by him, are changed daily more and more into the newness of the Spirit, even until they become a new lump, a lump wholly leavened. So it is that old things are passed away, and all things become new, that is—they are not of old Adam any more, but are all of God in Christ. They are all of the new nature and Spirit, which is righteous in the sight of God.

Now, this is what all should labor for and seek after—even the kingdom of God and his righteousness, to find an entrance ministered to them into the everlasting kingdom, and the righteousness thereof, that they might really put off the old man with his affections and lusts, and put on the new man, the new man's nature, image, spirit, and righteousness. All should seek the true wedding garment in which to be married to Christ, to be as a bride prepared for the bridegroom. Oh, it is precious for anyone to feel his soul in this state! And who would not travel and wrestle and strive and watch and pray and wait, that he might be thus fitted by the Spirit of the Lord for his Son Jesus Christ?

Oh, that such as take upon them the profession of Christianity might feel the power, and wait upon the power, and know what it is to believe in the power, and live in the power. For without this, the oppressed state of Christianity is but dead, dry, and cold, not having the true living sap and warmth in it. There are great deceits in the world about the imputation of righteousness and such things. But he that knows the truth as it is in Jesus, who has been visited by the power, gathered to the power, and abides in the power, he has found that which anoints the eye and heart, and strengthens against the most subtle devices and deceits of the transforming spirit. But whoever professes Christianity, and yet is not here, he is not safe, but the enemy has ways of bewitching and deluding him, which he cannot effectually withstand and avoid.

A Brief Question About Reading Scripture Aright

Question: What is the right reading of the Scriptures so as to benefit and profit the reader's soul?

Answer: He that reads the Scriptures in a true measure of life received from God, he reads them aright, and whenever he so reads, it is to his benefit. He that reads outside of that measure of life reads to his own hurt, for the nature that misunderstands, misapplies, and grows conceited, wise, and confident according to the flesh is still at work in him. This one is prone to set up his own interpretations instead of the meaning of God's Spirit, and also to condemn all that does not assent and agree with his own understanding.

The true birth is meek, tender, gentle, fearing before the Lord, waiting upon him, often crying to him, that it may not be deceived, that a wrong thing does not rise up in it, and that it receive nothing for truth except what God knows to be truth. And when the Lord is pleased to give the true knowledge, it is held in the Lord's righteousness, in his life, in his will, in his wisdom, etc. But the wrong birth is not so, but instead is subtle in searching and forming ideas, and holding them in subtlety, and drawing the wrong part in others to agree with and acknowledge that which it represents and holds forth as truth.

There is a wisdom in man which is against God. This wisdom opposes the wisdom of God in two ways: either in a direct and contradictory way, or in a secret, subtle, undermining way. Now, no man can come to God, or truly understand or receive the things of God, except as this wisdom comes to be confounded and destroyed in him by the light and power of God. All of its strongholds, all of its subtle imaginations, all of its reasonings and consultings must be dashed and brought to nothing before the truth of God can have full place and power in the heart.

Now, in the true discovery of this false wisdom, and in the soul's denial of it, watching against it, and turning to the true wisdom, a man may wait upon God aright, read the

Scriptures aright, and come to the true sense, understanding, and experience of them. But if at any time he is without this, he is liable to the enemy's snare, to the misunderstanding of Scriptures, and to the fleshly confidence that arises therein. So that, having taken up a misunderstanding of a Scripture, he will even boldly venture to speak evil of the heavenly and spiritual things which are of God. Oh how does this wisdom destroy and entangle! And how has it destroyed and entangled many in this day who think they are greatly for God in those things and practices wherein they are directly against him!

Now mark well: The Spirit, the truth, the life, the substance, is God's forever, and the unclean spirit cannot enter into it, nor can the unclean womb conceive it, or bring it forth. However, the letter, the shell, the outward figure, the outward relation and description of things—these the other spirit, wisdom, and nature in man may read, guess at, transform, receive, believe, and build up according to the flesh. And here is the foundation and rise of antichrist and Babylon in those who raise up a building, a knowledge, a faith, a hope, a church, a worship, duties, ordinances, justification, sanctification, etc., in the imitation of Zion. But these things are not the thing itself, but rather false representations of the thing—either such as were invented by man, or such as were once appointed and made use of by the Spirit of the Lord. For there is little difference between inventing a new thing, and making use of an old thing which once was of God, but is now understood, observed, and practiced outside of the sense, light, and guidance of his Spirit (in another spirit, and according to another wisdom).

Now, this is not the right way of reformation, namely, to return to outward and literal things, which were practiced by the Jews in their day, or by the former Christians in their day, but rather to return to the Spirit that they were in, and to feel (in the true life and leadings thereof) what it teaches and requires to be observed and practiced now. For there are things whose value is not in themselves, but in God's requiring of them, which the wrong spirit may get into. And the Lord may draw his people out of these things (as he did out of the outward court, into the inward building or temple, by his light and Spirit within, when he gave the outward court to the Gentiles. Rev. 11:1-2). And he that is found in these things after God has given them to the Gentiles, and drawn his people out of them, is no longer owned or accepted of God in them, though God may bear with him in the time of his ignorance. Yet if he abides in them after the rising of light and its testimony, the Lord will not so bear with him, but will condemn him, and deal with him as a transgressor of that covenant wherein life and peace with him is witnessed.

Therefore, in all things that concern God, whether in reading the Scriptures, praying, or observing anything called duties and ordinances, oh that you would approve yourselves Christians indeed, waiting to know your guide and leader, and the true limits which are set by God! For thus you may serve him in the true faith, Spirit, and understanding, even in that which God knows to be so, and not in that which you may falsely account so! For mark: if you are Christians, are you not in Christ, and is not Christ in you? And are you not to feel his life, and the guidance of his Spirit, so that you may live in the Spirit, and walk in the Spirit, read in the Spirit, pray always in the Spirit, believe in the Spirit, worship in the Spirit, and in the holy understanding of his truth, which is of him?

He that would be right in religion, must have a right beginning. How is that? He must begin in the Spirit, that is, his knowledge, his faith, his hope, his peace, his joy, his righteousness, his holiness, his worship, etc., must begin there. He must come out of his own spirit, his own wisdom, the counsels and thoughts of his own heart, and wait on him who begins the work of regeneration and life in the heart.

And afterwards, he must diligently watch against that spirit and wisdom out from which the Lord has led him, that it at no time enters him again. For it will be striving to lead him out of the way with likenesses and false images of things, with false knowledge, with a faith that is not truly of God, nor of the same nature with that which the soul first felt. It will present him with false hopes, false fears, false joys, a false righteousness and holiness, which are not Christ's, nor according to the Scriptures, but only such as man apprehends to be so. For a man, who once tasted the truth, and in some measure judged aright, may afterwards err in his palate and judgment, and then take the wrong for the true, not keeping to that which formerly gave him the true relish.

Now, he that would meet with the true religion, the religion of the gospel, must meet with the power, receive the power, believe, dwell, and act in the power. For Christ was made a king, priest, and prophet, "not after the law of a carnal commandment, but after the power of an endless life," and his covenant is not like the old, in word or letter, but in the same power and life. So the knowledge here, the faith here, the hope here, etc., are not literal, but living. He that receives this knowledge, receives living knowledge. This faith gives victory over unbelief, and over that spirit whose strength lies in unbelief. This hope purifies the heart, even as he is pure. And he that receives the righteousness of this covenant, receives a living garment, which has power in it over death and unrighteousness. The beginning of this religion, this power and holy inward covenant, is sweet, but the pure progress and going on of it is much more pleasant, as the Lord gives to feel the growth and sweet living freshness of it. Though there are temptations, fears, troubles, trials, oppositions, and great dangers, both within and without, the soul that keeps to the life (which it was first turned to) finds the yoke easy and the burden light, as the mind and will is changed by the power, and helped and assisted by the Lord in its subjection to the power.

So, may the Lord God of tender mercies remove the stumbling blocks, and lead the wandering souls (who are entangled in their own thoughts and reasonings about the letter) into that which is Spirit and life. For the Spirit and life was before the letter, and excels the letter (with its dispensation) in glory, and is to remain after the letter, and be the rest, joy, life, peace, and portion of the soul forever and ever. So honor the letter, in believing its testimony concerning Christ, who is the Shepherd, the way, the truth, the life itself, to whom the soul is to come, and on whom the soul is to wait for life. And having received life from him, then dwell, abide, and grow up into him who is the life. Do not go backward into anything that is literal, or without life, nor seek glory in the knowledge, or literal descriptions of things, but go forward into the spiritual, heavenly dispensation of life and power. The law was letter, the gospel is life and power. The law was a shadow of good things to come, but the gospel is the substance, the life, the virtue, the Spirit of what the law shadowed out. From here the Christian is to spring, the Jerusalem from above is to be its mother, and the Holy Spirit its begetter. And here the truth, sweetness, and fullness of words is known, felt, and witnessed, even in that which comprehends them, and gives them their due weight and measure. For none can possibly understand the words of the Spirit except he that is in the Spirit; and then he knows both the place of the words which came from the Spirit, and the

Spirit from whom the words came. Oh this is precious! But it will not be witnessed by the wise disputer, but only by the serious traveler, who is first broken and dashed to pieces in his own wisdom, and then afterwards is healed, led, and guided by the eternal Spirit of wisdom, which is the sure and unerring guide.

Chapter XV

Letters of Isaac Penington
Written between 1666-1679

* * *

To Friends in the Two Chalfonts

Dear Friends,

You have a deep place in my heart, and my cries are to the Lord for you, that you may live to him, and find his life springing up and abounding in you. What is it to have a distinct name, or distinct meetings from the world, unless the power of the Lord is felt in your hearts, and his presence is in your assemblies? Oh that the Lord would awaken you! Oh that the Lord would quicken you! Oh that it would please the Lord to raise up a strict watch in you against all drowsiness, carelessness, temptations, and snares of the enemy, that you may travel on your journey with your backs upon the world and your faces towards Zion. And may you never look back to the fleshly nature, desires, or lusts, to entertain anything of that anymore. For you have parted with such things in the demonstrations and leading of life, and must press on further and further, till you come to apprehend and be possessed by that for which you have been apprehended by God.

O my friends, there is a path of life in which you must

travel, even to the very end of it, or the crown of life is not to be received! Oh that you might travel on, and that nothing might stop you! Oh that you might every day wait for and feel the leader, and walk on with him in the simplicity, uprightness, and sense of his life, out of the reach of that wisdom which is always forming reasonings in the heart against it, and striving to darken and to make difficult the plain way of God.

May the Lord God of mercy watch over you, pruning and keeping down all the earthliness and corruption in any of you, and watering and cherishing his own plant in you all, that you may daily witness the dying and decrease of the one, and the quickening and growth of the other, even till death be perfectly consumed and swallowed up by the growth, power, and presence of the immortal life in you, and your souls safe and happy in your God. O my friends, prize the rich, tender mercy of the Lord in calling you out of this world towards his everlasting inheritance and fullness of life! And let not anything of this world come between him and you, but let all that is of this worldly nature, both within and without, be trampled upon by you. Let the prize of the high calling of our God in Christ Jesus be faithfully and earnestly pursued after, so that none fall short of the hope and glory set before you. And may everyone so run as to obtain and enjoy forever the dominion and reign of God over all that is contrary to him, and so sit down in the rest, joy, and peace of his nature forevermore. Amen.

Your friend and brother, in the meek, innocent nature of the Lamb, from my present place of confinement in Ayles-bury, according to the will of God, who is blessed, and to be blessed in all that he does, or allows to be done.

I. P.
22nd of the Third Month, 1666

To Friends in Truth in Chalfont and Thereabouts

Dear friends, whom I love in the Lord, and whose prosperity and growth in the truth I greatly desire,

This advice sprang in my heart to you this morning: Mind and keep watch to that which quickens and enlivens the soul towards God, and watch against that which flats and deadens it. For these are both near, and they both seek after you, the one for your good, the other for your hurt. I need not tell you what these are, nor where or how they appear, but in continual watching to the one, and against the other, is the diligence and care of your spirits daily to be exercised. Oh, at no time let your spirits be loose and careless! For the enemy waits to do hurt, and the Lord waits to be gracious, and to do your souls good. Watch therefore, and pray, that you enter not into the temptation of the enemy, nor miss the tender mercies and lovingkindness of the Lord, which are sure to the seed (and to all that are of and abide in the seed) forever.

And, my dear friends, mind your meetings together to wait upon your God with great seriousness and intention of spirit, everyone watching to feel life rise up in your own spirits. Oh, sit down (yes, breathe earnestly to the Lord to enable you to sit down) in the silence of flesh, and in the stillness of your spirits, waiting for the presence, appearance, and power of your God to be revealed in the midst of you. In this way your hearts will be searched more and more, and the pure judgment will be revealed against whatever would appear or rise up contrary to the holy nature and will of God, and that which is for death, will be brought into death more and more. Thus the impure will be kept down, and that which is pure (the plants and trees of righteousness) may thrive, flourish, and spread more and more, and you will sit down under the shadow of your own vine and olive-tree, partaking of the sap and fatness thereof. Oh that every one of you, in all your meetings together, might witness that scripture fulfilled in you—"They shall be abundantly satisfied with the fatness of your house, and you shall give them to drink of the rivers of your pleasure."

I beseech you, with a heart of tender love, to take heed of sluggishness, or carelessness, or deadness of spirit in your meetings. These things are in no way becoming of the Lord's people, nor of your professions of waiting upon the living God. You are to look up, to watch, wait, and breathe for the Lord, to be exercised by his Spirit before whom all things are naked and bare, and to offer up that acceptable sacrifice of a broken heart, of pure praises, of love, life, humility, thanksgiving, etc. You are to receive what the Father of mercies stands ready (in and through the Lord Jesus Christ, the Son of his love) to give forth unto you. Can you be exercised in this way while in a drowsy, sluggish, careless spirit? Do not such things dishonor the Lord, whose name you should honor? And is not the jealous God provoked and grieved by such things as these, with whom you should walk in all humility and tenderness of spirit?

I beseech you, therefore, watch against all things of this nature, and be diligent, that you may witness the law of the Spirit of life in Christ Jesus making you free, and fencing you in, against all things of this kind, that you may be a chosen generation, a royal priesthood, a holy nation, a peculiar people, a temple of living stones, wherein the living God may dwell, and walk, and sup with you.

There is one thing that yet remains with me, which I would eagerly have you grow to a true, sensible, and experiential understanding of, which is this—namely, what it means to "touch the unclean thing." The enemy will be stirring up and casting that which is unclean upon the vessels which God is purifying and preserving from all pollution. But there is a turning away from and shunning of evil, a forsaking of the vain, earthly mind and thoughts, and a receiving of such temptations and suggestions no more. Oh that you might all experientially know and witness what this is! I know many of you do in some measure, but may there be more of this knowledge, more of this experience! Indeed, my heart livingly breathes for myself and for you, that we may witness this Scripture abundantly fulfilled in our hearts, "Whosoever is born of God does not commit sin; for his seed remains in him, and he cannot sin, because he is born of God." Oh, feel the weight of this scripture! The Lord has made a new covenant, a living covenant, and he has prepared a new and living way for the ransomed to walk in without erring, that he might rectify all (within this new people) that was amiss in those under the first covenant.

Oh, let the Lord enjoy the design of his heart! And let his people so wait upon him that they may all be renewed in the spirit of their minds, that the Lord may have a generation of Calebs and Joshuas, who fully follow after him in all things. For if any draw back from the Lord, and from the holy commandment of life, the Lord's soul can have no pleasure in such. Oh that there may be none among you drawing back to perdition! Take heed of deadness, drowsiness, sluggishness of spirit, earthliness, fleshly wisdom, unbelief, etc. But grow in faith, with diligence, towards the saving of your souls (which is far nearer than when you first believed), which you shall be sure in due time to reap, even the salvation you wait for, if you do not faint or grow weary.

May the grace, mercy, love, and peace of God our Father,

and of our Lord Jesus Christ, be multiplied unto you, and fill your hearts from day to day, according to your several capacities,

I. P.
Reading Jail, 22nd of Third Month, 1671

To Catherine Pordage

Friend,

I observed yesterday that you did acknowledge the light to be the seed of life, and that you did affirm that those people with whom you walked also acknowledged it. Now, it is one thing to acknowledge the seed, and another thing to know it, feel its guidance, and be subject to it. It is a good step to acknowledge it in the comprehension, from an external testimony, but they that go so far may still never come truly to know and own the thing itself.

Oh, many have had some touches of the light, some true appearances and tastes of the glory. But who has been so united to the light so as to keep out of all that corrupts? There is something that still lives near, that would eagerly be mixing with the light, and drawing the soul higher than the pure light of life and truth. Oh how this leads out of the way, above the pure, true, innocent, and simple! How it makes haste to be spiritually rich and glorious, departing from that poverty of spirit wherein is the safety and preservation of the soul.

Come now, live no more; know no more of yourself. Instead, wait to feel the pure seed raised to live and know in you, and to feel its light enlightening you, and creating a new capacity in you. This will allow you to bear the pain of dying, and of taking up the cross, which will truly slay every life, appearance, and power that is not of its own nature. You have formerly taken up crosses in a way of man's wisdom, and according to a natural knowledge and judgment. Come now, learn to take up the seed's cross in the true foolishness. For there is not another thing that gives life besides the cross of our Lord Jesus Christ, which truly and really slays. And to whoever can discern and take up this cross, and live and walk under it, the yoke is easy and the burden is light. But that which finds the cross hard must first be brought under and destroyed, before the yoke and burden are known to be light. If you could come out of your own wisdom and consideration of things, into the simplicity of the seed, you would soon recover your lost ground again. And you would also see how the enemy, with his subtlety, has gained upon you, and into what great danger he has brought your soul.

The Lord searches and tries the heart, and what his light discovers is the true state of the soul. The mind outside of the light cannot apprehend its own state. Therefore, be still; do not justify yourself, nor condemn the judgment of others, till the Lord makes the thing manifest to you. If it then proves better with you than what others have said, that will be to your advantage. But if you then prove mistaken, and the judgment of others (which your heart has condemned) should stand, it will be your great loss and disadvantage.

This is in love and true friendship to your soul, in a deeper sight and sense of you than you are aware,

I. P.

26th of Third Month, 1671

To Nathaniel Stonar

Dear Friend,

There is something on my heart to express to you, in love and great goodwill, which is as follows:

Would it not be sad if you should perish from the Lord forever? If you err in heart from the living way, it may be so. Indeed, if your mind is not turned from darkness, inward darkness, to the inward light of God's Spirit, it cannot be otherwise. Now, if you feel the inward light, the power of the pure light, and are changed by it, you cannot speak against that light.

There was no true religion in the apostles' days without turning to the inward light, and the true ministry was then sent to turn men to it. And there is no true religion now without being inwardly turned to and walking in the same light, nor can man try any truth, or understand any scripture rightly, except in the light of God's Spirit. No one can understand the things of God except the Spirit of God. The Scriptures are holy words, and deal with the things of God, which no man can understand except in a light of the same nature from which they came. And when a man comes to the true understanding, he quickly finds that the understanding which he had of the same things before was but an understanding after the flesh, far short of the nature of the true understanding. And friend, consider if your knowledge, which you have hitherto had, has changed or does change the nature of your understanding and will. Or is your old understanding and will yet remaining, despite all your knowledge and practices in religion? Oh, do not dally in things of such great importance, lest you repent too late! For I do not tell you what I see concerning you in the light of God's eternal Spirit, but rather desire that your own eye, or rather the right eye in you, be opened and brought to see.

Now consider one scripture seriously concerning the church of Laodicea. Did not this church have the true knowledge outwardly, and a true church state, and right ordinances? Did it not believe in Christ, and look up to him for justification, etc.? What did it lack as to the outwardness of its state? But it lacked true sense, life, and warmth, inwardly. So that, if you had all ordinances and truths of the gospel light outwardly, yet lacked the inward power, you could not help but lack the tried gold, the white raiment, and eye salve. And so, even though you might think yourselves rich, etc., yet the shame of your nakedness would appear: Yes, indeed, the nakedness of such as are not clothed with God's Spirit does clearly appear to the Lord, and also to the eyes and spirits of his children which he opens in his own light, and who see with this eye. Truly the shame of their nakedness does appear, notwithstanding all the religious covers they put upon themselves. Oh that you had desires, living desires, after the nature of truth, and were acquainted with the new nature, which can be satisfied with nothing but the virtue, life, and power of truth!

Come friend; wait on the Lord to have the old nature, the old spirit, mind, wisdom, understanding, and will broken, and the old garment torn to pieces. Only then will you come to experience that which is new, pure, and living, and find the new vessel filled with that which is new. For if you will come into the ministration of the new covenant, you must come into the Spirit and power. You must know the letter of the Scriptures in the Spirit and power which wrote them, if ever you will know them aright. Yes, if you will become a son of God, you must receive power from Christ so to do; and if you will believe aright, you must feel faith wrought in your heart by that very power which raised our Lord Jesus Christ from the dead. All other faith falls short of the nature of true faith.

Now consider: the apostle speaks of the state of the Gentiles before they were turned from darkness to light, and from the power of Satan to God. Their understanding was darkened, being alienated from the life of God through the ignorance that was in them, because of the hardness of their heart. Even though what might be known of God was manifest in them, Rom. 1:19, their ignorance remained because of their hardness in not minding it, not turning to it, and so they became alienated from the life, and their understanding was not opened by it. In this state, men are without God, without Christ, strangers to the covenant of promise, and without any true hope of salvation. And in this same state are those who have a form of godliness without the power; they are even as the natural heathen. For nothing makes a true Christian besides the life and power; and he that does not hear the voice of Christ's Spirit in his heart is no better than a heathen and a publican. Yes, any church built up outside of the life and power is no better than a synagogue of Satan.

It is precious indeed to know the Spirit of the living God, and to be begotten by him in the life which is true and pure. It is precious to be separated from death and its power, and to be married to life and its power—to be married to the conquering Lamb, who triumphed over sin and death in his body of flesh, and who, by his Spirit and power, delivers his spouse from the strength and dominion of them. And it is precious to walk with the Lamb, and to follow the Lamb wherever he goes. For he always leads out of sin and unrighteousness, into ways of purity and righteousness, into the path which is prepared for the ransomed, where there is no danger of erring.

God does not strip his people naked, and gather them out of the spirit of this world, that they should be empty and desolate forever. No, he gathers them into, and fills them with, his own Spirit! He fills them with light, fills them with life, fills them with holiness, fills them with righteousness, fills them with peace and joy in believing and obeying the gospel! And in this Spirit is the kingdom known which is not of this world, the inward kingdom, the spiritual kingdom, the everlasting kingdom, where the everlasting throne is near, and the everlasting power is revealed. The Lord God Omnipotent reigns in the hearts of his, and other lords do not reign, but their horns are broken, and the horn of God's Anointed is exalted, who sits ruling as King on his holy hill of Zion. Truly those who have suffered with him, and gone through great tribulation, do reign with him. Blessed be his name forever!

I am your friend in the heartiness of true love, so far as the Lord pleases to make use of me towards you,

I. P.

7th of Fourth Month, 1671

To Nathaniel Stonar

O Friend!

It is a dangerous thing to resist God's Spirit; and yet it is very easy for man to do so, who has not received a true understanding from the Lord, nor is acquainted with the leadings and outgoings of Him who is pure. He that is tender and truly sensible may discern when he resists, when he quenches, or when he grieves the Spirit of the Lord; but he that is not truly enlightened, nor in the true sense, cannot do so.

The Scribes and Pharisees were interpreters of the law, and very strict in outward observations and ordinances, etc., and blamed their fathers for killing the prophets, yet, concerning these, said Stephen, "You stiff-necked, and uncircumcised in heart and ears, you do also resist the Holy Spirit; as your fathers did, so do you." For until the stiff will and stiff wisdom be brought down in a man, he cannot help but resist God's Spirit, and fight for his notions and practices, according to his apprehensions of the letter.

Paul walked blamelessly according to the letter of the law, yet resisted the Spirit which gave forth the law. He who would not be found resisting God's Spirit must know the Spirit, receive the Spirit, live in the Spirit, walk in the Spirit, and not fulfill the lusts of the flesh. But he that is only in the letter, and in the form of godliness outside of the inward life and power, he is of that birth, mind, nature, and spirit, which cannot do otherwise than resist God's Spirit. He does not know, and cannot heed, the Spirit's drawings, movings, light, and life—either in his own heart, or in the hearts of others.

Oh, wait to receive an understanding from the Lord, that you may come truly to know whether you have resisted God's Spirit or no—that you do not lose the opportunity of making peace with your adversary while you are in the way with him.

This, in very dear, true, and tender love, from one who most sincerely and heartily wishes well to you.

I. P.
17th of Fifth Month, 1671

To Catharine Pordage

Friend,

It is true, the way to life is so difficult and intricate that none can find it, except those who are enlightened by the Lord, and who follow the guidance of his Spirit. Christ, who preached the kingdom, and bid men seek it, yet said, "Narrow is the gate and difficult is the way which leads unto life, and few there are that find it." In a race many run, but one obtains the prize. Are you able to read what Christ said, "Except you eat the flesh of the Son of man, and drink his blood, you have no life in you"? This seemed a hard saying to some of his own disciples, many of whom left him. And truly, friend, as it is not an easy thing to come into the right way, so neither is it an easy thing to abide in the way, for many are the bypaths, many and great the temptations, both on the right hand and on the left. The way was always the same, surely as difficult and hard formerly as it is now. But the states and conditions of some make it harder to them than it is to others.

It is sad indeed that any should be convinced of truth and not come into subjection to it; yet it is very easy and common. For men cannot deny conviction when it comes in power, but they may deny obedience to that of which they are convinced. Some in the apostles' day went further, even to taste of the heavenly gift, and the powers of the world to come, and to partake of the Holy Spirit, and yet fell away. Was this not very sad? And yet sadness was not a well-grounded objection against the truth and way of God then. Indeed, I make little of the illumination of the understanding, without subjection to him that illuminates.

As for prayer, it is a gift. He that receives it must first come to the sense of his own inability, and so wait to receive it, perhaps beginning with but a groan or sigh from the true Spirit, and thus grow in ability from the same Spirit, denying the ability which is after the flesh. This fleshly ability abounds in many, who mistake and err in judgment, not waiting on the Lord to be enabled by him rightly to judge and distinguish between flesh and Spirit. Many times men are willingly ignorant in this particular, and it will cost them dear to come to a true understanding therein.

Has not all flesh had some manifestation of God's Spirit allotted to it? And is not God's light, God's gift, God's Spirit, the rule to all? Is any prayer required or accepted outside of this? Indeed, he that has the sense of being but a dog, as I may say, and not worthy to be counted a child, yet he may pray for crumbs, and be heard, and receive them. But what are prayers without the light and life of God's Spirit? Are they not prayers of the fleshly birth, fleshly will, fleshly wisdom? Can they that are in the flesh, or who pray in the flesh, please God? Oh, forsake your own wisdom, reasonings, will, and desires, that you may come to true understanding in this matter. A little praying from God's Spirit, and in that which is true and pure, is better than thousands of vehement desires in one's own will, and after the flesh. For as long as a man pray in the flesh, that which should die in him still lives in his very prayers. And how shall it ever be destroyed, if it gets food and gains strength there?

As to "stirring up the gift," 2 Tim. 1:6, Paul knew to whom he wrote. Timothy had a great understanding, and both knew the gift, and how to stir it up. But he that does not have a true understanding may stir up something else, instead of stirring up the gift, and so kindle a fire of his own, and offer up his own sacrifice with his own fire, neither of which are acceptable to the Lord.

As for Christ being a mediator and reconciler, it is by his death and life, both of which are partaken of in the light which comes from him, even in the grace and truth which he dispenses. For as God wrought all in him by the fullness which he bestowed on him, so he works all in those that are his by a measure of the same Spirit, life, and power. But why do you so desire to be able to comprehend and reason about these things? This is not your present concern, but rather to feel after, and be joined to, that whereby Christ renews and changes the mind, and wherein he gives the knowledge of his good, acceptable, and perfect will. Take heed of being exalted above measure, or desiring to know the things of the kingdom after the flesh. It is better to lie low, and as a child to enter the kingdom, and to receive the knowledge of the things of God there, than to be feeding that knowing mind, which is to be kept out and famished.

Oh watch, that you may not lose your Leader, and meet with the deceiver, instead of Him that is true. Take care that you do not go back from light, life, truth, and power, instead of going forward toward them. Indeed, this letter of yours makes me afraid, as Paul speaks to the Galatians, lest I have bestowed labor on you in vain. For there seems to be in you a strengthening of your mind towards returning back to that from which the Lord has been redeeming and gathering you. If you feel the right seed, and come to be of the right seed, the way of the seed will not be too hard for you; otherwise it will.

This is to you, in love and grief, from your soul's true friend,

I. P.

21st of Sixth Month, 1671

To Catharine Pordage and Another

Friends,

If I should say one word to you, could you bear it? And yet this counsel is with me towards you: Oh wait for, receive, embrace, and be glad of that which reproves you, and be afraid of that which comforts you in your present state! For you must come through the trouble, judgment, breaking down, plucking up, consuming, and burning of the contrary nature and spirit which yet deceives you. And truly, you must witness all the knowledge, profession, practices, beliefs, hopes, that are founded there, and spring up from there, confounded and destroyed, before you can possibly come into the true ministration of life and power. You must die to your own wisdom if ever you will be born of, and walk in, the wisdom of God. Yes, you must die to that part which is so active in the wisdom of man, and which would even labor in fire for that which is but vanity, if ever you will receive the knowledge which springs out of truth and life itself, which indeed flows over and covers the earth of God's heritage as the waters cover the sea.

When we were in desolation and great distress, indeed, unutterable, we had none of these helps and instructions which now abound towards you. Oh, what a day of mercy you have met with! But how great will be your condemnation if you become as deaf adders to the Spirit of the Lord, and so miss his salvation! And if you will ever know the Spirit of the Lord, you must meet with him as a searcher and reprover in your own hearts. Yes, you must first meet with the merciful God as a severe Judge, and an unquenchable, consuming fire against that spirit, wisdom, knowledge, and faith in you, which is but of a chaffy nature. Truly, friends, it is far better to be stripped of it, than to find any rest or pleasure in it.

I. P.
7th of Seventh Month, 1671

To an Unknown Recipient

Dear Friend,

Some Scriptures sprang up and opened in my heart towards you this morning. The first was 2 Cor. 10:4-6:

> *For the weapons of our warfare are not carnal but mighty in God for pulling down strongholds, casting down arguments and every high thing that exalts itself against the knowledge of God, bringing every thought into captivity to the obedience of Christ, and being ready to punish all disobedience when your obedience is fulfilled.*

That which was chiefly on my heart was about the fulfilling of obedience. First, there is a knowing the will of God, a waiting to know and understand from God what is his holy, good, perfect, and acceptable will. Then, as God gives the knowledge, he requires obedience, which is to be learned of God in the new spirit and life. For in the old nature, mind, and spirit, there is nothing but darkness and disobedience; and in the new creation there is the new obedience. So that there is first a beginning of knowledge in the Spirit, a beginning of faith in the renewing power, and a beginning of obedience (in the same) to him that calls. Then there is an increase of knowledge, of true, pure, living knowledge, an increase of faith, and a growing more and more obedient under the exercises, judgments, and chastisements of the Father's Spirit. And at length, the soul comes to witness a full readiness, skill, and strength (in and through Christ, in and through the measure of the gift of grace received from him), to obey in all things. When the new birth is thus grown up into strength and dominion, into the stature of a man in

Christ, then the senses, which have been long exercised in discerning between good and evil, grow strong, and there is a quick discerning in the fear of the Lord, and an authority in his name and power over the enemy and his temptations. Here every stronghold is broken down, every imagination and false reasoning concerning the truth is subjected and broken by the evidence and power of truth, every thought is brought under into captivity, even to the obedience of Christ, with a readiness to reject all unbelief and disobedience that so much as offer to rise up. Now, is not this the Christian state, which God would have his children aim and strive at? Are they not blessed who witness it? Does not the true ministration of the gospel light, Spirit, and power lead to it? And should any be at rest in their spirits in an easeful, formal, dry, dead profession without it?

Another Scripture was 1 Pet. 2:2-5:

> *As newborn babes, desire the pure milk of the word, that you may grow thereby, if indeed you have tasted that the Lord is gracious. Coming to Him as to a living stone, rejected indeed by men, but chosen by God and precious, you also, as living stones, are being built up a spiritual house, a holy priesthood, to offer up spiritual sacrifices acceptable to God through Jesus Christ.*

It is precious to witness the state of a newborn babe, to be begotten to God by the word of life and power, even by the word which God ingrafts into the heart. Oh, what living desires rise up after that which nourishes the birth of life, which God breathes from his own Spirit! Now as the birth is pure, so the nourishment is pure—pure milk from the pure word—sincere, unmixed milk from the word of life, from the breast of life.

Now, who is it that begets to God? It is the Spirit, the Word, the second Adam, he whose name is the Word of God. Who is the mother of these children? It is the heavenly wisdom, the Jerusalem which is above. ("The Jerusalem which is above is free, which is the mother of us all;" "Wisdom is justified of her children.") And who feeds these children? Who nourishes and brings them up? Why, the mother who bore them, she holds forth the breast of life to them, she yields to them the pure milk of the word. The newborn babes, they long for it, they cry for their food, they earnestly desire after it, and the tender mother gives it forth to them—even the milk of the breast of life from the pure word of life, and by this they grow.

But how came the babes to desire after such pure, sincere, unmixed food? Oh, they have "tasted that the Lord is gracious!" They have had the heavenly taste, they have tasted that which was living and pure from God, from his tender mercy and grace, wherein he ministers life and salvation. Indeed, the remembrance and sense of the sweetness of this is upon their palates! And how precious and living is it, when it comes new and fresh from him! The words which he speaks, they are still spirit and life to the soul. How can they help but desire that he minister unto them the pure food, that they may know and feed on the truth as it is in Jesus? Here they come to him as unto a living fountain, and a living stone, rejected by the builders after the flesh in all ages and generations, but chosen of God, and precious to all that have the true sense and understanding. Thus they come to him daily, and so are built up into a living house, or spiritual temple and dwelling place for God. He is the foundation stone, the corner stone, the top stone, the hope and crown of their glory. They are the living stones in him, quickened and kept alive in and by him, and shining in his light and glory.

Oh, little do you know the loving kindness of the Lord in visiting you with his truth, in giving you a sense beyond others, and in so tenderly drawing and inviting your heart! Nor have you yet seen what this will come to, if you faithfully give up, hearken to, and follow him.

I. P.

20th of Tenth Month, 1671

To Thomas and Ann Mudd

Dear Friends,

Of whose love to me I have been and am sensible, and to whom I bear true love.

When I was last at Rickmansworth, it was on my heart to visit you, and while I was there with you, true and living breathings did spring up in my heart to the Lord for you. Since then, I have often thought of you, and in my desires have wished well concerning you, even as to my own soul.

Your days here cannot be long, and what you sow here you must reap when you go out of this world. Oh that you may now sow to the Spirit of God in such a way that you may then reap from him life everlasting!

Last first day, my wife had a letter of George Fox's sent to her, which I read that night. In the reading of it, I had many thoughts respecting you, and a desire that you might sincerely, uprightly, and without prejudice, peruse it, and so I sent it unto you the next day for that end. Now, this morning you were upon my heart, and two things rose up in me in reference to you, as very necessary for you, that you may be safe, and that it may go well with you forever.

One was, that you keep steadfast in that holy testimony of truth, which was given forth among us at the beginning. For this truth is the same, and the testimony of it does not vary or pass away, but shall last throughout ages and generations, to redeem all that receive it, and are faithful to it. The testimony was this: to draw away from outward, dead knowledge, and out of dead practices and worships after men's own conceivings, into an inward seed, and into worship in Spirit and truth, both inwardly in the heart, and outwardly in the assemblies of God's gathering.

The second was, that you be daily exercised, guided, and your hearts opened and quickened, by the seed and Spirit of truth, so that you may know what it is to walk with the Lord, and to feel the power of the Lord, and enjoy the presence of the Lord, and be led by him out of, and away from, the mysterious workings of the power and spirit of inward darkness. For if, through a grievous mistake, you let this into your minds and spirits, instead of the Spirit of truth, you cannot help but call darkness light, and light darkness, truth error, and error truth, and so you will err from the true way and fall into something which, in God's sight, is not so. For there is a spirit of delusion as well as a spirit of truth. This spirit of delusion works in the heart as a minister of righteousness, in a seeming light, warming the heart with a wrong fire, bringing it into a wrong bed of rest. It administers to the heart a wrong peace, hope, and joy, setting up there a wrong sense, belief, and judgment concerning itself and others. And so it leads to separate from them that are true, and be joined to them that are false. It draws from the assemblies and worship of God's true gathering, and begets prejudices against, and hard thoughts about, those who are owned by the Lord, and are kept in their habitation by him who dwells in them, and they in him.

O my friends, may the Lord give you the true discerning of this spirit, and of his own Spirit! And may he deliver you out of the snare of the enemy by opening that eye in you to which he gives the sight of what is of him, and what is not of him. And may you be disjoined from all that is not of God, and joined to the Lord, abiding and walking in him.

I am a true friend to you both (in true and faithful love, as in God's sight), and a hearty desirer of your everlasting happiness.

I. P.

19th of Twelfth Month, 1672

To Colonel Kenrick

Dear Friend,

The gospel dispensation consists in Spirit and power. The kingdom which Christ and his apostles preached—which the true believers were to receive, and to wait for an entrance to be ministered to them into—stood not in word, but in power. Now there are four sorts of professors of the Christian religion in this our day, of which only one sort are truly acquainted with the gospel dispensation.

First, there is one sort who have been nurtured in a profession of Christianity by education, and have improved it by study, but have never known the power, virtue, and inward life. But as men, with the man's part, wisdom, understanding, and seriousness of mind, they have considered the truth and weight of things contained in the Scriptures, and so they have received something of the holy doctrine into their natural understanding, and given themselves up to the observation and practice thereof, according as they have apprehended and understood things. These have become more serious and excellent men than others, but still fall very short of the nature and state of Christianity. Yes, the strictest among these, many times, become the greatest opposers and persecutors of true Christianity.

Secondly, there are some who have had a taste of the true power, and have had living desires and breathings after it, and a sense of the preciousness and excellency of it, who have also felt the quickening Spirit, and begun therein. But afterwards, they have lost that sense, and landed in a literal knowledge and wisdom about those very things of which they once had some living experience. These are like salt which has lost its savor, and it is hard for them ever to be seasoned again. And from among these do rise the greatest persecutors and bitterest persecution against the life, truth, and power.

Thirdly, there are some who, though they never came to the distinct knowledge of the power, yet have had a great sense of their lack of it, and have abode in that sense. And in all the ways and forms of religion they have been, or are in, they still seek after it, and find no value in outward forms, except as the power (in some measure) appears in it. For the cry of their souls is daily after the power and life, and their waiting is for it. These, wherever they are, are of the true seed. These are of the birth of the heavenly Spirit and wisdom. These are sheep of the true Shepherd's fold, though they are not yet gathered home to the fold to which they properly belong. These are the broken, the bruised, the sick, the wounded, the captives, the distressed, the poor, the naked, etc., to whom the gospel of peace, the gathering, the salvation, and redemption belongs. And the bleating of these sheep is known. Yes, their longing and cry after the redeeming and gathering power of the Shepherd is felt, though they may be, at present, prejudiced against that very dispensation of truth, life, and power, whereby the Shepherd gathers.

Fourthly, there are some whom God has brought to the distinct sense and knowledge of the power. There are some whose minds God has turned to the inward light and power. There are some whom the Shepherd has gathered home to the Father's house, where there is bread enough, and to the true fold, where there is rest and peace enough. These have seen to the end of man's legal comprehendings and creaturely strivings after life, righteousness, and holiness, and at last have come to the commandment wherein is life everlasting. Now these indeed experience something of the gospel dispensation, and know the difference between being under the law and under grace. These can tell what the kingdom is which Christ preached and bade men seek, and what the gospel is which the poor in spirit receive, and what the healing is which drops from under the wing of the Savior and Redeemer. And these can distinguish between truth as testified in the letter, and truth as it is in Jesus; between the law of the letter, and the law of the Spirit, which is written in the new heart and mind, by the finger of God's pure and living power.

Now the knowledge of these, the faith of these, the peace, the joy, the justification, and sanctification, and redemption of these, differs greatly from all the former—from the two first sorts in nature and kind, from the latter in degree, clearness, and purity. For though all the sheep of the true Shepherd have something of the true knowledge, true faith, true justification, true sanctification, and may at times have some taste of true peace and joy, and have true breathings and supplications in their spirits towards their Father that begat them, still they are not clear, they are not pure, they are not unmixed. There is a great deal which is not true, which passes for true with them because they are not come to the anointing, to the eye salve which opens the eye, nor to the Spirit of judgment and burning, which separates inwardly in the heart, understanding, mind, and judgment, between the precious and the vile. So that when they speak of the heavenly things, they do but stutter and stammer. And even though truth can sometimes own their sense (yet, many times not their words), there is such a mixture of the dark, earthly comprehension in them, which they are not yet delivered and redeemed from.

But it is otherwise with those who are turned to the light and power of our Lord Jesus Christ, and have known it, and been exercised, fanned, and purged by it. For in these, the blind eye is opened and the deaf ear is unstopped. And to them, the pure understanding and language is given whereby they know and understand, not only words concerning Him, but he himself who is true, and they are in him that is true, even in Him who is the very God and life eternal.

Yet there are different states among those who are thus effectually called and gathered home, according to their growth in the truth, and their faithfulness to it. For if there is not a great care and watchfulness, there may be, in some, a neglecting to hear the voice of the Shepherd, and to walk with him. These can miss the pastures of life, and the pure rest, joy, and peace, and the garment or covering of the Spirit, which they who live and walk in the Spirit (giving up in everything to the Spirit, and denying all the lusts and fruits of the flesh) daily find themselves covered with. God does not "dwell in them and walk in them," as he does in those that remain separate from all evil (from which the Spirit of judgment and burning purifies and separates), and touch no unclean thing. Yes, they who grieve Christ's Spirit, and do not heed his call and knocks, do not partake of the river of life and wine of the kingdom as fully as those whose ear is open to him, and who are always ready to obey and follow him "wheresoever he goes."

I. P.
19th of Fourth Month, 1673

To Widow Hemmings

Dear Friend,

I think it long since I heard from you. I remember the sweet and precious savor that was upon your spirit the last time I was with you, with my dear friend, J.C. It has been my hope and desire that the Lord might preserve you therein.

The truth in the inward parts is of God. That is the thing which all are to mind, and in which acceptance with God is witnessed. Without the truth in the inward parts, there is no acceptance with God, let men profess what they will or can. For God never disowned the truth, nor any that are in it. Here, the flesh and blood which give life are fed upon. Here, the bread which comes down from heaven and the water of life are known. But outside of this they are not, nor can they be, known.

Oh my friend, that you might feel more and more truth in the inward parts, and be more and more established therein! What is the outward feeding, or outward supper? It is but a shadow. The inward feeding, or the inward supper, is the substance. And as the day dawns, and the daystar arises in your heart, the shadows will flee away, and the substance will be discovered, owned, and delighted in by you. The shadows reach but to the outward part, but the ministration of life, the ministration of the substance, reaches to the seed. And you must be more and more transplanted into the seed, that Christ may be formed in you, and you formed in him, and so grow up into his heavenly nature and image, out of the earthly, out of the natural. Oh, may the Lord God prosper his own seed and holy plantation in your heart! And may he keep you in the meek, lowly, humble, poor, and tender spirit, unto which is his mercy and blessing.

I expected to have heard from you, or at least from your daughter S., before this time, supposing I had a promise thereof from her. The Lord uphold, preserve, and bless her. Let her look not out, but only look within, for the will of the Lord; may she mind nothing else; and it will be well with her.

My dear love is both to you and her, who am your sincere friend,

I. P.
4th of Ninth Month, 1673

To an Unknown Recipient

Dear Friend,

I had a desire to have stayed a little while with you the last time I passed through Uxbridge, but was prevented. The occasion of my writing to you is something which was on my heart toward you.

Do you desire to know the Lord in the gospel covenant, and would you walk with him therein? I know you would.

Do you desire to have sin destroyed in you, and Christ reign in your heart? Do you desire to fight against your enemies so as to overcome, and to run the race so as to obtain the everlasting prize, the eternal weight of glory? Oh then, mind truth in the inward parts, even the grace and truth which are by Jesus Christ to whom God has given power! For he gives power to his own, by the grace of his Holy Spirit, over sin and corruption in the inward parts. Did not God conquer the enemies of the outward Jews in Egypt, in the wilderness, and in the good land also? And shall he not do so inwardly for the inward Jews?

Truly, there are enemies in Egypt, in the land that is (as I may say) wholly dark, and under the oppression of spiritual Pharaoh. There are enemies also in the heart, which is like a wilderness and solitary place. And there are enemies also in that heart which is in some measure renewed, and made good and honest. Now all the spiritual enemies, all the enemies of a man's own house, are to be destroyed by the power of the Lord Jesus Christ working by his grace in the heart. This grace, being received, subjected to, dwelt in, and obeyed, brings deliverance and salvation from them all. And when salvation is brought home to the heart, and wrought out there by the Lord, it is to be enjoyed and abode in, and the soul is not to return back again into captivity. Indeed, having been delivered out of the hands of its inward and spiritual enemies by the holy, inward, and spiritual covenant, the soul is to serve God in the dominion of his Son's life, in holiness and righteousness all its days here upon the earth.

O my friend, mind this precious truth inwardly, this precious grace inwardly, the precious life inwardly, the precious light inwardly, the precious power inwardly, the inward word of life, the inward voice of the Shepherd in the heart, the inward seed, the inward salt, the inward leaven, the inward pearl, etc., whereby Christ effects his work.

Distinguish between mere words concerning a thing, and the thing itself within. Then wait and labor to know, understand, and be guided by the motives, leadings, drawings, teachings, quickenings, etc., of the thing itself within. And take heed of being offended by anything either within or without. For offenses will come, but blessed was he that was not offended at Christ outwardly in the days of his flesh; and blessed is he that is not offended at his inward truth, and inward way of appearance in the day of his Spirit.

O my friend, how precious is the substance, beyond all words or testimonies! Oh that you may come to know it in yourself, and be sensible of God's ministering by it to you, and increasing it in you! Then you will experientially feel the seed in you, and find it growing more and more, till it come to be a tree. And then you will sit under its shadow, and be delighted with its defense, and partake of its sap and fruit. Oh that every day you might have a sense of the life itself, the truth itself, the power itself, the wisdom itself, the righteousness itself! And may you find the Lord Jesus Christ both unclothing and clothing you inwardly, sensibly, and experientially—that is, that you might find him taking away your sin, your iniquities, your unrighteousness, both within and without also, and filling you, and clothing you with his righteousness. Then, by his putting these on you, and forming them in you, you might find your heart filled and covered with the nature, image, and Spirit of the dear Son. And so you may indeed put off the old man with his nature and deeds, and put on the new man, and know the renewing and new-creating in Christ Jesus, in the spirit of your mind. And then you will have a certain understanding of the truth as it is in Jesus, and as he manifests it, gives power to it, and causes it to work in your heart. This is the desire of my soul for you. May the Lord guide you to it, and remove all obstacles and hindrances out of your way.

My dear and true love is to your husband. May the Lord manifest his pure and living truth in both your hearts, and gather both your minds to it, and make you one in it.

Your friend in truth, who heartily wishes well to your soul.

I. P.
Grove Place, 17th of Ninth Month, 1673

To Elizabeth Stonar

Dear Friend,

Whose life in the Lord, and prosperity in the truth, my heart greatly desires, even that you may come to the perfect service, and free and full enjoyment of your soul's Beloved. And truly, if I could be in any way helpful to you in this, my heart would greatly rejoice and bless the Lord.

This morning when I awoke, my heart was exercised before the Lord concerning you. Several things did spring up in my mind relating to you, which I may now signify to you, as the Lord shall please to bring them again to my mind, and open them in my heart in reference to you. I greatly desire to have you rightly understand, and be found doing, that which the Lord requires of you, that it may go well with you, and that your heart may be satisfied, and your soul blessed, in believing and obeying the truth as it is in Jesus.

A few scriptures, sweet and precious to my taste, sprang up in my heart to lay before your view, that you also might suck sweetness, and reap benefit through the living sense of them. The first scripture that sprang up in me to you was that of Rom. 12:2, "be not conformed to this world, but be transformed by the renewing of your mind, that you may

361

prove that good, that acceptable and perfect will of God." You must stand at a distance from the spirit of this world, you must not touch the unclean thing, but be a chaste virgin in heart, in word, in conduct, if you expect to be married to the Lamb, to become one spirit with him, to know his mind, and to enjoy the love and be the delight of his Father.

The next was Samson's riddle from Judges 14:14. "Out of the eater came forth meat, and out of the strong came forth sweetness." It is everlastingly true, both inwardly and outwardly, to the children of the Most High, who live in his Spirit, and walk in his Spirit, and are guided by the power and virtue of his life. For everything that seeks to devour and destroy them, the Lord destroys by the power and virtue of his life and Spirit springing up in them. And truly, out of that which is strong against them, which roars against them in the strength and power of darkness, the Lord brings forth sweetness in and to their spirits.

Then that of Luke 9:23-24 came before me: "If any man will come after me, let him deny himself, and take up his cross daily, and follow me. For whosoever will save his life shall lose it; but whosoever will lose his life for my sake, the same shall save it." Now, I beseech you, consider: do you take up the daily cross, and bear it faithfully for Christ's sake? Do you stand a faithful witness against the spirit of darkness, and works of darkness, where you live? Do you not comply with any worship there which your heart knows to be out of the truth and Spirit of life, in which all true, holy, living, spiritual worship can alone be performed? Oh take heed of shunning the cross in any respect! For then you give way to unbelief, and to that wisdom, thought, reasoning, and judgment which are not of the truth, but rather of the flesh. And then you shun that which God has appointed to crucify sin in the heart, and under which the seed is to spring up and live, which is the power of God unto salvation to all that abide under it and daily bear it.

Thus, my dear friend, in the most dear, tender, and true love have I opened my heart to you, as things sprang in me for your sake. And the desire of my soul to the Lord is that they may be serviceable to you, and that you may be led by the holy, leading Spirit more and more into truth, and live in truth, and feel the life of truth living and reigning in you. Oh that you would be delivered from the enemy's temptations, and the subtle twistings of the serpent, which your present condition will often meet with. May the Lord discover them to you, and preserve you from being ensnared with them.

Your constant friend in the dear love and service of the truth.

I. P.
Amersham, Bury End, 20th of First Month, 1675

To Catharine Pordage[1]

Ah, my poor, distressed, entangled Friend,

While you seek to avoid the snare, you deeply run into it! For you are feeding on the tree of knowledge by giving way to these thoughts, reasonings and suggestions which keep you from obedience to that which has already been made mani-

---

[1] Being that this letter to Catherine Pordage is a somewhat strong correction and warning, it seems appropriate to insert here a few words of John Penington, Isaac's Penington's eldest son, written upon the occasion of his father's death. He writes, "I have also observed, where he [Isaac Penington] has been engaged on truth's behalf to rebuke anyone sharply, who were declining from their first love, and deviating from the truth as it is in Jesus, it has been with so much reluctancy and averseness to his natural temper, as I never discerned the like in any. So that it may be safely said, he never used the rod, except with great compassion to reclaim. Truly it was in love that he was drawn to smite what the purest love could not allow to go unrebuked."

363

fest to your understanding. And it is no wonder you are feeble in your mind, while you are thus separated from Him who is your strength, and while you let in his enemy. Why should you not act, so far as God has given you light? Why should you not appear willing to obey him, even in little things, so far as he has given you light? What if I should say that all this reasoning is but the subtlety of the serpent's wisdom to avoid the cross, and is not that simplicity and plainness of heart towards God which you take it to be? What if you are unwilling to be so poor, and low, and small in the eyes of others, as this practice would make you appear?

And what a subtle device the enemy has put into your mind about prayer, which has no weight or truth in it as applied to this present case! For prayer is the breath of life, an effect of God's spiritual breathing, which no man can perform aright without the Spirit's breathing upon him. Therefore, the Spirit is to be waited upon for his breathings and holy fire, so that the sacrifice may be living, and acceptable to the living God. But the prayer you mention is mere language, as any man or woman uses in ordinary conversation, and does not require a motion of life to bring it forth, no more than to bring forth other words. And will you say that you truly long for and pant after the Lord, and the way of truth and righteousness, while you remain walking against the light which God has given you?

O my friend, you and your husband have dallied too long. The Lord has shown great love and mercy towards you. Take heed of dallying any longer. What more would you have the Lord do? How far has he worked towards bringing you into obedience in this thing! But you say you find an inability to abide therein. Do you abide in the faith where the strength is given, and out of the thoughts and consultations of the enemy? Oh take heed of murmuring against the Lord (as you have been too apt to do)! Consider rather what great matter of complaint the Lord has against you. What could he have done more for you, than He has already done? And have you not been turning aside from his convictions and drawings, into your own thoughts and reasonings?

I received your letter last night, and upon the reading of it was greatly burdened and grieved for your sake, feeling your spirit so exceedingly wrong in this matter, and your reasoning so crooked and provoking to the Lord. But this morning, my heart was opened and drawn forth in this manner to you. And now, may the Lord give you a present and a future sight of the enemy's working in this against the love of God towards you, and against the redemption and peace of your soul. My heart breathes to the Lord for you, and desires that He may manifest to you that nature, wisdom, and spirit, from which these things arise. Oh that the child may not always be stuck in the birth, but at length be brought forth into the light, into the life, into the faith which gives victory, and into the single-hearted and holy obedience, where the pure power is known.

Your friend in the truth, and in sincere love,

I. P.

Amersham, 25th of Ninth Month, 1675

To His Brother Arthur[2]

Dear Brother,

I have been a traveler after the Lord from my childhood, and great misery have I undergone because of my longing after him. That which I wanted was his Spirit, life, virtue,

---

[2] Arthur Penington, Isaac Penington's younger brother, was a Roman Catholic priest.

and redeeming power to be revealed in my own heart. And oh, blessed be the Lord, beyond my expectation, he has directed me where to wait for this within, and has revealed it in me! And now I can say in truth of heart, and in the sense of that birth which God has begotten in me, "Lo, this is my God whom I wanted, and for whom I so waited!" And indeed I find him stronger in my heart than the strong man, who possessed it before he cast him out from there, and made a spoil of his goods. And now, dear brother, how can I hold my peace, and not testify of the love, mercy, and goodwill of the Lord towards me, and invite others to the redeeming power of which the Lord, in his goodness, has made me a partaker? Now, brother, a few words with respect to your response to what I sent you—not for contention's sake (the Lord knows my dwelling is in that life and peace which shuts that out), but in the tender love and care of my heart concerning the eternal welfare of your soul, which I would not, by any means or device of the enemy, have eternally deceived.

All sides may agree in notions about the regenerating power, but all do not receive the regenerating power, or are truly regenerated in the sight of God. Nor do all come to witness the head of the serpent inwardly crushed, and his works destroyed, and his kingdom laid waste inwardly by this power, which must be witnessed before a man is translated out of the kingdom of darkness, into the kingdom of the dear Son. There is an inward kingdom of darkness, where the unbelieving and disobedient to God's Spirit and power dwell. And there is an inward kingdom of light, wherein the children of light dwell with God, and walk in the light as he is in the light.

But that the work of regeneration is only begun in this life, and not finished till the other life, that is a great mistake. For the Scriptures testify that salvation is to be wrought out here, and not hereafter. Christ had all power in heaven and earth, and he sent forth his Spirit and power to work out the work here, by his sanctifying Spirit and power which is able to sanctify throughout, in soul, body, and spirit. And the gifts of the ministry are for perfecting the saints, till they all come in the unity of the faith, unto a perfect man, that they may be presented to God perfect in Christ Jesus. The holy leaven is put into the lump here, and it is able to leaven the lump here. So that holiness is not only to be begun, but perfected in the fear of God, as the apostle exhorts, who did not exhort to a needless or impossible thing. And the whole armor of God is able to defend the whole man from all the assaults of the wicked one; for greater is He who is in the saints, and who preserves from sin, than he that tempts to sin. Oh, how precious is it to war with the enemy in this conquering faith, and to resist him therein, and to watch him flee from God's power and sword, which will pierce him and can easily over-come him.

There is a state where the spirit is willing, but the flesh weak. But it is not so where the spirit has become strong in the Lord and in the power of his might. The flesh will be rebelling against the Spirit until it be destroyed by the cross of our Lord Jesus Christ. But when a man is really crucified with Christ and dead to sin, then sin has no more power over him, for Christ lives in him and reigns in his heart over sin and its temptations. When the God of peace treads Satan under the feet of the soul that was once taken captive by him, there it is known to whom belong the kingdom and the power and the victory and the dominion.

And this is true blessedness begun, carried on, and upheld by the pure, sanctifying power of the word of life in the heart. Indeed, the birth which is born of God knows this to be no delusion, but rather the truth as it is in Jesus. These are obedient to the true church of God, and to the holy ministry which he has brought out of the wilderness, and they also know of what nature the churches and ministries have been which have appeared and been set up in the world. For the devil has long transformed himself into the likeness of an angel of light, and cheated and beguiled souls. Indeed, the false church has reigned, with antichrist sitting in the temple (the man-child having been caught up to God, and the true church hidden in the wilderness), and men have generally put darkness for light, and light for darkness. But blessed be the Lord, the true light which shone in the apostles' days now shines again! This light discovers the mystery of iniquity, and the golden cup of abominations with which the earth has been made drunk, and Satan falls down like lightning before the power of Him upon whom the true church leaned when she came out of the wilderness. And upon him she still leans, and will lean forever, and the gates of hell shall not be able to prevail against her.

Blessed be the Lord who has brought many wanderers and distressed ones to the knowledge of the true church, and to a delightful obedience to her, whose voice is not different than Christ's, but one with it. These are in fellowship with the Father and Son, and with the saints who dwell in the light. They are clothed with the Lamb's innocency and righteousness, and do not dwell in darkness or sin, having crucified the old man with his affections and lusts, and put off the body of the sins of the flesh by the circumcision of Christ, and put on the new man which is created in Christ Jesus, in the righteousness and holiness of truth. They that are here dwell not in notions and preferences, but in eternal life, in the pure pastures of life, where the Shepherd of the inward and spiritual Israel feeds his holy flock day by day.

As for the Roman Catholic Church, or any other church

built up in the apostasy from the Spirit and life of the apostles, the Lord has given me to see through them, to that which was before them, and will be after them. And O dear brother, if you could but rightly wait for and meet with the holy, regenerating, purifying power (which in tender love I testified to you of), it would lead you to that which is the true church indeed, which has been persecuted by the dragon and false church, who are made drunk by the blood of the true seed.

The Lord has made me your brother in the line of nature; oh that you were my brother in that truth which lives and abides forever! Oh that you knew the church of the firstborn, who are written in heaven, and the Jerusalem above, which is free, and is the mother of all who are born of the regenerating virtue and power!

I. P.

20th of Seventh Month, 1676

To Sir William Armorer[3]

Friend,

The weighty sense of an eternal condition after this life has been upon my heart from my childhood, and it is often with me that I must give an account to God (when I pass out of this transitory world) of all things done in the body. Then

---

[3] About this man, Thomas Ellwood writes, "Penington's sixth imprison-ment was in the year 1670, in Reading Jail, where he went to visit his friends that were sufferers there for the testimony of Jesus. Notice being given of his visit to one called Sir William Armorer, a justice of the peace living in the town, he was forthwith brought before him and committed to the jail, thereby becoming a fellow-sufferer with those he had come to visit." This imprisonment lasted about twenty-one months.

indeed I shall enter into eternal rest and blessedness, or eternal woe and misery.

This causes me to call upon the Lord daily, for grace and wisdom from him, that my conscience, being cleansed through the blood of his Son, may be kept void of offense, both towards him and men. And truly (I speak not boastingly, but in the fear of the Lord, and in the sense of his goodness and tender mercy to me), my heart is preserved in love and innocency towards those who most injuriously, and without provocation on my part, have taken away my liberty, as far as I know, for my whole lifetime. What you further intend towards me, the Lord knows, to whom I have committed my cause. But this is on my heart to express to you, because, when I was with you, you spoke words to this purpose—that we wished you hanged, or we would be glad if you were hanged. God, who knows my heart, is witness, that I wish you no evil, neither to you nor your family. Indeed, I wish you may avoid all such things that may bring his wrath and curse upon you, either in this world or the world to come.

And, friend, do not provoke the Lord by afflicting those that fear him. Rather, cease to do evil, learn to do well, and this will please the Lord, and is more acceptable to him than all the worship that can be offered up to him without this.

I have sent you a little book as a token of my love, desiring you to peruse it seriously. Oh do not endeavor to bring me into such a condition as is there related! In the light I have seen that I ought not to swear, but to give the "Yes" and "No" of truth, which comes from the Christian nature, and is of far more certainty and assurance than swearing. For the man that swears may easily break his oath, but he that keeps to the truth cannot alter his yes and no, but it stands in the truth. And this our Lord and Master has set above, and instead of, swearing—which if we should vary from and deny, we would deny him who has taught us not to swear.

Friend, God has given you an immortal soul, and does require of you righteousness towards your fellow-creatures, and temperance and moderation of spirit, and sensibleness of the judgment to come after this life. You are stricken in years, and you have but a little moment left remaining of your time, and then it will be determined concerning your soul, what or how it shall be forever! Let the words of love, truth, and innocency from me, prevail upon you to be serious, and to let in the sense and fear of God upon your heart. You have spent much time in serving man; oh, spend a little in serving and fearing God! There is something which is pure, and of God, and appointed by him to exercise the conscience towards him. You have this thing near you. Oh that you might know it, and be joined to it! For until then, you can never truly serve or fear the Lord, but may spend your time here in a vain show, and at last be judged and condemned by the Lord, and lie down in eternal sorrow. Truly, it is the desire of my heart that this be not your portion from the hand of the Lord.

This is from a sufferer by you, who never gave you the least cause or provocation to so deal with me.

I. P.
Reading Jail

To the Lady Conway

Dear Friend,

I have heard both of your love to truth, and of your great afflictions outwardly, both which occasion a sense concerning

371

you, and breathings to the tender Father of my life for you. My earnest desire is that your heart may know and be joined to the truth, and that you may live and walk in it, reaping the sweet comfort, support, and satisfaction, which God daily ministers in and through it to his gathered and preserved ones. Oh that you may be led to where the Comforter does daily delight to supply the afflicted and suffering ones with comfort, whether inwardly or outwardly.

Now, my dear friend, take heed of that wisdom and knowledge which is not of the seed, and which can be held in the mind, without the springing life of the seed. The first day I was convinced, I was not only convinced in my under-standing concerning the seed, but I felt the seed in my heart, and my heart was enraptured with the sense and feeling of it. And my great cry to the Lord was that I might faithfully travel through all the sufferings and death of the natural part, into union with an enjoyment of the seed, and that the wisdom which was not of the pure living root and nature might die in me. Now, how I have been exercised and taught since that time is hard for me to utter. What poverty, what weakness, what foolishness I have been led into! How I have learned in the true sense, out of the reach of the comprehending, knowing mind! How tender I have been of every secret shining of light in my heart! How the Lord has taught and enabled me to pluck out my right eye, and cut off my right hand, and cast them from me, that I might not see with that eye, nor work with that hand, but be greatly maimed in the sight of men, and in my own sight too.

O friend, wait daily to feel the seed, to feel the seed live in you, and let the most pleasing part of your nature die, as it can live outside of the seed. Oh that you could exchange all old knowledge for that which is new and living! The seed is the well; receive the seed and you receive the well. Let it spring; wait for its springing; wait to know its springing. Bear all the trials and judgments which the Father of life sees necessary to prepare the heart for its springing. And learn to feel that which limits and subdues your thoughts, and brings them into captivity and subjection! Be not exercised in things too high for you. David, the man after God's own heart, who was wiser than his teachers, was not. Rather, come out of knowledge into feeling, and there you will find the true knowledge given, arising, springing, and covering your heart, as the waters cover the sea. And wait to be taught of God, to distinguish between the outwardness of knowledge —the notional part as it can be comprehended in the mind— and the life of it, as it is felt and abides in the heart.

May the Lord God of my life be your teacher, and point your mind to the pure seed of the kingdom, and open it in you. And let him make you so little, that you may enter into it, and keep you so low and poor that you may abide in it, managing these troublesome times in the outward for your advantage in the inward. Then the city and temple of the living God may be built within, and you will know him daily dwelling and walking therein. Thus may you be married to the Lord, and become one spirit with him, finding him to remove all that must be removed by the mighty arm and pure operation of his Spirit, till all that is contrary is done away. Then may your soul dwell with its Beloved in fullness of joy, life, and peace for evermore.

This is from the tender love, and fresh breathings of life, in your soul's true friend, and most hearty well-wisher,

I. P.
17th of Third Month, 1677

To James Eeles[4]

Friend,

God is my witness, to whom I must give an account of all my actions, that it is my desire to be found in all true love, courtesy, and righteousness, in my dealings towards all men, and I would by no means deny any man his just due, which he can by any just law or right claim from me.

Now, with respect to tithes, the payment or refusing of them is to me a matter of conscience, weighty on my heart before the Lord, and I desire to do therein as he might justify, and not condemn me. I know tithes were ordained by God to be paid to the Levitical priesthood under the law, but the same power that ordained them under the law, annulled them under the gospel. See Heb. 7:12 and 18. Here is God's power and authority for annulling them. Now, to suggest that any man has a true right, power, or authority to require payment under the gospel for what God's power has annulled —indeed, I do not see in Scripture. Nor can I be subject to any human authority or law in this thing without sinning against God, and incurring his wrath upon my soul, which I have formerly found very dreadful, and would not, for fear of sufferings in this world, expose myself to bearing it. Besides, Christ says, "He that denies me before men, him will I deny before my Father." He is the substance of all the figures under the law; he has put an end to them. Truly he is King, Priest, and Prophet in the church of God. All power in heaven and earth is given to him, and he sent forth his ministers without tithes. Now, tithes were set up in the dark time

---

4 James Eeles with either a magistrate or a priest who demanded tithes from Penington.

of Roman Catholicism, and not by the gospel light. Those who know the gospel light dare not be subject to that which was set up by the dark power of Rome, in the time of darkness.

I was willing to give you this plain and naked account that you may see how weighty the thing is with me, and how dangerous it would be for me to do what you require of me. For in so doing, I would lose my peace with God, I would be unfaithful to the testimony he has given me to bear, I would dishonor his name and truth, and bring his sore wrath and displeasure upon my soul and conscience. Judge for yourself in this matter, whether I had not better expose myself to any outward sufferings, though ever so great (either from you or any you shall make use of), than expose my soul to so great inward misery and sufferings for disobedience to the Lord in this particular. Consider Ralph Trumper,[5] a just, tender, honest-hearted man—how much he has suffered in this respect, to keep his conscience clear in this thing. But I believe he would rather suffer all his former losses ten times over again than suffer what he did for paying tithes after he was convinced of the evil and unlawfulness of it. I do not contend with you by the law of the land; but I must be subject to the law of God, who shows me from what root tithes came, and that they are not the maintenance of the ministry of Christ, or allowed by Christ, but rather the maintenance of a ministry that Rome's power set up. And truly this ministry and its maintenance are to be denied and witnessed against by those whom he calls forth to testify to his truth.

So, at present, I say no more, but remain your friend,

---

[5] Ralph Trumper was one of thousands of Quakers who had corn, cattle, and other goods taken by force to pay obligatory tithes to the Church of England. He was later imprisoned on at least two occasions for the same offense.

ready to do you any good, though I should suffer ever so deeply from you.

I. P.

25th of Fourth Month, 1677

To Dulcibella Laiton

Dear Friend,

Concerning whom I feel a travail, the following is the sense of my heart in relation to you.

There is a pure seed of life which God has sown in you; oh that it might come through, and come over all that is above it, and contrary to it! And for that end you must wait daily to feel it, and to feel your mind subdued by it, and joined to it. Take heed of looking out, in the reasonings of your mind, but dwell in the feeling sense of life, and then that will arise in you more and more which makes you truly wise, and gives power, and brings into the holy authority and dominion of life. Many that have been long traveling are now entering into their possessions and inheritance, which the Lord is daily enlarging in them, and to them. Oh that your lot may be among them, inwardly witnessed and possessed by you! Prize inward exercises, griefs, and troubles, and let faith and patience have their perfect work in them. Oh, desire to be good, upright, and perfect in God's sight, and wait to feel the life, Spirit, and power which makes you so! Come out of the knowledge and comprehension about things, into the feeling of life, and let that be your knowledge and wisdom, which you receive and retain there. This will lead you into the footsteps of the flock, without reasoning, consulting, or disputing.

Oh wait to be taught and enabled by God to take right steps in your travels, and to take up the cross and despise the shame in everything where that wisdom, will, and mind of man (which is to be crucified) would be judge! For the wisdom from below will judge amiss and lead aside if it be hearkened to by you.

You must be very low, weak, and foolish, that the seed may arise in you to exalt you, and become your strength and wisdom. You must die exceedingly, again and again, more and more, inwardly and deeply, that your life may spring up from the holy root, and you may be more and more gathered into it, spring up into it, and live in the life, virtue, and power of it. The travel is long, the exercises many, the snares, temptations, and dangers are many, and yet the mercy, relief, and help is great also.

Oh that you may feel your calling and election, your sinking down, springing up, and establishing in the pure seed, in the light and righteousness thereof.

Your friend, in the most sincere, tender love,

I. P.

11th of Fifth Month, 1677

To Sir William Drake

Dear Friend,

You expressed to one of my youngest sons, as he related to me, that you had a desire I should visit you, that you might have some discourse with me about religion. That is the most profitable kind of discourse that can be, if it be ordered in the fear of the Lord, and in a weighty sense and dread of him. I am very serious in reference to religion, and desire not to mistake or miscarry in it by any means. And if I might be helpful to you, or to any man, as to the truth and power of religion, it would be a matter of gladness to my heart, and of praising and blessing the Lord, in the sense of his stretching forth his hand towards the saving of any.

Now, that our meeting and discourse may be the more solemn and advantageous, I have written below a few plain propositions to consider, which I do not only find signified in the Scriptures, but the Lord has also written them on my heart. And if these things are plain to you, and you also are in the serious sense of them, it may tend towards the making of our discourse the more easy and profitable.

First, there is a holy, righteous, living, powerful God, who made heaven and earth, and all things therein, and at last made man in his own image, and set him over the works of his hands, to have dominion, and rule in his wisdom and power over them. Now, in this state, God was pleased and took delight in the works of his hands, and in man above all.

Secondly, man, sinning against his Maker, lost this image, which was his glory, and became brutish in understanding, and an enemy to God in his mind, and liable to the wrath of God's holy and righteous nature.

Thirdly, there is no reconciliation to be had between God and man, except by the change of this nature in man. For God is unchangeable; he is light, he is life, he is holiness unchangeable, and he will never be reconciled to, or have fellowship with, darkness, or with that which is dead and unholy—which man in his fallen state is. So man must be begotten again unto God and changed and renewed from his evil and sinful nature into a good and holy nature. He must be turned from evil works and become the workmanship of God, created anew unto good works.

Fourthly, nothing can produce this change in man except the Spirit and power of Christ, except the grace and truth which is by Jesus Christ. Therefore, a man must be sure that he receive this Spirit and power, and that he feel the operative, changing virtue of it, and be really changed thereby, being created anew, begotten anew to God, in the holiness and righteousness of truth. He must be sure that he is made a son and servant to the living God, or he can never know what belongs to true reconciliation with God, and to fellowship with him in the light and life of his Son.

Fifthly, all the religions and professions upon the face of the earth which fall short of this Spirit, life, and power, and wherein this new creation in Christ Jesus is not witnessed, nor power received to abstain from what is evil, and to become sons to God—these are not the pure, powerful, gospel religion, wherein the divine virtue and power of life operates. Rather, these are religions which men, in the earthly wisdom, have formed without life. And all religions that have but a form of godliness, and not the power, are to be turned away from, and witnessed against, by such as are called forth to be witnesses to the true gospel religion and way of worship, which stands in Spirit, life, and power.

Sixthly, this religion and worship, which stands in Spirit, life, and power, is the religion and worship which Christ set up about sixteen hundred years ago. John 4:23-24, 1 Cor. 4:20, Rom. 6:4. And this is the religion which God has revived and set up again, as they that receive the gospel now preach it. And those who believe in the power, which is both outwardly testified of, and also inwardly revealed, have the witness of it in their own hearts. Rev. 14:6-7, 1 John 5:10-12, Isa. 53:1. Oh, how sweet are these scriptures when they are rightly read and rightly understood. May the Lord give the right understanding, and lead into the true experience of them!

I remain an acknowledger of your kindness, and a

desirer for you that you may obtain from God the knowledge of himself and his Son, which is experienced (by them that receive it) to be life eternal.

I. P.

19th of Fifth Month, 1678

To the Women's Meeting at John Mannock's

Dearly beloved and honored in the Lord,

Blessed be the Lord, who has gathered you, and given you hearts to meet together, to feel his precious presence and power, and to wait to do his will therein.

Oh what could the Lord do more for his people, than to turn them to that pure seed of life which will make them all alive, and keep them all in life and purity, and then to make use of every living member in the living body as his Spirit shall breathe upon them, and his power actuate them? And indeed, there is need of all the life and power to the body, which the Lord sees good to bestow on any member of it. Every member of the body has life given it, not only for itself, but also for the use and service of the body. Only dear Friends, here is to be the great care, that every member keep within the limits of life, wherein its capacity and ability for service lies. For apart from this, it can do no real service for God or to the body. Oh, therefore, keep the eye fixed upon the life, upon the power, upon the presence of the Lord with your spirits! Then he may go along with you, and guide you in every thought you think, in every word you speak, in reference to his work and service.

And mind, Friends, what is now upon me to write to you: It is one thing to sit waiting to feel the power, and to keep within the limits of the power there; and it is another thing, yes, and a harder one, to feel and keep within the sense and limits of the power when you come to act. For then your reasonings, your wisdom, your apprehensions, have more advantage to rise up in you, and to put themselves forth. Oh therefore watch narrowly and diligently against the forward part in you, and keep back to the life, which, though it rise more slowly, yet acts more surely and safely for God.

Oh, wait and watch to feel your Keeper keeping you within the holy bounds and limits, within the pure fear, within the living sense, while you are acting for your God! Then you will be his instruments alone, and will feel him acting in you. Therefore, everyone wait to feel the Judge risen up, and the judgment set in your own hearts, so that what arises in you may be judged, and nothing may pass from you publicly except for what has first passed the pure judgment in your own breasts. And let the holy rule of the blessed apostle James be always upon your spirits, "Let everyone be swift to hear, slow to speak, slow to wrath." Oh, let not a talkativeness have place in any of you! Rather, abide in such gravity, modesty, and weightiness of spirit as becomes the judgment seat of the Spirit and power of the Lord. You can never wait too much for the power, nor can you ever act too much in the power, but you may easily act too much without it.

And as for this troublesome, contentious business in some, may the Lord teach you to consider and manage it in a wise, tender, and healing spirit. You must distinguish in judgment between enemies and erring friends. And take heed of the quickness and strength of reason, or of the natural part, which avails little. But wait for the evidence and demonstration of God's Spirit, which reaches to the witness in others and does the work. Are they in a snare? Are they overtaken in a fault? Are they in measure blinded and hardened, so that they can neither see nor feel aright? Retire, sit still awhile, and travail for them. Feel how life will arise in any of you, and how mercy will reach towards them, and how living words, from a tender sense, may be reached forth to their hearts, deeply, by the hand of the Lord, for their good. And if you find them, at length, bowing to the Lord, oh let tender compassion help them forward! Then what has been so troublesome and dissatisfactory in their progress, may at length have a sweet issue for their good, and for our joy and rejoicing in the Lord.

So, my dear friends, the Lord be with you, and guide you in this, and in all that he shall further call you to. And may he multiply his presence, power, and blessings upon you, and make your meetings as serviceable to the honor of his name, as he himself would have them, and as you yourselves can desire them to be.

Your friend and brother in the tender truth, and in the pure love and precious life.

I. P.

19th of Fifth Month, 1678

To Those Who Drink of the Waters at Astrop Wells

Dear Friends,

There is a great God, the Creator of all things, who gave man a being here in this world, to whom every man must give an account when he goes out of this world.

This great God, who loves mankind, and would not have them perish, is near unto man, to teach him the fear which is due from him to God. The man that learns this pure fear of

God is daily exercised by it in departing from evil, both in thought, word, and deed, and in doing that which is good in his sight.

There is likewise another teacher near man, who is also ready to teach such as do not know or fear God. This one teaches to dishonor the great God who made man a vessel of honor for his glory. They that learn of this teacher learn not to fear God, or to do good, but rather to please themselves in doing evil, both in thought, word, and deed. Oh, what account will all such give when they go out of this world, and come to be judged by the great God (who is of pure eyes, and cannot behold iniquity), when all their sins are set in order by him before them, and just judgment is proportioned out by him? Oh, why do men forget God their Creator days without number, and instead hearken to him who first deceived them, doing the will of the deceiver and destroyer of souls, and not the will of the blessed Creator and Savior?

Oh, hearken to wisdom's counsel, when she cries in the streets of your hearts against that which is evil, and contrary to the nature, life, and will of God, lest a day of calamity from God come upon you! For then you will cry unto the pitiful and tender God, but his tender heart will be turned against you, and refuse to show you mercy! Read Prov. 1:20 to the end of the chapter, and may the Lord give you the weighty consideration and true understanding of it for your soul's good, and for the reclaiming of you from anything that is evil, and destructive to your souls.

This is written in tender love unto you, from one who pities and loves you, and desires your prosperity in this world, and your everlasting happiness with God forever.

I. P.

Astrop, 15th of Sixth Month, 1678

To Such as Drink of the Waters at Astrop Wells

Dear Friends,

I entreat you to consider what I have included for your eternal good. Oh be not deceived by the enemy of your souls, in things of an everlasting concern! Here are some questions, propounded for your consideration, in the tender melting love of my heart towards your everlasting welfare.

First question: Is not God light? Is he not pure light, spiritual light, eternal light, in whom is no darkness at all? 1 John 1:5.

Second question: Is not man, in his natural, unregenerate, corrupt state, darkness? And can he possibly, in that state, have any union or fellowship with the great God and Savior? See Eph. 5:8, 2 Cor. 4:6, 1 John 1:6.

Third question: Does not the great God, in his tender love to mankind, cause his pure, heavenly light to shine in man's heart, in this his dark and corrupt state? 2 Cor. 6:6, John 1:5.

Fourth question: What is the purpose of God's causing his pure light to shine in man's corrupt heart? Is it not that man might be turned from darkness, and from the power of Satan (who keeps him in darkness), to the light which God causes to shine in him, and to God from whom this light comes? See Acts 26:18. So that, following Christ, and not walking in darkness, he might obtain the light of life? John 8:12.

Fifth question: Does man, in his natural corrupt state, love this light when it shines in him? Or does he rather hate it? And can he hate this light without hating God from whom it comes, and whose nature it is?

Sixth question: Why does man, in his natural, corrupt state, hate this light? Is it not because his deeds are evil, and because he would prefer to continue in his evil deeds, without being disturbed or reclaimed by this light? John 3:19-21.

Seventh question: What does the light of the pure God do for them that receive and obey it? Does it not bring them out of darkness and change their nature, so that they become children of the light, and "light in the Lord," and no more children of darkness, as they were before? John 12:36, Eph. 5:8.

Eighth question: How shall it fare with those who receive the shinings of this light of Christ in their hearts, hearkening to the reproofs of it, and fleeing from that which it shows to be evil? Shall they not receive the remission of their sins from God, and an inheritance among the saints in light? Acts 26:18, Col. 1:12-13.

Ninth question: But what will become of those who do not mind the shining of God's light in their hearts, nor are turned to it, nor changed by it, but rather spend their time in what pleases the corrupt part in themselves? Will they not be separated, when they go out of this world, from God, who is light, and have their portion with dark spirits, in utter darkness? 2 Thess. 1:6-10. See also Matt. 25:30.

Oh, consider these things, while you have time, for your souls' eternal good, so that you do not miss the holy way of life and salvation, and so perish! For God does not desire that any perish, but stretches forth his hand of love by his inward "light of life," effectually to save your souls.

I. P.
Astrop, 20th of Sixth Month, 1678

To One Who Sent a Message from Astrop Wells

Friend,

I had no purpose in writing or sending those papers besides true love to your immortal soul, that you might seriously consider them, and be found in the practice of them, and so be happy forever. For as Christ said to his disciples, so it is with me in this case towards you, "If you know these things, happy are you if you do them." I have felt the sweetness and great benefit of the practice of them, which I heartily desire you may also experience.

I here send enclosed a token of my love to you in particular, which your courteous message drew from me. It contains, in a few words, the true pathway of salvation, which, though you may know already, yet the reading and serious consideration thereof may be serviceable to you.

THE PLAIN PATHWAY OF SALVATION

The Lord Jesus Christ is the only Savior.

Grace and truth comes by Jesus Christ.

The Lord Jesus Christ saves by the grace and truth which comes by him.

For it is the grace of God that brings salvation, and it is the truth, as it is in Jesus, which makes free indeed.

He, therefore, that desires to be saved from sin and condemnation, must wait for the inward manifesting and revealing of the grace and truth in his heart, and must receive it, and be subject to it, learning of the grace to deny ungodliness and worldly lusts in every kind. And he must learn of the truth as it is in Jesus, to deny whatever is contrary to the life, nature, and Spirit of Jesus. He must likewise learn of the grace and truth to fear God, to turn from all false, invented worships and ways of men, and to worship God, the Father of spirits, in spirit and in truth. And as he learns and practices this, he will also learn of the grace and truth to live soberly and righteously in this present world, yes, and godly also, even as the holy God would have him. Titus 2:11-12. For God would have men live no otherwise than as his grace and truth teaches them. Now God's grace and truth, and the law of the Spirit of life in Christ Jesus (which is written in the inward parts), do not only teach that which is good, and to deny and depart from that which is evil, but they also give ability so to do. "My grace is sufficient for you," said God to Paul. And the truth of Jesus, revealed inwardly, has virtue and power in it, insomuch that they who receive the grace and truth which comes by Jesus Christ, receive power to become sons of God. For grace and truth are not notional things, but indeed have in them the virtue and power of life, and also the power of mortification. They that truly receive these, partake of their virtue and power in operation, and a true exercise of them in their hearts, and are thereby really made dead unto sin, and alive unto God.

So then, he that knows the grace and truth which comes by Jesus Christ, and receives it, learns of it, is subject to it, and partakes of its virtue and power, this one knows Christ unto salvation. But he that knows not, receives not, is not subject to the grace, and does not experience the sufficiency of the grace, nor witnesses the ability and power through it to become a son of God and to do the will of God—this one does not yet know the Lord Jesus Christ unto the salvation of his soul, regardless of what he may profess or believe concerning him.

I am your friend, in true love and desires for you.

I. P.

Astrop, 28th of Sixth Month, 1678

To the Women Friends
that Meet at Armscot in Worcestershire

Dear Friends,

In your meetings together to do service for the Lord, every one of you be very careful and diligent in watching to his power, that you may have the sensible, living feeling of it, each of you in your own hearts, and in the hearts one of another. Be careful to keep within the limits of it, and not think, or speak, or act beyond it. And wait more and more to know how to keep that silence which is of the power, so that in every one of you, whatever the power would have silent, may be silent. Oh, take heed of the forwardness of the flesh, the wisdom of the flesh, the will of the flesh, the talkativeness of the flesh! Keep them back; oh let them forever be kept back in every one of you, by the presence and virtue of the power!

The power is the authority and blessing of your meetings, and therein lies your ability to perform what God requires. Be sure you have it with you! Keep back to the life; keep low in the holy fear, and you shall not miss it. You will find it easy to transgress, easy to set up self, easy to run into sudden apprehensions about things, and then one will be of this mind and another of that. But feel the power keeping down all of this, and keeping you out of it, while everyone watches to the life, when and where it will arise to help you. Then you will be sensible of it when it does arise, and not (in the wrong wisdom) oppose it, but rather be one with it. And thus, if anything should arise from the wrong wisdom in anyone, you will be sensible of it, not defiled or entangled with it, but abiding in that which sees through it and judges it. Thus, life will reign in your hearts and in your meetings, above that which seeks to be forward and rise up over the life.

So the Lord God of my life be with you, and season your hearts with his grace and truth, and daily keep you in the savor thereof. Then you will be blessed by him, and be a blessing in his hands, and all that is evil and contrary to truth will be kept down in your own hearts, and you will be fit to keep down evil in the minds and hearts of others. And if anything be unsavory anywhere, it will be searched into, judged, and cast out, and the soul that let it in can be sought out, and if possible, recovered and restored. Then, you will know the joy of seeking out and bringing back the lost sheep.

There is that near you which will guide you. Oh, wait for it, and be sure you keep to it! Then, being innocent and faithful in following the Lord in the leadings of his power, his power may plead your cause in the hearts of all his tender people hereabouts, and they will see and acknowledge that your meetings are of God, and that you are guided by him into that way of service, in his holy fear, in which he himself is with you. Be not hasty either in conceiving anything in your minds, or in speaking it forth, or in anything you are to do. Rather, feel him by his Spirit and life going along with you, and leading you into what he would have any of you to do. If you be in the true feeling sense of what the Lord your God would have done, and join with what is of God as it rises in any, or against anything that is not of God as it is made manifest among you, then you are all in your places and proper services, obeying the blessed will and doing the blessed work of the Lord your God.

I had something upon me yesterday to you, but my weakness was great. This morning, this lay as a weight upon my spirit to lay upon yours; may the weight of it come upon you, to weigh down whatever is light or chaffy in any of you, that the seed of life may come up over it, and you may be weighty before the Lord, in the weighty seed of life. May the Lord make you rightly serviceable to him. You will find a great work to keep one part down, so that that which is pure and living of God may come up in you, and you act only in it, not exceeding its limits.

I. P.

Written at John Hawford's, 7th of Seventh Month, 1678

To S. W.

Dear Friend,

I ever had a love to you, and a deep sense of the serious work of God upon your heart, and the upright desires of your soul after Him. And it is wonderful in my eyes that the Lord should yet preserve you alive, in the midst of so great and languishing weakness. I have often inquired concerning you, and was glad to find a letter from your own hand, upon the reading of which, in the retired sense of my heart, I felt love arise to you, and breathings to the Lord for you. Oh that you may fully feel, and be joined to the seed of life, the seed of the kingdom, of which our Lord Jesus Christ, in the days of his flesh, prophesied.

O my dear friend, let not any part of your life lie in notions above the seed, but let it all lie in the seed itself, in your waiting upon the Lord for its arisings in you, and in feeling its arisings. Oh what becomes of flesh, and self, and self-righteousness, when the seed lives in the heart? My religion (for which I now daily bless my God), began in this seed, and when I first felt it, and discerningly knew it to be from the Lord, my cry to him was, "Oh, this is what I have longed after and waited for! Oh, unite my soul to you in this seed forever! This is your Son's gift from you, your Son's grace, your Son's truth, your Son's life, your Son's Spirit! I desire no more than to be made nothing in myself, that he may be all in me." And now, what I meet with and witness here, what I feel the Lord Jesus Christ to be made to me here, none knows, or possibly can know, except they that have felt the pure power of the Spirit of life, and have been led by it into the same holy and blessed experience.

Ah, sin has no share here in this blessed seed, but is excluded by the life and power which is stronger than it. Here Christ is formed in the soul. Truly, here the black garments of unrighteousness, yes, of man's righteousness too, are put off, and the white raiment is put on. Here the holy image is brought forth in the heart, even the image of the dear Son, which partakes of the divine nature of the Father. Here the soul is newly created in Christ Jesus. Here is no deceit of any kind met with, but only truth from God, even the true life, light, virtue, power, of the Lord Jesus Christ, as livingly felt in the heart, and as effectually operating there, as ever the power of sin did previously. Oh that you might daily discern this, and feel this to grow up in you more and more, and die to all notions, even notions of the heavenly things themselves which are held outside of this. Then your soul may fully live in the life, Spirit, and power of the Lord Jesus Christ, and nothing but his life, Spirit, and power may live in you, to the glory of God the Father, and to the great joy and gladdening of your heart in his presence! Amen.

Your friend in the true, sincere love of the heavenly, everlasting seed.

I. P.

13th of Twelfth Month, 1678

To the Lady Conway

Dear Friend,

In tender love, and in a sense of your sore afflictions and exercises, I do most dearly salute you, and I desire for you that the work of the Lord in your heart may not be interrupted by any devices of the enemy. Oh may it go on and prosper in you, in the springing up of the pure seed of life in your heart, and in the powerful overturning, by the mighty arm of the Lord, of all that is contrary to it in you. Oh that you may daily feel that holy birth of life, which is begotten by the Father, and lives by faith in him! May you daily feel it living in you when temptations and trials increase on every side. Oh, feel the birth of life, which will cry to the Father, "Lord, increase my faith!" Though sorrows, heaviness, and faintings of heart increase ever so much, yet, if your faith increase also, it will bear you up in the midst of them.

Oh that you might come to feel the daily wasting away of sin and death, and the daily springing up of life and holiness in your heart. The pearl is worth thousands of worlds, together with the greatest earthly glory and pleasure imagin-able. Oh that you may be taught of God to discern it more and more, and to buy it, and to come into the enjoyment and possession of it! May the Lord manifest Zion more and more to you, and show you the glory of it, and set your feet towards it, and put into your heart to seek the way to it, renewing you more and more in the spirit of your mind, whereby the way comes clearly to be discerned, and faithfully walked in. Then you will witness daily the everlasting covenant of life and peace, even the sure mercies of David.

The desire of my soul is that your afflictions (which, however grievous they may be, are but momentary), may fit you for, and work out, an eternal weight of glory, for your soul to inherit in another world, forever.

I remain a sympathizer with you in your sufferings, and desire that all blessings from the God of my life may come to you, which hardships, temptations, and trials prepare the heart and make way for.

I. P.
14th of 12th Month, 1678

To S. W.

Dear S. W.

I have ever had a love to you, and have many times been filled with earnest desires for you, that you may know the Lord in his own pure teachings, and travel into and dwell in the fullness of the kingdom of his dear Son.

In order to arrive here you must wait to know God and Christ in the mystery of their Spirit, life, and power, and here you will find the secrets of the mystery of darkness searched and purged out, and the mystery of godliness opened and established in your heart in its place. You must know Christ formed inwardly, the soul formed, yes, and created inwardly anew in him. You must know a real transplanting into his death, and a real feeling of his springing and rising life in all of its sweetness, safety, and virtue. So you must be only what you are made and preserved to be in the light, grace, life, virtue, and power of the Lord Jesus Christ, and must feel him remove anything that is unrighteous, and clothe you with his pure life, Spirit, and righteousness.

Oh this is indeed the pure, precious, living knowledge of the Lord Jesus Christ, which all outward knowledge must lead to, and where it is comprehended and finds its end. This is the excellency of the knowledge of Jesus Christ our Lord, which Paul was so ravished with, and for which he counted all things but dross and dung.

Now, that you may obtain this, mind the inward appearance, the root, the fountain, the rock within, the living stone within. Mind its openings, its springings, its administering life to you, and take heed of running into the outwardness of openings concerning heavenly things, but keep in the inwardness of life within! This is the everlasting habitation of the birth which is begotten and brought forth, bred up and kept alive by the presence, power, and operation of the living Spirit alone. The Lord Jesus is that Spirit, as really as he was once Man, even the holy, heavenly, immaculate, spotless Lamb of God. And in this state, life reigns in the heart, and the horn of the Holy One is exalted, the head of the serpent crushed, yes, Satan is trodden underfoot by the God of peace. For the Lord desires that his children dwell in the sweetness and fullness of the gospel, in the peace, life, righteousness, and joy of his blessed Spirit and power.

Oh, who would not desire after and wait for and walk with the Lord towards the obtaining and possessing of these things? All the promises in Christ are yes and amen. Inward victory is promised; the inward presence of God is promised;

God's dwelling and walking in the soul is promised; Christ supping with the soul, and the soul with him, is promised; putting the law in the heart, and the writing of it there, and putting the pure, living fear into the heart, and the holy, powerful Spirit which can cause it to walk in God's ways, and to keep his righteous judgments and do them—all of this is promised. Yes, the Lord is able to do this work in the heart, for what cannot the Spirit of judgment and burning consume and burn up within? Indeed, all these things are promised. He can cause the soul to rejoice in the Lord, and work righteousness, and to remember the Lord in his ways, as some were taught and enabled to do in former times. Isa. 64:5. Yes, he can bring into the way of holiness, the King of glory's highway, into which no unclean thing can enter. And truly, they that are kept undefiled in the way taste of the sweetness, blessedness, purity, and holy pleasure.

Certainly, if that is indeed put off wherein the enemy's power lies, and that indeed is put on wherein the strength of the Lord Jesus is revealed, and if the soul is really in the possession of, and abides in this state—how can it not be strong in the Lord and in the power of his might? How will it not witness the good pleasure of the Lord fulfilling his good work, and the work of faith going on with power, daily, more and more? A little measure of this kept to, removes the mountains inwardly, and gives strength over the enemy.

O my friend, there is an ingrafting into Christ, a being formed and newly created in Christ, a living and abiding in him, and a growing and bringing forth fruit through him into perfection. Oh, may you experience all these things! And that you may do so, wait to know life, the springings of life, the separations of life (inwardly) from all the evil which hangs about it, and would be springing up and mixing with it, under an appearance of good. I desire that that life may come to live fully in you, and nothing else. So sink very low, and become very little, and know little. Yes, know no power to believe, act, or suffer anything for God, except as it is given to you by the springing grace, virtue, and life of the Lord Jesus. For grace is a spiritual, inward thing; it is a holy seed, sown by God, springing up in the heart. People have a notion of grace, but know not the thing. Do not concern yourself with the notion, but feel the thing, and know your heart more and more plowed up by the Lord, that his seed's grace may grow up in you more and more, and you may daily feel your heart as a garden enclosed, watered, dressed, and delighted in by him.

This is a salutation of love from your friend in the truth which lives and changes not.

I. P.

27th of Twelfth Month, 1678

To M. Hiorns

Dear Friend,

I received two letters from you lately, whereby I sense your great love to me, and the Lord's great goodness to you, in administering that which rejoices and refreshes you.

Now, this advice arises in my heart: keep cool and low before the Lord, that the seed, the pure, living seed, may spring more and more in you, and your heart be united more and more to the Lord therein. Coolness of spirit is a precious frame, and the glory of the Lord most shines therein, in its own luster and brightness. When the soul is low before the Lord, it is near the seed, and preciously (in its life) one with the seed. And when the seed rises, you will have liberty in the Lord to rise with it. Only take heed of that part which will be outrunning it, and getting above it, and so not ready to descend again, and keep low in the depths with it.

O my friend, I have a sense that this has been the error of that people with whom you have formerly walked, and I yet observe in your spirit a liability to it. May the Lord give you to watch against it, that you may come to a pure observation and discerning of the everlasting, unchangeable seed in your own heart. And may you daily feel your mind bowed down to worship in this seed, and become wholly leavened into it, and be perfectly changed and preserved by it.

We are here but a little while in this world, for the Lord to make use of us, and to serve himself by us, and to fit us for the crown of glory which he will give us fully to wear in the other world. Now, feel the child's nature, which chooses nothing, but desires the fulfilling of the Father's will. I cannot desire to enjoy anything (says the nature of the true birth), except as the Father is pleased to give me to enjoy. There is a time to need, as well as to abound, while we are in this world. And the times of need, as well as the times of abounding, are greatly advantageous to us. How should faith, love, patience, meekness, and the excellency and suffi-ciency of God's grace shine, except by, in, and through the many exercises and varieties of conditions wherewith the Lord visits us? Yes, the greatest in the life, power, and glory of the Lord, have the greatest trials and exercises, which is to their own advantage, as well as for the good and benefit of others, and to the great honor and glory of the Lord. Oh, at all times, and in all conditions, take heed of a will, take heed of a wisdom, which is above the seed's will, and above the seed's wisdom.

Let the Lord alone be all in you, and make you every day what he pleases. In due time, you shall know a life—even the seed's life, the Son's life, whom all of the angels are to worship—as it is revealed and brought forth! So, be still, quiet, and silent before the Lord, not putting up any request to the Father, nor cherishing any desire in you, except in the seed's lowly nature and purely springing life. And may the Lord give you the clear discerning, in the lowly seed, of all that springs and arises in your heart.

You did read precious things of the seed when you were here, written outwardly; oh that you might read the same things written inwardly in your own heart! This you may do, if you become as a weaned child, not exercising yourself in things too high or too wonderful for you. Every secret thing, every spiritual mystery, besides what God opens to you, is too high and wonderful for you. And if the Lord at any time opens to you deep mysteries, then fear before the Lord, and go no further into them than the Lord leads you. The error is still in man's comprehending, knowing mind, but never in the lowly, weighty seed of life. For the greatest, as well as the least, must be daily taught by the Lord, both in their ascending and descending, or they will miss their way. Yes, they must be daily taught of him to be silent before him, and know what it is to be still in him, or they will be apt to miss in both.

This from your friend,

I. P.

Amersham, Woodside, 4th of Fifth Month, 1679.

To Sarah Elgar

Dear Friend,

The child which the Lord has taken from you was his own. He has done you no wrong in calling it from you. Take heed of murmuring; take heed of discontent; take heed of any grief, except what truth allows you. You have yet one child left. The Lord may call for that too, if he please, or he may continue and bless it to you. Oh, mind a right frame of spirit towards the Lord in this your great affliction! If you mind God's truth in your heart, and wait to feel its seasoning, it will bring you into, and preserve you in, a right frame of spirit. The Lord will not condemn your love and tenderness to your child, or your tender remembrance of him. But still, in this be subject to the Lord, and bow before his will and disposal, and let not the will of your nature rise above it. Retire out of the natural, into the spiritual, where you may feel the Lord your portion, so that now, in the needful time, you may daily receive and enjoy satisfaction therein. Oh, wait to feel the Lord making your heart what he would have it to be, in this your deep and sore affliction.

And now, let the world see how you prize the truth, and what truth can do for you. Feed on it; do not feed on your affliction. The life of truth will arise in you, and raise you up over your affliction, to the honor of the name of the Lord, and to the comfort of your own soul.

I. P.
Nunnington, Sixth Month, 1679

To Sarah Bond

Dear Sarah,

I have had many thoughts of you in this my imprisonment, wherein I have seen in spirit your error and miscarriage, and also a hope and expectation in your heart which will deceive you.

Oh, how much precious time have you lost, wherein you might have been traveling far on your journey, while you are disputing in your mind, and wandering in the deceitful reasonings of your heart! And indeed, it will never be as you imagine, but you must begin low, and be glad of a little light with which to travel out of the earthly nature, and be faithful therein. And in faithfulness you may expect additions of light, and as much power as may help you to continue on. And though you may long be low, weak, little, and ready to perish, yet in the humble and self-denying state, the Father will help you, and cause his life to shoot up in you, and in this shooting up will be your redemption.

But oh, hasten out of the earthly nature while you have time, and still have any visitations from the Spirit of the Lord! And do not, in your wisdom, limit him, but accept whatever at present comes from him; for the flood is breaking out, and will swallow up and drown all that are not found in the ark. Therefore enter, enter quickly! Mind that which checks you in your heart. And mind also that which reasons against those checks, to hold you still in captivity, and to keep you from traveling out of the earthly nature, spirit, wisdom, and practices. Oh, come out of the spirit and way of this world, that you may live and not die. For none shall live except those that walk in the way of life, and leave the paths and course of the dead, in which you are yet entangled. Do not limit the Holy One of Israel in your desires or expectations, but thankfully receive the smallest visitation that comes from him to your soul, for there is life and peace in it, and death and perplexity in turning from it. Therefore, receive the day of your visitation, and be turned in it from the darkness of the earthly mind and nature, into the light of all living and redeemed souls!

And this is my tender counsel to you—wait for and gaspingly receive the checks of the Most High, and take heed of reasoning against them. As these (though in a low and mean and despicable way to your wisdom) draw and lead you out of any earthly thought, word, custom, or practice, follow diligently, waiting to have your reasonings subdued to the smallest motions and lowest guidance of life in you. For I know that life is near you, even the life that would effectually redeem you. But now the life is bowed down and held captive under the dominion of the earthly wisdom. So it is that your redemption (which is to be wrought out by the life) is hindered, and will be hindered, until your heart is persuaded to join to the life and become subject to it without reasoning, consulting, or disputing. For I certainly know the light manifests in you, but the darkness puts off the present manifestation of the light, and expects another; and this is in the will of the flesh, which the Father will not answer. O friend, in this will and expectation you will perish; but your help, life, and salvation are in being subject to the present manifestation of light, and parting with, and departing from, what you already know to be of the earth, and not of God.

In doing this, more will be made manifest in the Lord's season, and power will be given to become a child (after some entrance into the childlike nature). But the will and expectation of the flesh in you shall never be answered. It has been long written in my heart concerning you, but I dare never utter it to you. Oh that it may be now uttered, to the melting and advantage of your heart! For indeed, I love you, and have travailed for you, and desire the salvation of your soul, as of my own. Oh that you may be led out of that wisdom which destroys, into that which saves, where (in humility of heart) you will receive instruction daily, according to your need. But truly you must come into, and come under, that which crucifies your nature and wisdom. Here only (in the season of God's wisdom, who answers the desires of his own Spirit in the heart, but regards not the flesh) will you meet with life and power, but nowhere else.

I am your friend, and a dear lover of that in you which desires the Lord. Oh, that it might rise up in you, and be severed from the earth, that your soul may live!

I. P.

To Friends in the Truth at Lewes

My Dear Friends,

The God of truth plants his truth in the hearts of people, that it might grow there, and bring forth fruit to him. O my dear friends, feel it grow in every one of your hearts, bringing forth the proper fruits of its growth to the Lord.

Mind what arises from the truth, what truth brings forth, and wait for and receive your nourishment from the Lord, that it may be brought forth in you. And whatever the Lord has made barren in you (you who have experienced his right-eous judgments), let it be kept so by the same power which made it barren, that no more fruit may be brought forth to sin and unrighteousness. Then you will live the life of truth, and dwell and walk in the truth, where there is no greater joy, delight, or peace to be desired or enjoyed.

O my dear friends, know, and every day experience, Enoch's life—a being translated out of the kingdom of dark-ness, into the kingdom of the dear Son, and of walking with the Son in his kingdom. Then you will walk with the Father also, and know the heavenly paths of life, joy, righteousness, and peace in the pure light of life, which is no less than a paradise to the renewed soul.

I would eagerly have seen you together, had the Lord made a way, but let me feel you in the hidden life, and meet you at my Father's throne. This is the salutation of my love to you, which so lay upon me that I could not pass it by, who am your friend, in the everlasting, unchangeable truth of our blessed God and Savior.

I. P.

To an Unknown Recipient

Friend,

Because my not praying in my family, according to the custom of professors, seemed to be such a great stumbling-block to you, it sprang up in my heart to render you this account thereof.

I did formerly apply myself to pray to the Lord, morning and evening (besides other times), believing in my heart that it was the will of the Lord I should so do. And this was my condition then—sometimes I felt the living spring open, and the true child breathe towards the Father, but at other times I felt a deadness, a dryness, a barrenness, and only a speaking and striving of the natural part. Even then, I felt this was not acceptable to the Lord, nor any profit to my soul, but I apprehended it to be a duty, and I dared not but apply myself to it.

Since that time—that is, since the Lord has again been pleased to raise up what he had formerly begotten in me, and feed it by the pure giving-forth of that breath of life which begat it, which is the bread that comes down from heaven daily to it—the Lord has shown me that prayer is his gift to the child which he begets. I have seen that true prayer stands not in the will, or time, or understanding, or affectionate part of the creature, but in the Lord's own begetting, in which he first breathes upon the soul, and it breathes again towards him. The Lord works this at his own pleasure, and no time can be set when he shall breathe, or when he shall not breathe. When he breathes, then is the time of prayer, then is the time of moving towards him, and following him who draws. So that all my times, all my duties, all my graces, all my hopes, all my refreshments, and all my ordinances, are in his hand, who is the spring of my life, and conveys, preserves, and increases life of his own good pleasure.

I freely confess, all my religion stands in waiting on the Lord for the riches of his Spirit, and in returning back to the Lord (by his own Spirit, and in the virtue of his own life), that which he pleases to bestow on me. I have no faith, no love, no hope, no peace, no joy, no ability to do anything, no refreshment in anything, except as I find his living breath beginning, continuing, answering, and performing what it calls for. So that I have become exceedingly poor and deso-late, except in what the Lord pleases to be to me by his own free grace, and for his own name's sake, and in his rich mercy. And if I have tasted anything of the Lord's goodness sweeter than ordinary, my heart is willing (so far as the Lord pleases) to faithfully point any others to the same spring, and not to discourage the least desire after God in them. But where they have lost the true living child, and another thing has risen up in its stead (which, though it may bear the image of the true to the eye of flesh, yet is not the same thing in the sight of God), and where this nourishes itself by praying, reading, meditating, or any other such like thing, feeding the carnal part with a kind of knowledge from Scriptures—this, in love and faithfulness to the Lord and to souls, I cannot but testify against, wherever I find it, as the Lord draws forth my spirit to bear testimony.

This I know from the Lord to be the general state of professors at this day. The Spirit of the Lord is departed from them, and they are joined to another spirit, as deeply and as generally as ever the Jews were in their day. And their prayers and reading of the Scriptures, and preaching, and duties, and ordinances are as loathsome to the soul of the Lord, as ever the Jews' incense and sacrifices were. And this is the word of the Lord concerning them: You must come out of your knowledge, into the feeling of an inward seed of life, if ever you will be restored to the true unity with God, and to the true enjoyment of him again. You must come out of the knowledge and wisdom you have gathered from the Scriptures, into a feeling of the thing there written, as it pleases the Lord to open and reveal them in the hidden man of the heart.

This is what you must wait for from the Lord, and not to boast of your present state, as if you were not backslidden from him, and had not entered into league with another spirit which keeps up the image of what the Spirit of the Lord once formed in you, but is without the true, pure, fresh life.

From a faithful friend and lover of souls.

I. P.

To E. Terry

Friend,

If the Lord has extended favor to you and shown you mercy, I therein rejoice on your behalf.

Your desire—that what you wrote may be looked upon as

nothing, and that no contest may be raised from it—I am fully content to oblige. Indeed, my love flows to you, for I take notice of your seriousness, and of whatever I have unity with in your letter, and I overlook the other.

With regard to disputes, indeed, I have no love for them. Truth did not enter my heart that way, nor do I expect to propagate it in others that way. Yet, sometimes a necessity is laid upon me, for the sake of others. And truly, when I do feel a necessity, I do it in great fear, not trusting in my spear or bow (I mean in strong arguments or wise considerations, which I, of myself, can gather or comprehend), but I look up to the Lord for the guidance, help, and demonstration of his Spirit, that a way may be made thereby in men's hearts for the pure seed to be reached. Only in this is there a true conviction, and a thorough conversion of the soul to God is witnessed. I had far rather be feeling Christ's life, Spirit, and power in my own heart, than disputing with others about it.

Christians that truly fear the Lord have a proportion of the primitive Spirit, and if they could only learn to watch and wait there (where God works his fear), they would daily receive more and more of it. Only by this will they come to understand more and more of the true intent and precious-ness of the words of the Holy Scriptures. He that will truly live to God, must hear wisdom's voice within, at home, in his own heart, for he that will have her words made known, and her spirit poured out to him, must turn at her reproof. Prov. 1:23. Indeed, I never knew, and am satisfied that none else can know, the preciousness of this lesson till they are taught it of the Lord.

There is one thing more on my heart to express, occa-sioned by your last letter, which is this: I have more unity in my heart and spirit before the Lord with the Puritans, than with the churches and gatherings which men have built up and run into since. The seed of life and truth was near me, as well as others, in that day, but I wandered from it into outward knowledge, and, with great seriousness, into a way of congregational worship, and thereby came to a great loss. Then, at length, for lack of the Lord's presence, power, and manifestation of his love, I became exceedingly sick at heart. But now, the Lord, in great love and tender mercy, having brought me back to the same seed, and fixed my spirit therein, I discern the truth and beauty of that former estate, (along with my several runnings out from it), and I find what was true or false there uncovered to me by the holy Anointing, which appears and teaches in that seed. And friend, it is not a notion of light which my heart is engaged to testify of, but rather that very light which enlivens, which opens, which gives the heart to see, and that wherein the power of life is felt. For truly, in the opening of my heart by the pure power, I was taught to see and own the principle and seed of life, and to know its way of appearance. So that I can faithfully and certainly testify, that that which is divine, spiritual, and heavenly, is nearer man than he is aware, as well as that which is earthly and selfish.

O friend, if you cannot yet see and own the principle and seed of Christ's life and Spirit, nor discern his appearance therein, yet take heed of fighting against it. For, indeed, if you do, you fight against no less than the Lord Jesus Christ himself.

I. P.

To Richard Roberts

Dear R. R.

You did acquaint me that Timothy Fly, the Anabaptist teacher, did charge me with denying Christ's humanity, and also the blood of Christ which was shed at Golgotha, outside the gates of Jerusalem, and that I acknowledge no other Christ except he that is within men.

Certain I am that neither Timothy Fly, nor any other man, did ever hear me deny that Christ was born of the Virgin Mary according to the flesh, or that it was his blood which was shed outside the gates of Jerusalem. And the Lord, who knows my heart, knows that such a thing was never in my heart. No, for I do greatly value that flesh and blood of our Lord Jesus Christ, and witness forgiveness of sins and redemption through it. Yet, if I should say that I do not also know nor partake of his flesh and blood in spirit, I should not be a faithful witness to the Lord. For there is the mystery of God and of Christ, and it is the soul's food which gives life to the soul, even the living bread and the living water. There is a knowing Christ after the flesh, and there is a knowing him after the Spirit, and a feeding on his Spirit and life; and this does not destroy his appearing in flesh, or the blessed ends thereof, but rather confirms and fulfills them.

Indeed, the acknowledging of Christ being inwardly in his saints does not deny his appearing outwardly in the body that was prepared for him, unless Timothy Fly can prove this —that the same Christ that appeared outwardly cannot appear inwardly. "Do you not know yourselves that Jesus Christ is in you, unless indeed you are disqualified?" 2 Cor. 13:5. "And if Christ is in you, the body is dead because of sin," etc. Rom. 8:10. "Christ in you, the hope of glory." Col. 1:27. "Behold, I stand at the door and knock; if any man hear my voice and open the door, I will come in to him." Rev. 3:20. "I will come again," says Christ; you are now in pain, as a woman in travail, full of sorrow for the loss of my outward, bodily presence, but I will come to you again in Spirit; see

John 16 and John 14:17. "He that dwells with you, shall be in you," and then, when the Bridegroom is inwardly and spiritually in you and with you, "your heart shall rejoice, and your joy no man will take from you." John 16:22. And so, the apostles and primitive Christians did "rejoice with joy unspeakable, and full of glory," 1 Peter 1:8, because of the spiritual appearance and presence of the Bridegroom. And yet, there is no other bridegroom, who now appears in Spirit, or spiritually in the hearts of his own, than He who once appeared in the "body prepared for him," to do the Father's will therein.

I. P.

To the Independents at Canterbury

Dear Friends,

I have been a seeker after God, and a worshipper of him, from my childhood, according to the best of my understanding. And for a time, I sat down in that way which is called Independency, believing it to be the way of the gospel, and entering into it with much fear and seeking of God. In this time, the Lord had regard to the uprightness and tenderness of heart, which he himself had formed in me.

But, at length, the Lord's hand fell upon me, breaking me all to pieces as to my inward state. For what cause, I had then no knowledge of at all, but I mourned before him unutterably, night and day, and lay panting and languishing after him who was the only Beloved of my soul. Many pitied me, but none could reach my state, and after much serious discourse with me, they greatly wondered. Some said it was a unique case, and would doubtless end in goodwill and mercy from the Lord to me. I parted from the Independents in great love and tenderness—they expecting my return to them again (the love between me and them being so exceedingly great, and I having let in no prejudice against them), and I knowing nothing to the contrary.

But it pleased the Lord, after many years, when my hope nearly failed, to visit me in a wonderful manner, breaking my heart in pieces, giving me to feel his pure, living power, and the raising of his holy seed in my heart thereby. Then I cried out inwardly before him, "This is he, this is he whom I have sought after, and so much wanted! This is the pearl, this is the holy leaven! Do what you will with me, afflict me how you will, and as long as you please, so that at length I may be joined with this seed, and become one with it!" So the eye of my understanding was from that day anointed, and I saw and felt the pure life of the Son made manifest in me. Indeed, the Father drew me to him, as to a living stone, and has built my soul upon him. He brought me to Mount Zion, the holy city of our God, where the river of life sends forth its streams which refresh and make glad the holy city, and all the taber-nacles that are built on God's holy hill. And truly, from this holy hill and city, the law and word of life does issue forth, and the inhabitants of the rock of life hear it, and are friends to the Bridegroom, and glad of the Bridegroom's voice. These follow the Lamb, the Shepherd and Bishop of their souls, wheresoever he leads. And he leads them into the pastures of life, and the folds of pure rest, and gives them eternal life to feed upon.

O you Independents, whom I have loved above all people! I never had thoughts of departing from you, but was forcibly taken by the hand of the Lord out of your Society, and yet not without a desire to return to you again, if the Lord pleased to make any way thereto. O beloved Indepen-dents, that you could hear the sensible, experienced testimony that is on my heart to you concerning my Beloved, concerning his appearance, concerning his church, concerning his way, his truth, his kingdom! It is nearer than you are aware, and above all that you can comprehend concerning it. Oh that you might inwardly know these things! Turn in, turn in! Mind what stirs in your hearts, what moves against sin, and also what moves towards sin. The one is the Son's life, the Son's grace, the Son's Spirit; the other is the spirit and nature which is contrary to it. If you could only come to the sense of this, and come to a true, inward silence, and waiting, and turning at the reproofs of heavenly wisdom, and know the heavenly drawings into that which is holy and living, then you would soon find the Lord working in your hearts, to stop the issues of death, and to open the issues of life. You would find yourselves anointed daily by the Lord (for there is not a day that we do not need to see, nor a day where the Lord does not give sight), and an understanding also would be given you to know Him that is true, and an abiding in him that is true, even the "eternal life." 1 John 1:2. And abiding here, you cannot fail to receive power (from him who ministers according to the power of the endless life), not only to overcome sin and your souls' enemies, but to become sons to God, with delight performing his will. Then the yoke, which yokes down and subdues sin in you, will be easy. Yes, it will be the ease, pleasure, and joy of your souls.

May the Lord open an ear in you to hear, that you may become experiencers and possessors of these things. For, of a truth, the Lord is arisen to shake terribly the earth, and to build up his Zion, and to give unto his people "a peaceable habitation and sure dwellings and quiet resting places" upon Mount Zion. Isa. 32:18.

I. P.

To Francis Pordage

Friend,

There is a mind which can never know nor receive the things of God's kingdom, and yet, this mind is very busy in searching and inquiring after them.

The Scribes and Pharisees were questioning Christ, and desiring satisfaction about the kingdom, and about his doctrine and miracles, and the practice of his disciples, but they could never find satisfaction. Yet, the disciples themselves were many times afraid to ask Christ questions, there being a dread of God upon their spirits, and a limit to the knowing and inquiring part in them; for indeed, the true birth learns under the yoke.

This, therefore, is precious—to come to feel that which limits the natural mind, which is forward and inquisitive without the true nature and sense. Indeed it is good for that mind to receive the yoke, and to be limited by it and famished; for famine is appointed for that mind and birth. It is written, "I will destroy the wisdom of the wise, and bring to nothing the understanding of the prudent." Now, this is precious and greatly needful—that a man know, discern, and watch against that wisdom and understanding in himself which God will destroy and bring to nothing. For, to be sure, while he is learning and striving to know with that mind, God will never teach him, but rather hide the mystery of life and salvation from him. And what is all man's knowledge worth, that he learns of himself without God's teaching? What good is that which man receives into the understanding which is to perish and be destroyed? In the new understanding, God sets up the true light; but in the other understanding there are false lights set up, which do not give a true distinction of good and evil, but they call good evil, and evil good, and put darkness for light, and light for darkness. Indeed they cannot do otherwise, for the light in them is darkness, not being the gift of grace whereby they see and judge, but a light of their own forming, according to their own comprehension of things, in the dark and false understanding.

Now, the Lord has taught us the difference between all these lights, and the light of his grace, which purely teaches, livingly teaches, not in the reasonings of the mind, but in the evidence and demonstration of God's Spirit in the soul and conscience. When we came to see in this light, we found that which we had called good, according to our former apprehension of things, was not so in the true balance. And what we thought had pleased God, was abominable in his eyes. And truly, all that have not come to this light offer that which is abominable to God, and yet think it pleases him. Oh what a gross and dangerous mistake this is! Indeed, all such things are no better than acts of man's own will, which are done outside of the light, life, virtue, and power of God's Spirit. For the root must be good, or the fruit cannot be good. The mind must be renewed, or the knowledge is but old, dead, literal, and fleshly. The fleshly understanding seeks to comprehend and receive knowledge, but can never know or receive what is spiritual.

Truly, the Lord has led us a great way in our journey, and has done great things inwardly for and in our spirits. Yet, if we were not kept under the yoke, and that part in us still had liberty to know, live, act, and worship, we should yet perish, and be cut off from the land of the living.

I. P.

In Reply to an Answer of I. H.

Dear Friend,

Indeed, to speak properly, the church of the gospel, or the new covenant church, is invisible. The persons in whom the church is, are visible; yet the new covenant church is not a society of men, but rather of the invisible life within men. It is a fellowship in the faith, in the Spirit, which is the bond of their unity and of their peace.

The life is breathed invisibly into the hidden man, John 3:8, and is there nourished and built up invisibly into a spiritual, invisible temple, house, or church, and in that is the unity and fellowship. So the church is a mystery, and the fellowship is a mystery, which is hid from every eye but the eye of life. There is no having fellowship one with another except by coming to that, and keeping in that, wherein is the fellowship. 1 John 1:7. The church is built of inward Jews, whom God seeks to frame his new house of worship under the gospel. John 4:23. Now, of such stones as these, the Lord builds up a temple for his Spirit to dwell in, a house for his life and presence to manifest itself in, even a church for the living God. This building is by the Spirit, in the Spirit, and of that which is spiritual. This building is one with the foundation, and therefore is the pillar and ground of Truth, which none is but Christ, and that which is married to him, and so one with him. 1 Tim. 3:15.

It is the candlestick within persons—that is the church. It is not any outward meeting of persons, or joining together by covenants, or receiving or practicing of ordinances, that can make a church, but rather the eternal life in believers, formed by the Spirit into a candlestick, to hold the eternal lamp or light, with the everlasting oil of salvation. The light thus shining in this candlestick, continually refreshed by this oil—here is a flourishing temple, wherever it is found. Here is the church of the living God. Here is the spouse married to the Lamb, her Husband. But if you grieve the Spirit, quench the Spirit, despise the prophesying thereof, and light a candle of the fleshly wisdom and knowledge of the things of God instead of these, then the oil soon fails. When the oil fails, the lamp goes out. And the lamp, or light, being gone out of the candlestick, the Lord soon removes the candlestick. And once the candlestick is removed, the very same persons may meet together often, and hold up the form, performing things mentioned in the Scriptures concerning a church, and observing such things as they may call the institutions and ordinances thereof, but they are far from continuing to be a church. Take away the faith, what is left of a Christian? And take away the candlestick, what is left of a church?

It is the Spirit alone that can square stones and fit them for the building of a church. He alone can build them up into a house when he has squared them. Eph. 2:22. And after he has built, he can also pull down again, and bring into a wilderness state. For there is a wilderness state of Christianity, as well as a built state. Rev. 12:6. And just as it is dangerous to be out of the church in its built state, so too it is dangerous remaining in that building which the Spirit of the Lord has forsaken. Now, if the Spirit be the builder, surely then he will take in no stones except such as he has first squared and fitted for the building.

The church is a body gathered in the Spirit, and watching to the Spirit. And the Spirit is present there with his pure, searching, discerning eyes, so that nothing that is impure can enter (each stone watching to the Spirit, according to the order of the gospel). There is not one counterfeit Jew. There is not so much as one false apostle, though they clothe themselves ever so like angels of light. Rev. 22. But if they are negligent, and come off from the watch, not waiting for the guidance of the Spirit, then that which is corrupt may creep in, and endanger the body. Jude 4.

I. P.

To Bridget Atley

Dear Friend,

I am sensible of your sore travail and deep distress, and how hard it is for you to meet with that which is comfortable and refreshing, and how easily again it is lost. And I know from where this arises, even from the working of the enemy in a mystery of deceit in your heart, wherein you do not perceive or suspect him, but instead swallow down his baits, and so he smites you with his hook, and thereby draws you back into the region of darkness. Then he enters that part in you which is in nature one with him, filling it with his wickedness, and laying loads of accusations upon you, as if they were true. These are not strange things to the travelers after the Lord, but such as are usually met with in the like cases. But if your eye were made single and opened by the Lord, you would see those baits, and turn away from that which you now so readily swallow down, and so avoid the stroke, and keep your place in the light and mercy of the Lord. You must not look so much at the evil that is near, but rather at he who stands ready to pity and help, and who has pitied and helped your distressed soul, and will pity and help it again. Why is there a mercy seat, but for the sinner to look towards in time of need?

Neither must you hearken to the questionings of the ensnaring questioner, but rather cleave to that which shuts them out, keeping to the sense of the love and mercy when the Lord is kind and tender to you. When the enemy entered your habitation again, and broke your rest, peace, and enjoyment of the Lord, he then drew you into the pit of darkness, where the remembrance of life, and the sense of mercy and love vanishes. Here there is no help for you from anything you can do or think. But be patient, till the Lord's tender mercy and love visit you again. And then, look up to him against this and such like snares, which would come between you and the appearance of the Lord's love, so that you may feel more of his abiding with you, and the sweet effects thereof. For, these things are not to destroy you, but rather to teach you wisdom, which the Lord is able, through many exercises and sore trials, to bestow upon you. And my soul will exceedingly rejoice to hear that your heart has been rid of all that burdens you, and filled with all it rightly desires after.

Your faithful friend,

I. P.

To Abraham Grimsden

Friend,

You have made some profession of truth, and at times have come among us, but whether you have been changed thereby, and been faithful to the Lord in what has been made manifest to you, belongs unto you diligently to inquire. There is no safe dallying with truth. He that puts his hand to the plow must not look back at anything of this world, but rather take up the cross and follow Christ in the single-hearted obedience, hating father, mother, goods, lands, wife, yes, all for his sake, or he is not worthy of Him. The good hand of the Lord is with his people, and he blesses them both inwardly and outwardly. They that seek first the kingdom of heaven, and the righteousness thereof, have other things also added. But they that neglect the kingdom, and are unfaithful to truth, seeking the world before it—the hand of the Lord goes forth against them, and they many times also miss the world for which they seek and labor.

Truth is honorable. Oh take heed of bringing a reproach upon it by pretending to it, and yet not being of it, in the pure sense and obedience which it begets and brings forth in the hearts and lives of the faithful. Oh, consider rightly and truly! It had been better for you if you had never known truth, nor been directed to the seed and path of righteousness, than, after being directed there, to turn from the holy commandments, and deny obedience to the righteous One. May the Lord give you a true sense and repentance, if it be his holy pleasure, and raise you out of this world's spirit, to live unto him in his own pure Spirit. It is easy to profess and make a show of truth, but hard to come into it. It is very hard to the earthly mind to part with that which must be parted with before the soul can come to possess and enjoy it. Profession of truth without the life and power is but a slippery place, from which men may easily slide. Indeed, if men are not in the life and power, they can hardly be kept from that which will stain their profession. The Lord, who searches the heart, knows how it is with you. Oh, consider your ways, and fear before him, and take heed of taking his name in vain, for he will not hold such guiltless!

I am, in this, faithful and friendly to your soul, desiring its eternal welfare, and that it may not forever perish from the presence and power of the Lord.

I. P.

To an Unknown Recipient

Friend,

God breathed into man the breath of life, and man thereby became a living soul to God, to whom, by transgression, he died. But Christ (who was before Abraham, and, in due time, took up that body prepared by the Father) is the resurrection and the life, who, from the Father, breathes life into man again, and so he comes to live again. And man, being quickened by Christ, is to rise up from the dead, and travel with Christ into the land of the living. And Christ is all to believers, in whom dwells all fullness. The circumcision is in him, the baptism is in him, the righteousness, rest, and peace also are in him; yes, in him are all the treasures of wisdom and knowledge. Truly Christ is made unto those that believe in him, wisdom, righteousness, sanctification, and redemption.

Now, it is very precious to feel this, but of little value to imagine or comprehend apprehensions about this. For the end of words is to bring men to the thing itself, but the Scribes and Pharisees, by their apprehensions upon the words given forth by the Spirit, missed the thing (though they thought they did not miss, but rather were blessed in their knowledge of the law). This same spirit is alive in many that profess truth now, who, by their understanding of Scripture words are kept from the thing of which the Scriptures testify. What did Christ come in the flesh and suffer for, but to unite and reconcile to God? And what is the anti-christian way of erring from the truth, but to extol the appearance of Christ in the flesh, his sufferings, resurrection, ascension, etc., in that spirit wherein the true union and reconciliation is not witnessed? If we receive the light, and walk in the light, as

God is in the light, then we have a share in his Son's death and atonement, and his blood cleanses us from unrighteousness, but not otherwise.

Oh that all who truly desire salvation, might know the way here, and receive from God that which cleanses and keeps clean! Amen.

I. P.

To an Unknown Recipient

Dear Friend,

I received your letter kindly, and in the tenderness of love which desires your enjoyment of the Lord in this world, and the eternal welfare of your soul with him forever.

It is a great matter to have the mind rightly guided to that wherein God appears, that the soul may wait at the posts of wisdom, to hear wisdom's voice. And what says wisdom to he that hears and observes her voice? "I will pour out my spirit unto you; I will make known my words unto you." Prov. 1:23.

You have read in the Scriptures of the kingdom of God, which, Christ told the Pharisees, was within them. In parables he also expressed what it was like—even like a grain of mustard seed, like a pearl of great price, like a lost coin, or piece of silver, like a treasure hid in a field, like leaven, etc. Now, it is my desire that you might come to the discerning of this. Is there any such thing in you? Surely, there is. Do you know it? Are you in union with it? Has it grown and enlarged in you? Is there room made for it, and does it overspread your heart?

You say the covenant, the new covenant, is contained in the Scriptures. There are, indeed, descriptions of the covenant in the Scriptures, but the covenant itself is an agreement of life and peace made with the soul in the Lord Jesus Christ, upon believing in His power, and obeying His voice. For thus says the scripture, "Hear, and your souls shall live, and I will make an everlasting covenant with you, even the sure mercies of David." Isa. 55:3. Now, this is what the soul is to wait for—even to feel the power of life breaking the bonds of death, and opening the ear to the voice of God's Spirit. Only then will the soul receive his impressions, and feel the new creation inwardly, the new heart, the new mind, the new law of life, written within by the finger of God's Spirit, even the law of the Spirit of life in Christ Jesus. And then this law is the inward rule, even as the outward law was the rule to the outward Jews.

You think me somewhat too sharp and severe in my sentence concerning the ministers of this day. I have received great mercy, and I desire not to be sharp or severe towards any. If, therefore, any such thing was written by me, be assured it was in faithfulness to the Lord's requirings. All sorts of Christians own Christ in words, but all do not distinguish, discern, nor are subject to, the appearances of his Spirit and power. Instead, many resist, gainsay, and oppose, through error and mistake, till at length they come to hardness. These are the builders who refuse the cornerstone. The builders rejected Christ's appearance in the flesh, in the days of his flesh, and the builders again refuse his appearance in Spirit, in this day of his Spirit. Oh, that any who are tender among them might be sensible of it! Then they might not draw down God's severity and sharpness upon their heads, which if they do, it is not our joy, but a matter of grief to us. Whatever is of God in any of them, my heart cannot help but own. But many take that to be of God (that fear, that faith, that love, those prayers, those hopes, that peace, that joy, etc.), which is not truly of him. Oh, how precious is that light which truly and rightly distinguishes! "My sheep hear my voice." The voice of the Shepherd distinguishes every deceit and every deceiver.

But whereas you say, "The spirits are to be tried by the Scriptures," I have found it otherwise in my experience. The Scriptures may indeed try words, but nothing can try spirits except for the Spirit. "I will know," said the apostle, "not the words of them that are puffed up, but the power." Deceivers may come with Scripture words, but they cannot come with the true power of God. Therefore, the Apostle John, who bade the believers to try the spirits, told them they had an anointing from the Holy One, and pointed them to that. 1 John 2:20, 27. But who can judge this, except he that has the anointing, and is taught by the Lord to try things by it? This one knows how it tries, and what a certain judgment it gives concerning the nature of things, and concerning every voice and every appearance. The Spirit of God searches all things, discerns all things, discovers all things—every snare, every device of the enemy, even the net spread ever so secretly. Blessed are they whose eyes are opened and kept open by him.

Oh, wait to know that wherein the Lord inwardly appears! And take up the cross of our Lord Jesus Christ to everything that is contrary to God, so that it all may be cruci-fied in you, and that your soul may live in the abundance of life and peace. And be not discouraged because of any weakness, or because of your age. Your weakness is not your disadvantage, but rather your advantage, for the weaker you are in yourself, the fitter are you to have Christ's power revealed and manifested in you. Only wait to know that wherein God appears in your heart, even the holy seed, the immortal seed of life, that it may spring up in your heart, and live in you, and gather you into itself, and leaven you all over with its nature. Then you will be a new lump, and may walk before God, not in the oldness of your own literal knowledge or apprehensions of things, but in the newness of his Spirit.

May the Lord appear to you, in the light and demonstration of his Spirit in your heart and conscience. May he touch you, quicken you, lead you, guide and make you sensible of every appearance of his, so that no motion or drawing of his Spirit may be quenched in you, nor any motion of the contrary spirit, under any deception, be hearkened to. Then you may travel on faithfully, and come to the end of your travels with joy and full peace, reaping the sheaves in life everlasting, of all that you have sown to the Spirit.

This is the earnest and single desire of my soul for you, who am your true and faithful friend, and a hearty well-wisher to you and yours.

I. P.

To Ruth Palmer

My Dear Friend,

Whose love I am sensible of, and to whom I entirely wish well, and desire that you may purchase and possess the pearl of great price, and so know and enjoy Christ Jesus, the Lord, and witness him to be eternal life to your soul.

I received a letter from you, which occasions my writing to you. With regard to election, we do believe it, according as the Lord has taught us, and as the Scriptures express it. But such an election as shuts out any from the salvation that God has prepared for the sons of men, we cannot own, because the Scriptures expressly testify that God "would have all to be saved, and come to the knowledge of the Truth." Yes, we also know it to be his nature. It is the nature of the destroyer to destroy—he would have none saved. But it is the nature of God, the Savior, to save—he would have none perish. There is indeed a "making the calling and election sure," but there is first a coming into the elect seed. And, as we are chosen in him, and come into him (out of darkness into his marvelous light, out of death into his life), so we must abide in him, for the promise is to the one that continues unto the end.

As for that place of Rom. 11, it is manifest that there is an election, and that this election is not of works, but of grace. Yet, there must be a hearing of the voice, "Today," said the apostle, "if you will hear his voice," etc. So there must be a coming to Christ, and an abiding in him, and a walking in the strait way, for this is the way God chooses. God has chosen Christ, and the soul in him, and the message is to invite all to come to him, and abide in him to the end. The condemnation is upon rejecting him, and the salvation is to them that receive him—which is not of man's self either, but men are made willing so to do in the day of God's power. And this power is not far from any, or lacking to any, in the way that the Lord has appointed it.

The falling away is not because persons were not elected, but because they let in that which is contrary to the election, and they cleave to it. So there is the "heart of unbelief," in which men depart from the living God, and make shipwreck of faith and of a good conscience, and the ground of their falling is their hearkening not to the Lord, but to the voice and temptations of the enemy.

Yes, there are called, and faithful, and chosen. These are

states to be come into, and abode in. Many may be called who never come to be faithful, nor chosen. To witness the peculiar choice of God, this is precious, and then one should not be content with a touch of the calling, or a touch of the election, but rather to "make them sure." There is no choosing except in the seed, so if you make sure of that seed, you make both your "calling and election sure." For indeed, "many are called, but few chosen." And yet, when a man comes so far as to know himself chosen, is he quite out of danger? Did not Paul know his election sure? Yet, was he not afterwards careful "lest," says he, "when I have preached to others, I myself should be a castaway."

You say, "Whom God once loves, he loves to the end." Did he not once love all men, even the whole world? Did he not manifest it in sending his Son for them? And they that come into his Son, they come into his love. They that come into his love must continue in his love and in his goodness. For, it is not persons ("God is no respecter of persons"), but the seed, God loves. "In your seed shall all the families of the earth be blessed," and in that seed they are loved, and contin-uing there, they continue in the love. It is true, God's grace appears, and thereby many are gathered. And when any fall, the grace of God appears again, and thereby many are restored. But if any become hardened by "the deceitfulness of sin," that they hearken not to the voice of grace when it comes to restore, are they restored by it? Indeed, God's compassion did not fail to Israel of old, nor to Israel now, yet were not many consumed then, who, though they came out of Egypt, yet rebelled, and lusted, and tempted Christ, etc., and so were destroyed by the destroyer? And so, let none make shipwreck of faith now, for it is by faith that any stand, as the apostle expresses in Rom. 11:19-22. Read, and consider. And the apostle, in a true sense of things, cries, "Oh, the depth!"

etc. Love in severity, mercy in severity! If it be stopped one way, it will break forth more abundantly in another way. And, "who has known the mind of the Lord," or given him counsel, which way he should manage his love and mercy? Romans 11:33-34. Indeed, all salvation is to be ascribed to God, and is ascribed to God by all that receive salvation from him. But still, God saves in the way he has appointed (in man coming into the way, in abiding in the way, in walking in the way). Here alone is safety; but out of it is death and destruction forever.

All our best righteousness is as filthy rags, it is true. However, the gift of God is not as filthy rags; the righteousness of his Son revealed in the heart is not as filthy rags. The pure offerings and incense which are offered up to God in the times of the gospel are not as filthy rags. Oh, what a state of blindness many are in that they cannot distinguish between what is of themselves and what is of God in them! And so they cannot avoid offering up a corrupt thing, nor can they offer up that which is holy and pure, even the holy sacrifice, with the holy fire, upon the altar of God! Consider the 3rd chapter, 3rd verse of Malachi, and tell me, if you know, what an offering in righteousness is, and whether it be as filthy rags, or no. Consider that place, John 3:21, "He that does the truth comes to the light, that his deeds may be made manifest, that they are wrought in God." And what are those deeds that are wrought in God? Is not God holy and pure? And is anything wrought in him except what is holy and pure? Therefore, we should wait rightly to distinguish things, and not jumble the precious and the vile together, as if they were all one.

As for a method of speaking, I have none of my own, but wait for the method and words which God's wisdom teaches. Indeed, when I speak of the light, and the life, and the power,

I do mean Christ Jesus, who is the light, life, and power, but it is a great matter to come to know him so revealed in the heart. For where he is so revealed, darkness, and death, and the power of Satan, are scattered and put to flight by him. Yes, Satan falls like lightning before the power of his kingdom, where it is revealed.

This is a blessed experience, and these know Christ indeed. The Lord grant that you may so know him, which is the hearty desire of your soul's true and faithful friend.

I. P.

To Joseph Wright

Dear Friend,

I entreat your son to acquaint my brother Arthur, that I took very kindly and was very glad of his affectionate expressions towards me. I have been somewhat concerned that, though my religion had enlarged my love towards him, yet his religion might have diminished his to me. I bless the Lord on his behalf that he enjoys his health so well. And for myself, though I have been exceedingly weak formerly, yet the inward life and comfort which the Lord daily is pleased to administer to me increases the health and strength of my natural man beyond my expectation. Blessed be my tender and merciful Father, who has visited one so distressed, miserable, and helpless as I was for so many years!

And whereas he says he is like me in speech, but most unlike me in opinion—I pray tell him from me, that my religion does not lie in opinion, but in that which puts an end to opinion. I was weary and sick at heart of opinions, and if the

Lord had not at last brought to my hand that which my soul so needed, I would have never meddled with religion more. But as I felt that in my heart which was evil and not of God, so the Lord God of my life pointed me to that of him in my heart which was of another nature, teaching me to wait for and know his appearance there. And in subjection to this, I now experience him stronger than the strong man that was there before, and by his power, he has separated me from that within which separated me from him before. And so being separated, I truly now feel union with him and his blessed presence every day, which, what this is unto me, my tongue cannot utter.

I would be glad, if the Lord saw good, that I might see my brother before I die, and if I did see him, I would not be quarreling with him about his religion, but rather embrace him in brotherly love, and in the fear of the Lord. As for his being a Roman Catholic, that does not damp my tender affection to him. If he be a Catholic, I had rather have him be a serious than a loose Catholic. If he has met with anything of that which brings forth a holy life in him, then he has that far met with something of my religion, which teaches to order life aright, in the light, and by the Spirit and power of the Lord Jesus. My religion is not a new thing, though it is newly revealed more fully than in many foregoing ages. Truly it consists in that which was long before the Romish church was, and will continue when it shall be no more. And he that would rightly know the true church must know the living stones whereof the true church is built, against which the gates of hell cannot possibly prevail. Oh, the daily joy of my heart in feeling my living membership in this church! Here the true "gold," the "white raiment," the pure "eye salve" (with which the eye, being anointed, sees rightly), are received and enjoyed inwardly, by such as the world knows not, but rather despises. Blessed be the name of the Lord!

I desire my sincere, entire affection, as in God's sight, may be remembered to my dear brother.

I. P.

* * *

The following testimony was written by Mary Penington, the wife of Isaac Penington, upon the death of her dear husband in 1679.

While I keep silent concerning you (oh you who are blessed of the Lord and his people!) my heart burns within me. I must make mention of you, for you were a most pleasant plant of renown, planted by the right hand of the Lord. Indeed you took deep root downwards, and sprang upwards. The dew of heaven fell on you, and made you fruitful, and your fruit was fragrant and most delightful.

Oh, where shall I begin to recount the Lord's remarkable dealings with you? He set his love on you, oh, you who were one of the Lord's peculiar choice! Your very early childhood days declared of what stock and lineage you were. You desired the "sincere milk of the word as a newborn babe," even in the bud of your age. And who can declare how you had traveled towards the Holy Land in the very infancy of your days? Who can tell what your soul felt in your travel? Oh the heavenly, bright, living openings that were given you! God's light shone round about you. Such a state as I have never known of in any other, have I heard you declare of. But this it did please the Lord to withdraw, leaving you desolate and mourning, weary of the night and of the day, naked and poor in spirit, distressed and bowed down. You refused to be comforted, because you could not feed on that which was not bread from heaven.

In that state I married you. My love was drawn to you, because I found you saw the deceit of all notions. You remained as one who refused to be comforted by anything that had only the appearance of religion, until he came to his temple who is truth and no lie. For all those shows of religion were very manifest to you, so that you were sick and weary of them all.

This little testimony to your hidden life, my dear and precious one, in a day when none of the Lord's gathered people knew your face, nor were in any measure acquainted with your many sorrows, have I stammered out, that it might not be forgotten. But now the day has broken forth, and you were so eminently gathered into it, and a faithful publisher of it. I leave this other state of yours to be declared by the sons of the morning, who have witnessed the rising of the bright star of righteousness in you, and its guiding you to the Savior, even Jesus, the First and the Last. Let those speak, who are strong, and have overcome the evil one, and are fathers in Israel. You have declared of your life in God, and have published it in many testimonies.

Ah me, he is gone! He that none exceeded in kindness, in tenderness, in love inexpressible to the relation of a wife. Next to the love of God in Christ Jesus to my soul, was his love precious and delightful to me. My bosom one! My guide and counselor! My pleasant companion! My tender, sympathizing friend, as near to the sense of my pain, sorrow, grief and trouble, as it was possible! Yes, this great help and benefit is gone, and I, a poor worm, compassed about with many infirmities, through mercy was enabled to let him go without an unadvised word of discontent or inordinate grief.

And such was the great kindness the Lord showed me in that hour, that my spirit ascended with him the very moment the spirit left his body, and I saw him safe in his own dwelling place, and rejoiced with him there. From this sight my spirit returned again, to perform my duty to his outward tabernacle.

This testimony to Isaac Penington is from the greatest loser of all who had a share in his life.

—Mary Penington

Made in the USA
Charleston, SC
15 April 2015